# Praise for *Fall in Love, Stay Put, Save the Pl[a]*

"Frank Schaeffer excels at understanding his own experiences and how they reflect our world. He is smart, thoughtful, and funny, too! Wonderful book."

—**Jane Smiley,** Pulitzer Prize–winning novelist, essayist, and biographer

"In *Fall in Love, Have Children, Stay Put, Save the Planet, Be Happy* —Schaeffer's new tour de force—he makes the bold argument that we should focus on living meaningful lives rather than making money and seeking validation from our jobs. Schaeffer's argument takes him down paths that will surprise, delight, and even shock readers. This is an essential read. I hope it starts a new movement."

—**Charlotte Gordon,** author of *Romantic Outlaws: The Lives of Mary Wollstonecraft and Mary Shelley,* winner of the National Book Critics Circle Award

"Frank Schaeffer's book *Fall in Love, Have Children, Stay Put, Save the Planet, Be Happy,* has all the ingredients for a successful life, but is the opposite of what is being sold in our culture. May we see a transformation in our lifetime, if not, in our children's lifetime, and for future generations, as we cannot continue down this path of isolation, struggle, and greed."

—**Johanna (José) Zeilstra,** CEO, Gender Fair, a Public Benefit Corporation; board member and former Wall Street executive, specializing in helping companies improve on gender equity and diversity

"Frank Schaeffer has written a revolutionary manifesto for our deeply troubled world. Reading this book feels like time spent with a wise, challenging, sometimes cantankerous friend who, like Rilke's 'Archaic Torso of Apollo' is looking back at you with a simple demand: Change your life."

—**Laura Dawn,** filmmaker; founding cultural director, MoveOn.org; founder and CEO, ART NOT WAR

"You've really got something here. Hope everyone recognizes how badly *Fall in Love, Have Children, Stay Put, Save the Planet, Be Happy* is needed by the rest of the country now more than ever. I really like it! Basically, *love,* dummy!"

—**Myrna Perez Sheldon,** professor of Classics and World Religions, Women, Gender and Sexuality Studies, Ohio University; editor of *Cosmologics Magazine*

"Frank Schaeffer has been an important voice to me personally on so many topics, from religion to politics to how to bring up children. But Frank is also a deeply committed father and grandfather, and his insights on family connections are profound. Frank's book encourages us to push back against the ideals of our culture, to prioritize time and connection over 'success' and ego. In *Fall in Love, Have Children, Stay Put, Save the Planet, Be Happy*, Frank makes his compelling case through both research and deeply touching anecdotes from his life as a doting grandfather. This book is a deeply needed and timely exploration of what it means to be a good human."

—**Kristen Howerton,** marriage and family therapist, author of *Rage Against the Minivan*

"Reading Frank Schaeffer is a journey into a mind and heart shaped by powerful religious forces few of us can imagine. Liberated from a fundamentalist Christian past, Frank refuses to be angry and bitter. Instead, he uses his awesome gifts (as filmmaker, painter, poet, blogger, columnist, TV personality, and bestselling author) to confront and condemn the evil 'family values' he inherited and at the same time—as in this book—help us imagine a whole new set of real family values built on love that are absolutely necessary if we are to survive the next wave of fundamentalism sweeping our nation."

—**Mel White,** leader in the LGBTQ
community and author of *Stranger at the Gate:
To Be Gay and Christian in America*

"Frank Schaeffer is one of my favorite authors. He brings wisdom, wit, and warmth to whatever he writes. His new book goes to the heart of everything, really, inviting us to fall in love with what matters most. It's like a feast of sanity in these crazy times."

—**Brian D. McLaren,** speaker, activist,
and author of *Faith After Doubt*

"When the cerebral power and control structure of the nepotistic sidekick meets up with the heartfelt longing to nurture vulnerable living beings with openness, spontaneity, humor, and protectiveness, *Fall in Love, Have Children, Stay Put, Save the Planet, Be Happy* is inevitable. Who knew that a pandemic could so profoundly alter a human being's definition of success? Motherhood comes in many forms and bodies, and Frank Schaeffer's lived experience is that capitalism has ripped the mothering impulse from so many hearts and bodies, especially men. For the sake of our children, our planet, and the deepest humanity in all of us, it must be reclaimed, championed, and practiced. None of the directives in the book's title can be fully experienced unless we allow nurturing care to redefine our identity, our values, and our purpose for being alive on this Earth. As a feminist and a recovering evangelical, I am deeply indebted to you for writing this book."

—**Carolyn Baker,** author of *Confronting Cristofascism: Healing the Evangelical Wound* and *Sacred Demise: Walking the Spiritual Path of Industrial Civilization's Collapse*

# FRANK SCHAEFFER

Bestselling author of *Crazy for God*

FALL in Love

HAVE children

STAY PUT

SAVE the Planet

BE HAPPY

Health Communications, Inc.
Boca Raton, Florida

*www.hcibooks.com*

**Library of Congress Cataloging-in-Publication Data**
**is available through the Library of Congress**

© 2021 Frank Schaeffer

ISBN-13: 978-07573-2411-6 (Paperback)
ISBN-10: 07573-2411-8 (Paperback)
ISBN-13: 978-0-7573-2412-3 (ePub)
ISBN-10: 07573-2412-6 (ePub)

HCI, its logos, and marks are trademarks of Health Communications, Inc.

Publisher: Health Communications, Inc.
          1700 NW 2nd Avenue
          Boca Raton, FL 33432-1653

*Cover design by Larissa Hise Henoch*
*Interior design by Larissa Hise Henoch, formatting by Lawna Patterson Oldfield*

*This book is dedicated to my wife,
my three children, five grandchildren,
daughter-in-law, son-in-law, and
granddaughter-in-law: Genie, Jessica,
Francis, John, Amanda, Ben, Lucy,
Jack, Nora, Becky, Dani, and Claire.
They are the **only reason**
this book (or I) exist.*

# CONTENTS

# ACKNOWLEDGMENTS

Thank you to the friends and family who read and reread this book offering notes, critiques, and new information during a five-year process while I researched and wrote twenty-seven drafts.

Thank you:

David Higgins, supporter of progressive causes, who provided the grants that allowed me the time to research this book;

Jennifer Lyons, my agent and friend of twenty-plus years, for sticking with me;

Christine Belleris, my talented and kind editor at HCI, who provided so much support and asked all the right questions;

Lindsey Mach, my tireless publicist at HCI;

Christian Blonshine, vice president of HCI, who has been so supportive and personally involved in helping to turn this book into a reality;

Thank you, Larissa Henoch, for a brilliant book cover and interior design;

Mary Ellen Hettinger, HCI copyeditor, who went the extra mile by not only copyediting this book but asking useful and inspiring questions that helped me clarify what I am trying to say;

Anders Lindgren, musician and friend, who read the very first rough draft many years ago and encouraged me to keep going;

Paul Hawley, provider of fresh editorial eyes looking over many drafts;

Myrna Perez Sheldon, friend, scientist, and university professor, who read four drafts and inspired, edited, and added;

Claire Depit, my granddaughter-in-law and political science student, who read the book two times and gave me great suggestions;

Genie Schaeffer, my partner in everything for fifty-one years: wife, lover, first and last reader of all my books, wise counselor, and best friend;

John Schaeffer, my son (and co-author of another book with me), who read this book twice and offered notes and encouragement;

Alexandra Torres, scientist and friend, who offered encouragement and gave me permission to quote some of her personal correspondence at length;

Charlotte Gordon, a writer's writer, a pal for the better part of forty years, winner of many writing awards, and reader of an early draft, who encouraged me to stick with it;

Ernie Gregg, dear friend, graphic designer, confidant, manager, producer, and my collaborator and facilitator on so many online projects;

Kristin Breiseth "KB," artist, teacher, and friend, who read the book and offered vital suggestions;

Samir Selmanović, leadership and life coach and friend, who encouraged me to write this book and who lent me his kitchen table in NYC to write on during many visits;

Benedetta Friso Bellemo, artist and illustrator, who encouraged me by saying this book "is for me" early in my writing process;

Ilyse Hogue, scientist, writer, and friend, and progressive activist, who offered encouragement;

Johanna (José) Zeilstra, CEO, Gender Fair, a Public Benefit Corporation, board member, and former Wall Street executive specializing in helping companies improve on gender equity and diversity, added notes and gave encouragement;

Laura Dawn, filmmaker, founding cultural director of MoveOn.org, and founder, and CEO of ART NOT WAR. No one has been more interested in my work or more supportive or offered better suggestions;

Daron Murphy, friend and co-founder of ART NOT WAR, a writer, producer, director, musician, and creative director, whose friendship encouraged this book;

Rod Colburn, my friend who has intervened numerous times in my life in ways that helped make this book a reality;

Tiffany Kimmel, screenwriter, producer, animator, and director, who read the book and provided terrific notes;

Dave Krysko, of Disney Club Penguin fame, a culture-making man who also builds housing for people in need, has been kind to me and supportive of my work in creative and generous ways;

The Waring School in Beverly, Massachusetts, is an example of (and incubator for) many of the ideas expressed in this book about educational values. It is the high school I wish I'd been to, and the faculty and Tim Bakland (Head of School and Music Teacher) are the best "door-openers" to students I've encountered.

"I used to think I was the strangest person in the world but then I thought there are so many people in the world, there must be someone just like me who feels bizarre and flawed in the same ways I do. I would imagine her, and imagine that she must be out there thinking of me, too. Well, I hope that if you are out there and read this and know that, yes, it's true I'm here, and I'm just as strange as you."

**—Frida Kahlo**

"At the same time that a pandemic was underway, another global movement was unfolding, this one beautiful and life-giving and perhaps even offering an antidote to the other crises. It was a movement of courage and creativity in which masses of people discovered and lived into an interdependent relationship with the ecosystem and with humans locally and around the world. It believed in the vision of beloved community, it non-violently opposed supremacist narratives and aggressive individualism, and it acted for a more equitable, peaceful, beautiful society."

**—Gareth Higgins**
*(How Not to Be Afraid: Seven Ways to Live
When Everything Seems Terrifying)*

"Good writing, like good physics, should not be perfect, simplified, flawless, or devoid of humanity. It should be as complicated as it needs to be, and only when we allow it room to be unlike anything we've ever seen before can we possibly begin to understand a larger truth."

**—Tiffany Kimmel**
*(screenwriter, writer, movie producer, director, animator)*

# INTRODUCTION

What matters most? An exchange with my granddaughter Lucy, when she was four, helped me focus on my answer to that question. I was on a brief break at home during an especially hectic book tour of colleges. Lucy could see that I was exhausted and asked me plaintively, "But, Ba, *why* are you traveling *so much*?"

"To sell my latest book," I said. "I earn my living as a writer."

She thought about this for a few moments and then stated emphatically and with the candor only a child could muster, "You should write *less*!"

Lucy's question got me thinking about our evolutionary history and what—at the most profound emotional level—makes most of us tick. Her suggestion that I stay home more and write less was, ironically, the genesis of this book and doing lots more writing about . . . writing less. Go figure.

It seems to me that Lucy had already gotten one thing right: she intuitively knew that family connections are more important than career, let alone a quest for prestige—such as trying to be a successful author (whatever that is). When Lucy questioned why

I would willingly travel so much when I complained about our spending too much time apart, she was mirroring our species' deepest longing for meaningful, loving connection to others: the only real "how-to" for a happy life.

Eight years later, when Lucy was twelve, we experienced the coronavirus lockdowns together. She'd gotten her wish; I wasn't traveling at all. No one was.

I found my life stripped to the essentials. What I was doing full-time career-wise wasn't about career at all. It was about being a full-time father of three, grandfather of five, and husband of one. I found during the year-plus of stay-at-home sheltering that I was living in tune with the most basic evolutionary prime directive of all, which I'd been researching for this book for five years: *the survival of the friendliest.*

That's a fancy way to say that—as a sixty-eight-year-old White heterosexual "okay boomer" father and grandfather—I had discovered something surprising about myself: I'd rather be a mother.

I'm using the word *mother* (or *mothering*) as a verb describing the practice of providing nurturing, creative, joy-filled childcare as a shared, luminous gift given a child by any person of any gender. Whether they're a biological parent or grandparent, an adoptive parent, professional caregiver, uncle, aunt, or teacher, Black, White, or Brown isn't the point. And, of course, the practice and experience of mothering is open to all people of any age, no matter how they identify themselves.

That's to say, the pandemic intensified my "mothering" experience. I'd already been doing lots of childcare for the three youngest of my wife Genie's and my grandchildren—Lucy (twelve), Jack (ten), and Nora (seven)—since Lucy's birth back when she and her parents were living with us. Two years after that, Lucy and her family moved across the street, where they've been ever since. The pandemic intensified that experience. It also made something very clear: family was and is the center of my life. Careers fade. Priorities change. Our closest relationships are what last and define us. And our culture that has put business and career ahead of relationships has made a big mistake. Maybe that's because men have been in charge.

## We weren't the only people whose lives changed

As my daughter, Jessica, who is the CEO of a green-energy investment company in New York City, put it: "Businesses were established by men. They pretended they had no families. Families and women stayed home. When women joined the workforce, the deal was we pretended we didn't have a family either and played by men's rules. Then came Covid, and business meetings were on Zoom. Everyone was working from home. Family life was out in the open. Babies ran through online meetings. Toilets flushed in the background. I was meeting with the president of a bank on Zoom yesterday, and he whispered, 'I have to talk quietly or I'll wake the baby. She just went down for a nap.' Not only were families suddenly visible, people seemed to be getting used to the fact they didn't have to hide them and could even admit they had kids. Suddenly, the worlds of work and home had mixed. Everyone is rethinking their priorities and how they balance work and life, Dad."

Lawyer and activist Christie L. McEvoy-Derrico describes women who feel pressured to keep family life hidden in order to be taken seriously at work. In an email to me she wrote, "This issue was brought to my attention at a 'Women in Innovation' event held at the Rye, NY, art center several years ago. During a panel discussion featuring several prominent women leaders, the point was made that, as women, we need to 'stop lying about where you are.' I was interested to learn that other women also sometimes feel they need to lie when our location relates to family and children. Whether it's a doctor's appointment or maybe a school event, when I'm on a professional call I find myself not wanting to admit where I am. For instance, I say I'm at the office, not doing a school pickup. I wouldn't say that I've completely stopped doing this but these days, after Covid, I'm much more forthright about my actual life and priorities."

In his introduction to *The Power of Giving Away Power* by Matthew Barzun (a book I'll be quoting later), his publisher, the author Simon Sinek, explores some of the reasons we've ignored the human side of living for business only "ethics." Sinek writes:

> Our society has overindexed on rugged individualism. . . . We emulated the big personality leaders who presented an image of the "strong man," the genius in the room. As the "high-performing individual" became the standard, company structures transformed to feed the beast. They adapted their incentive and reward systems to recognize individual performance almost exclusively. Ethics, teamwork, and leadership qualities seemed to fall to the wayside when we evaluated people for promotion. Even our business schools became complicit. Over the years, they adapted their curricula to serve the market rather than teach leadership as it should be taught. However, if it's long-term results, stability, or innovation we're hoping to achieve, this model of leadership simply doesn't work.

**An important lesson about what matters most**

I've learned the hard way that a happy life is not about career success. It's about using the time we have to experience the simple things that bring us joy. But we all have a problem: our society is designed to deny this joy. We have another problem, at least I do: I've made such big mistakes they haunt me. Everything I do is mostly second best compared to my ideal.

That said, do you think it's fair that American capitalism forces most parents to choose between spending time building their careers or being with their preschool-age children? I don't. Worse: we have also become more materialistic—possibly because capitalism has coerced us into thinking we need more stuff.

This book is my plan for making life fairer—for everyone. It is a blueprint for happier lives through better family and romantic, sexual, and pair-bonded relationships, along with a legislative agenda to help make those possible. It is also a very personal account of how and why I serendipitously stumbled upon this evolutionary fact: *we evolved to feel happiest when caring for others, not when seeking power over them.* I wish I'd known and believed that decades ago.

**Human babies' brains got big**

As we shall see, we evolved to love first and strive second. That's because (as I'll go into in more detail in Chapter 2) as we evolved, human babies' brains got so big that they couldn't complete their growth in utero. Unlike most other mammals, we humans had to birth babies with huge heads and still survive. Human babies' skulls remained flexible in order not to kill their mothers, but that wasn't enough. So—*big fact here, please take note*—just about everything that most of us feel about connection, bonding, spirituality, fairness, empathy, art, and love comes down to this: human females started to give birth to *premature* babies.

If our babies had developed in the womb to the same point as, say, newborn monkeys, they would need to gestate for two and a half years. With their heads fully grown to accommodate our big human brains, they'd *kill* all their mothers at birth rather than just kill many of them. So human babies evolved to be born when their brains are less than 30 percent the size of an adult human brain. We continue our outsized brains' development outside the womb, with our brain doubling in size in our first year. Thus, we needed intensive parental care for years and years to grow our brains. This is (as we shall see) why we love.

## Who feeds the mother while she's feeding her big-brained baby?

Why do any of us crave balance in our lives between work and love? Because our species' babies needed at least two caregivers—in fact, an entire community—to survive. That community and the baby's parents, friends, and relatives had to stick together for the years and years it took to raise their big-brained baby to adulthood. And helping raise children meant males had to stick around, too. A new kind of male evolved (drum roll please): *the father*. And a new kind of living arrangement evolved (drum roll please): *communities*. And a new type of human activity evolved: *parenting*. And parenting wasn't limited to only biological parents. Indeed, "it takes a village."

Communities took responsibility for seeing that their children survived. In fact, as we'll see, evolution made this so by giving people who care for kids feelings of love. In fact, fathers evolved to secrete hormones that strengthen bonds with their newborn infants just as much as biological mothers do. As studies show (we'll look at these in some detail), *it's the closeness of relationship, not gender*, that triggers hormones that strengthen bonds. That means that anyone doing parenting can experience these bonds.

Brain networks that govern parental response to infants have been studied with imaging techniques over the last twenty years. The interaction of thoughts and behaviors required for good parenting enables the formation of each person's first social bonds and shapes development. This pattern is not only a "female thing." Gay men who give their child individual, loving parental attention form hormonal bonds similar to biological mothers. And primary-caregiving fathers exhibit high amygdala activation, the region of the brain that processes emotion, similar to mothers while interacting with their children; as we shall see, this has been demonstrated by several important studies.

## So this book is for . . . *everyone* because in one sense we can all be mothers, even if we're not parents

This book is for every parent fighting for more time with their children; every grandparent who cares about their grandchildren; anyone thinking about having children; gay, straight, and non-binary people trying to balance career and family; high school and college students trying to figure out relationship strategies; anyone in love who wants a "how-to" on how to stay in love; feminists looking for an unlikely male ally; and legislators looking for support and ideas related to crafting family-friendly legislation.

This book is also for some of us who regret our choices about family relationships, having kids "too early" or "too late," or not at all. Those choices are behind us. There's not a damn thing we can do to take them back and start over.

I have a pal who addresses the issue of regret well. In an email I asked my friend Chef, Leadership Coach, and Facilitator Samir Selmanović, "What about those of us who have missed the boat in terms of some aspect of our lives we wish had been different? Those who have fallen off the wagon? Cut down by injustice or blind fate?" Samir emailed back this:

> Mystics have been custodians of a superpower that every human being has: bridging the inner and outer world and learning to experience life that is larger than our own. This can happen in an instant. Suddenly our neighbor's kids become our own. I missed the artist caravan, but looking at your paintings I exclaim, "Look at us, artists!" Portals to our unlived lives are all around us. You did not have children? Let me tell you about my daughters. They are beautiful and powerful, and they are yours too. I have never had a chance to care for my parents in their old age. May I help you with yours? The moment I allow my heart to feel this void, to have this conversation, a miracle occurs. Past, present, and future collide. This crazy shit makes people lose their minds only to become sane for the first time. Of course we belong to each other! So, you have missed the boat, fell off the wagon, and were cut down? Where has your love gone? It has gone to those children playing while you were walking by, it has gone to causes your life has never given an opportunity to understand, it is going to the grass that will grow from your body soon enough. If you want to, before you go, you have an entire life span ahead of you. Take a mystic jailbreak. You are way more than just the "you," you think you are.

Maybe you are like me and are feeling regretful and (in my case) ashamed of some past actions. But guilt isn't a good place for change to come from. For instance, I can't go back and have kids at twenty-eight instead of doing what Genie and I did—getting pregnant as teens. Worse: I can't go back and be a better father. I was a kid myself and an angry misinformed one at that. I'd been groomed to be mean. And when I learned to do better, I'd fall back into old ways and was still a jerk more often than I ever want to admit to myself. I can blame others for what I was told. I can't blame them for doing things I'd woken up to as being wrong. Those are my fault. I know what shame feels like.

I was raised in an evangelical theological tradition (what's called Reformed Calvinism) that brought out all my worst bullying instincts and insecurities. Women were to be kept in their places! Children were to be punished! People not like me were "lost!" I slapped my daughter Jessica. I spanked my sons. I screamed at my wife. If I met that "me" now, I'd want to kill him. Correction: I would kill him. Correction: In fact that other me has sometimes haunted the present-day me with such guilt and depression that I've been tempted to kill myself.

**I'm only here because of the love of others**

My experience of redemption is in spite of horrible mistakes for which I feel shame. This book is in spite of those mistakes, too. That is one reason I want to share the redemptive feeling of being galvanized to make good (or at least better) choices going forward. I want to help my reader make their life happier—in spite of the fact that maybe you (like me) sometimes have a hard time forgiving yourself for the way you shaped your life, for past wrongs, and mistaken past priorities.

## What qualifies very flawed me to write a pro-love road map?

Perhaps with my mistakes comes some wisdom in hindsight. For instance, I've learned to be grateful for my failures (at least in theory). Looking back, I know that if I'd always gotten what I wanted, this would have resulted in unmitigated disaster for my family and for me. I might be a top evangelical political flake now. In fact, what I most bitterly regret these days are some of my successes. As I'll explain in a moment, some of these achievements damaged our country. They also damaged me. They hurt my children. They hurt my wife.

## Wrong from the start

I was raised in an American evangelical mission located in Switzerland called *L'Abri*. It was founded by my parents, Francis and Edith Schaeffer, in 1954, when I was two. It shaped and (almost) ruined my life.

I'm a survivor of polio and of an evangelical/fundamentalist childhood; an artist and author of fiction and literary nonfiction who overcame dyslexia to become a writer (ironic, given I couldn't spell); and a self-taught movie director of 1970s religious documentaries that were highly influential in the evangelical world and four 1980s low-budget Hollywood "slasher" action, comedy, and horror movies that were all pretty terrible. I'm also someone who was very lucky. I married Genie. (I'll describe how we met later in the book.) The lucky part wasn't Genie's and my unintended pregnancy, but that counterintuitively, fifty-one years later, we're happy, in love, and grateful for being parents and grandparents.

We've learned a few things. For instance, that you can't change another person, but if you love them, *you can slowly change yourself for them.* And if the person you commit to loves you back, they will reward you by making some changes, too. It's called growing together instead of apart. And this takes time and is hard to do. It also takes luck.

Why does Genie's and my marriage work? We're sometimes asked this question by people we meet who know we've been together fifty-one years and are (as they put it) "still happy." Here are a few reasons (other than Genie serendipitously kicking my ass as I'll describe later): We were lucky that we failed with our projects enough times to never become wealthy. Here's another reason: I happen to wake up at 3:00 AM to write each day. Genie wakes at about 6:00 AM. Most mornings when Genie wakes up, last night's dishes are done and the kitchen has been cleaned. Why? Did she give me some speech about shared housework? Never. But when I make my 5:00 AM third cup of coffee, I take a fifteen-minute break from my Big Fancy Self-Important (often delusional) Writing Career and clean the kitchen. Why? Because I love Genie! That's the only real reason to do anything in life: love of self is love of others. It's the only reason that Genie makes our beds and vacuums our house. It's why I do most of the cooking seven days a week and Genie stacks four cords of firewood every year for our wood-burning stove. This is not complicated. Genie is happier walking into a clean kitchen. I write better knowing that while I do my "important" work, the kitchen sparkles and Genie's day is starting with her feeling loved. I am happier because I don't have to do all the heavy lifting on our property because Genie stacks truckloads of wood when she's not busy in her clothing design and sewing studio. Result? We both feel cared for—because we are. Duh!

## The religious documentary series I directed featured my famous evangelical evangelist father, Francis Schaeffer: the movies were destructive

In my early to midtwenties, I collaborated with my father and produced and directed two documentary movie series—*How Should We Then Live?* and *Whatever Happened to the Human Race?* Taken together, these series (and their book companions) provided the toxic ideological incentive for millions of Christians in the evangelical subculture to turn into a xenophobic aggrieved and perpetually angry mob. In other words, we set out to make them into people as immoral as us. That is to say, our series pushed evangelicals into the antichoice, misogyny-enforcing cult known as the "pro-life" movement. Forty-plus years later, this cult helped elect Donald Trump.

Back in the 1970s, after my father wrote the books our documentaries were based on (he did this together with C. Everett Koop, who later became the Surgeon General under Ronald Reagan), we three (Koop, Dad, and I) toured the USA and launched the movies in twenty cities. We spoke to tens of thousands of evangelicals. Millions more watched our movies in churches, Christian schools, colleges, and homes.

We claimed we were standing up for what we called "family values." These were cynical, fake family values. *What we were really selling was misogyny, pure and simple.*

Some forty years later, our followers and/or the people they'd influenced could be found either among those who stormed the Capitol on January 6, 2021, or else supporting and enabling the insurrectionist rioters while believing Trump's Big Lie—that he'd won reelection and that victory was stolen from him through an intricate network of liberal conspiracy, fraud, and corruption.

My only excuse is that back in the 1970s and early 1980s I was young, poisonously indoctrinated, and greedy, too. But by the late 1980s the ugliness and stupidity of what I had been born into—the religious right—started to sink in. By my early thirties, I'd fled the evangelical movement. I wanted to save my children and marriage from the monster my leadership in that movement encouraged me to be.

## I'd changed "sides" in our so-called culture wars

It was after I'd fled the evangelical world and the big bucks of the Big-Time God business that I found myself scraping out a living while directing four crappy feature films over a ten-year period. I got those inglorious Hollywood jobs by cutting out all the God bits from my religious documentary work and presenting a show reel to agencies. I found an agent, scripts were sent to me to read, and I got jobs. I never "made it," rather, I made it just far enough in Hollywood to be the director of second-rate B movies. It was a living (as they say) and better than selling my soul back to the devil: in other words, returning to the well-paid God Business.

Then (at Genie's urging) I wrote a novel. It was modestly successful. Then I wrote more novels. These works of humor (*The Calvin Becker Trilogy*) questioned the false certainties I'd been raised on. *Portofino*, *Saving Grandma*, and *Zermatt* were critically and commercially fruitful enough to get me branded by my former evangelical allies as a persona non grata, a hated critic of and outright enemy of the evangelical right. The novels also gave me permission to keep writing for the next thirty-plus years.

I'm still writing, and these days, you'll sometimes find me on TV, radio, Facebook, Twitter, and Instagram, or hear me on other people's podcasts ranting about the nefarious relationship of the

White American evangelical subculture to American politics. My ranting is informed by an insider's knowledge of the conspiracy-addled, hypocrisy-riddled subculture I fled.

I am very, very sorry that my greed and ambition, anger, and stupidity kept me in the blighted evangelical movement a few more years, even after I began to know better. This book is another step in my forty-year project of trying to make amends.

Please forgive me.

## Real family values are science based, not a bludgeon with which to bully women and children into subservience

It took me a long time to get over the fact that I'd been mutilated by evangelical religion. I'm still trying to get the ringing out of my ears. Bluntly: to be a man in the religious Right is to be, become, or remain an asshole by divine right.

A theology of male domination is all the evangelical movement is at its heart. Genie would not put up with this shit, and (very luckily) I loved her enough to try to change. That process continued through working at being a better father than the disciplinarian thug evangelicals trained men to be.

Through all the twists and turns and horrible mistakes I regret, I've found that—my changing beliefs, careers, and politics aside—I'm the fortunate man who is still married to Genie. She remains my point of orientation, my link, my reference, the only continuity I have while trying to make sense of a chaotic life. I'm also the lucky father of Jessica, Francis, and John and the fortunate grandfather of Jessica's grown children, Amanda and Ben, and these days, I'm also John's kids'—my three youngest grandchildren's—happy nanny. You will get to know Lucy, Jack, and Nora in these pages. Suffice to note here that they are the light of my daily life as I do childcare for them.

## Parenthood in modernity has become a choice

Parenthood has been a healing experience for me, especially as it has extended to hands-on grandparenthood. But given the way that parenthood is threatened by career-oriented capitalism, it is a fraught subject these days. So as a choice, I think parenthood "means we have to be more intentional about our motivations, reasons, needs, wants, and fears," as my friend, writer, and movie producer Tiffany Kimmel wrote to me after she kindly provided notes on this book. Her view is that, "If I choose to be a parent, I must acknowledge that the child I bring into the world or adopt from it may not bring me joy, nor is it their responsibility to bring me joy."

Procreativity is not just for parents. "Having children" is not merely to be taken literally. Every life is called to be generative toward others, to make something with their lives. We must honor the procreativity in us all: both those of us who have wanted but not been able to have literal children and those who have chosen not to. As we'll see in this book, the role of parenting is open to us all.

It seems to me that Tiffany is correct: parenthood can be a difficult path that may bring anguish because a human child some parent just brought into this world is not something that parent can or should control. Children are not clones. Nor are children containers to fill up with our unfulfilled wishes and desires. They are separate beings. That said, caring for children saved me. Loving Genie (as you may get tired of hearing me repeat in this book) did, too. So I'm biased in favor of pair-bonding.

I got married young. I am monogamous. I've had passionate crushes on some wonderful women I've met or worked with over the years and (assuming any of them would have had sex with me,

which is doubtful) only stayed faithful to Genie for these reasons:
I love Genie more than I wanted to have sex with other women;
I was raised by "you'll burn in hell" evangelicals who (to put it
mildly) enforced a knee-jerk instinct to not fuck around, and Genie
was, is, and remains the sexiest, most beautiful, and most fulfilling woman I ever met. Also—Genie has explained to me very
carefully and in rich, vivid, well-expressed, colorful expletive-
laden, somewhat personalized, and even surgically precise detail:
she'll kill me (and/or deftly remove several body parts) if I do
fuck around.

That said, the family is my thing. But this thing isn't easy.
And parenthood seems very screwed up these days. There are
plenty of articles about "helicopter parents" and now, the "bull-
dozer parent," who clears all obstacles out of the way for their
children to become fearful, entitled, and incompetent adults who
can't fend for themselves. This is especially the fate of those unfor-
tunate enough to be the children of the wealthy and/or famous.
The children of the upper classes and their future success become
all-consuming to many parents. This is not about children's
well-being but about some upscale parents' fear of missing out
and looking to their children to validate them. I know this. I've
made all these same mistakes and more.

**The healing and enlightening experience of being a
grandfather has helped undo some of my worst mistakes**

All the drawbacks of parenting notwithstanding, as a result
of caring for my youngest grandchildren as their full-time nanny
for the last twelve years, I'll be doing my best to be arguing for
authentic family values rather than the fake family values that
Dad and I once pitched. I'll be trying to share what I've learned

the hard way as a parent, too. I'll also be sharing notes written to my granddaughter Lucy for a reason.

These notes are about our life together, a personal childcare diary of sorts, written while caring for her from her birth forward. I'll be sharing these to provide the personal context in which the social, political, and scientific studies I explore here make sense to me because becoming my grandchildren's nanny has been the most rewarding experience of my life.

## So . . . this book is my love letter to anyone who loves loving and being loved

Don't look for footnotes. I'm not an academic. In fact, I have an inferiority complex about that. When I was invited to speak at Harvard's Kennedy School of Government about the military family experience in wartime—this was back when my son John was in the Marine Corps and we'd just written a bestselling book together (*Keeping Faith: A Father-Son Story About Love and the United States Marine Corps*)—he joked, "Dad, see if they'll give you an honorary high school diploma." The joke became a recurring family meme trotted out each time I headed off on yet another college speaking tour.

So while I consider myself a lifelong learner, a scholar I am not. I ran away from a private British boys' boarding high school (what the Brits call a "public school") and then dropped out of every other place I studied. I never completed my art school training or even my "A-Level" tutorials in English literature. My mother's experiments in homeschooling were failures. That's why I finally got sent to boarding schools. I could hardly read at age nine.

Before boarding school I knew the Bible. That was about it. I could not read it very well, but Mom read me many chapters every night. And I know that I'm not the only homeschooled person trying to get the ringing out of my ears from childhood overexposure to the bizarre collection of Bronze-Age-to-Roman-Era short stories my family called "The Scriptures." I know this because I've received thousands of emails and notes in response to my writing about the impact of religion—even when that impact has been thinly disguised as fiction in my novels—from people who were also raised by parents with a zealous sense of mission and who, like me, once believed that every single word of the Bible is true.

**My weird religious upbringing still influences me and thus my views expressed in this book**

As Christine Belleris put it (she's my very kind and very smart editor at HCI books): "You allude to your harsh evangelical upbringing, but that left me with more questions than answers. Just a little more info about your parents' mission of *L'Abri* would be helpful. It shaped you, it shapes the narrative and your message. What exactly happened to give you PTSD and put you in such a foul mood at Christmas?"

My Christmas story comes later, but for now I'll take a moment to briefly offer some background information I've previously covered in more detail in my memoir, *Crazy for God—How I Grew Up as One of the Elect, Helped Found the Religious Right, and Lived to Take All (or Almost All) of It Back.*

**L'Abri**

Before I was born, my family moved from the US to Switzerland as missionaries, Dad never learned to speak any other language besides English, notwithstanding his forty-year sojourn in Europe. So my parents mostly ministered to American, British, and other English-speaking visitors. Then in 1954—after yet several *splits* with the home mission board—Mom and Dad were led (another way of saying they had to figure something out when they were kicked out of their mission over a theological dispute) to start their own ministry. *L'Abri* (The Shelter) came into being.

My parents theoretically acknowledged that there were other real believers, but (many church splits later) there seemed to be no one besides our family that they wholeheartedly approved of. We were *different* and (at least in the early fundamentalist incarnation of our beliefs) sometimes smug in the rightness of our difference. Since our family and my parents' ministry represented the only truly theologically sound configuration of believers this side of Heaven, my sisters stuck around L'Abri even after marriage. Nepotism was our thing. My three sisters encouraged their husbands—who had wandered into L'Abri as young men, got "saved," and married a Schaeffer daughter—to join "The Work." Like my sisters, I was meant to "feel God leading" me to spend my life in our clan—maybe even lead it someday.

### Dad

Dad—the mere moon to Mom's sun, the short, somewhat dour-looking James Cagney–type only child of working-class parents with a hardscrabble life story of modest success extruded from an unlikely beginning—was a man who was "led by God" to become a pastor. But Dad's natural interests tended to art history, when he was not indulging his taste for full-contact "true believers versus liberals" theological blood sports. In the end these blood sports made him one of the most effective founders of the White (angry) religious right. Dad was also a solitary person, thrust—by both his and Mom's zeal for God—into a people-oriented ministry where he was swarmed day and night by strangers.

## Mom

Mom—Edith Schaeffer—was also in the wrong profession. She should have been a dancer with a Broadway career. This isn't a guess but reflects something she's often told me. My mother had wanted to be a dancer until her missionary parents put a stop to all such worldly notions. The strange thing was that Mom told me this several times *with a sigh while at the very same time passing on the exact same guilt-inducing indoctrination to me that she'd been programmed with by her missionary parents in a sort of unstoppable generational curse.*

## As for me, I was outnumbered from the start

I was an American expatriate missionary kid wearing a post-polio leg brace (like some sort of ball and chain designed to invite curious or mocking stares) being raised in foreigner-hating Switzerland, an Evangelical fundamentalist in a world filled with (what we called) "The Lost," *and* I had three older sisters who were much "closer to the Lord" than me. Mainly what I did was *not* go to school but "sacrifice for the Lord" along with my parents. We had no car. I had no real schooling (until age ten, when I was sent away), and these sacrifices were a sign of God's blessing. What we *didn't* have or *didn't* do loomed large and proved (to us anyway) that we were following God's Plan for our lives. We were not being "seduced by the world."

## Discipline had to be maintained

Both of my parents were spankers. They used belts, wooden spoons, hairbrushes, and hands. Dad sometimes hit Mom, too.

Mom's feeble spankings were a family joke, whereas Dad's (mercifully infrequent) whippings raised welts. My older sister Susan was beaten more than the rest of us (mostly before my time) and even put in a sort of straightjacket Mom concocted out of a sheet in which toddler Susan would be tightly wound until she was cocooned head to toe and then left on a bed—in the dark—for hours, to calm down—in other words, cry herself to sleep.

Our spankings—a nice catchall term to cover what were actually mostly passionless, "this-hurts-me-more-than-it-hurts-you" beatings by Dad—were done in the open and accepted by all of us as normal, as such "discipline" was also accepted as normal by many people during the 1950s. There was no shame in a "firm hand," as my parents' version of child-rearing was called. Mom and Dad often even used to tell "amusing" stories about how they had punished Susan (who was far and away our family's most "difficult child," or so Mom always claimed) for misbehaving in church as a little girl of five, when Dad was still a pastor in the States. When Mom failed to stop Susan from talking during his sermons, Dad would stop preaching, march into the congregation, pick up Susan, and head to the church basement, where he'd thrash her with a wooden spoon and then return to the pulpit. Mom said how pleased the congregation was to have such a "fine disciplinarian," a "real man of God" leading them as their pastor, and she talked about the churchgoers' amusement at the "cute" sound of Susan's wailing during these little demonstrations of male authority.

**To this day, hiding behind notions of religious liberty, an entire evangelical subculture in America is still awash in church-sanctioned brutality and neglect**

A lot of brutality is out of sight in the so-called homeschool movement. Across the country, children suffer violent punishments in the name of God. So do many wives. These aren't the exception in the evangelical "family values" far right but the norm.

There is an entire evangelical publishing industry pushing how-to books on disciplining children including detailed instructions on what to use for beating a child and for how long. There is an even bigger movement endorsing wives "submitting" to their husbands and approving all women (married or not) being led by men as "God's plan."

The parents beating their children have powerful friends on the present-day Supreme Court and in Congress, who themselves are, or have been, religious fanatics or are at least attuned to the fundamentalist fanatics' demands—and what they need to do to keep getting their votes. So right-wing legislators and judges are ready to do battle on behalf of the spankers, hitters, beaters, homeschool women-dominating tyrants "sheltering" their children "from the world," (and from science, among other things) while demanding the right to educate children their way. All this is done in the name of religious liberty. And these same people also claim religious liberty as an excuse for discriminating against the LGBTQ community. They claim the religious liberty rights of "conscience" to deprive their employees of health insurance coverage for contraceptives, too. And the list of religious liberty rights exempting religious Americans from an obligation to simple decency and the shared duties and values of being law-abiding citizens is getting longer.

The religious liberty lobby even got the Supreme Court (dominated by right-wing extremists) to allow them to disregard health regulations that asked them to forgo church services to stop the spread of Covid. In other words, religious liberty not only trumps science and women's health but also the health of all Americans. Enabled by the Supreme Court, churches used their "religious believer's rights" to become super-spreader centers of disease. And sadly, my dad's books were a big factor in launching the present-day wave of right-wing activism that seeks to turn America into what would amount to a Christian theocracy.

**Life was not all spankings, however**

Most of the time our family thrived on a somewhat hysterical diet of "miracles" that provided a constant high. In the 1950s, when my parents' L'Abri Fellowship ministry was just being established, Mom and Dad never asked donors for money, and yet—*miraculously*—the Lord "moved people's hearts" and we were sent gifts to "meet our needs." So we *knew* that (cue Charlton Heston's booming voice) From Before The Creation Of The Universe God had planned that in 1954 the Schaeffer family would found the American mission of L'Abri, located in Huémoz, Switzerland, conveniently near the ski slopes of Villars and the tearooms of Montreux (*and* only eight hours by train from Portofino, Italy), with stunning views of the towering mountains in every direction, which He'd *created expressly* for our pleasure.

Mom said that our job, and thus the *reason* for both L'Abri's and our existence, was to "*prove* the existence of God to an unbelieving world." We Schaeffers did this by praying for the gifts needed to run our faith mission. God provided the exhilarating life-affirming "proof" of His being out there somewhere by answering our prayers and sending us just enough money—*no more and no less*—so that His Work might go forth and so that I'd grow up eating cheese and various other ingredient-stretching casseroles to sustain my life *while* praying for meat!

**Then, the Lord answered my prayers for more protein and fewer casseroles!**

I got more protein, and the Lord also changed the course of American history. You see, in the late 1960s Dad published the first of many bestselling evangelical books. My parents both became famous evangelical authors and leaders. By the early 1970s my parents were unexpectedly awash in book royalties and speaking invitations. We ate better.

When they toured evangelical colleges and churches all over North America, I often accompanied them. I was along for the ride as Mom and Dad were being elevated to Evangelical Protestant sainthood, what the *New York Times* later referred to as "evangelical royalty," in an article about me leaving the movement. I was also absorbing all I needed to know to soon become a nepotistic, carbon-copy striver.

Our status meant that when a few years later Dad took a "stand" on the issue of abortion, a powerful evangelical-dominated movement inspired by his leadership was formed. The evangelical-led "pro-life" crusade was born.

**Ilyse Hogue**

As biologist and political activist Ilyse Hogue illustrates in her book *The Lie That Binds*, far more was involved in the formation of the antichoice cause than the Schaeffer family. Hogue describes how powerful right-wing figures such as Richard Viguerie, pioneer of targeting political direct mail and a political conservative writer, were waiting in the wings to manipulate those of us who were (at first anyway) sincere—if horribly mistaken—about becoming antichoice crusaders.

Nevertheless, sincere or not, what we Schaeffers provided to the far right was the missing link to the domination of the Republican Party. We helped enable the takeover of the Republican Party because we brought along millions of evangelical voters (Dad's and Mom's fans) to the GOP that we helped others goad into an activist and radicalized voting bloc.

"Our" voters were motivated and united by the cry, "Take America back for God!" and Dad's and many other leaders' bogus claims that America had a "Christian foundation." Dad said we had to "return to this foundation or perish." That this foundation was a *White*, slave-holding racist and murderous, woman-trashing, gay-persecuting quagmire didn't get mentioned much. Christians' belief that the Earth was created for human exploitation (and it turned out for utter destruction) and that this was "ordained by God" was also implicit in our pitch.

## My father is still a hero to many religious right leaders

Dave Andrusko (former editor of the *National Right to Life News*) writes in his review of two books on the history of the antiabortion movement that the antichoice movement "attracted people by building on the foundation established by theologian Francis Schaeffer." He continues, "It is difficult to exaggerate the importance of [Schaeffer's] book *Whatever Happened to the Human Race?* and [the 1970s] twenty-city film and lecture tour [undertaken] to awaken the evangelical community." And this quote by Joel Belz, founder of the evangelical magazine *World*, pretty much sums up the Evangelical establishment's view of my father: "Go to any evangelical Christian gathering and ask twenty people the simple question: 'What single person has most affected your thinking and your worldview?' If Francis Schaeffer doesn't lead the list of answers, and probably by a significant margin, I'd ask for a recount."

## My inglorious White entitled legacy

Even after my flight from (and repentance of) my involvement in far-right politics, my inglorious privileged White male legacy still shapes what I have experienced and what I have *not* experienced—i.e., what Black men undergo in our country's criminal justice system daily, up to and including routinely being harassed and even murdered by White police officers. Nor do I suffer what members of the LGBTQ and nonbinary communities undergo in the bigotry and violence they encounter. Nor do I face what all women are confronted by in the context of navigating our culture's everyday sexism—not to mention the challenging and sometimes life-threatening experiences of pregnancy, childbirth, and motherhood.

## My hero Nicole Lynn Lewis

When I compare my journey to that of many other people who faced struggles and young parenthood in less privileged circumstances, I feel ashamed to even describe my life as a struggle. For instance, a hero of mine is Nicole Lynn Lewis. Lewis serves as the chief executive officer of Generation Hope, an organization she founded in 2010. She is author of the memoir *Pregnant Girl: A Story of Teen Motherhood, College, and Creating a Better Future for Young Families.*

Generation Hope's mission is to surround teen parents and their children with the mentors, emotional support, and financial resources that they need to thrive in college. This supportive compassionate vision is the result of Lewis's own struggle as a young parent, which she describes so movingly in *Pregnant Girl*.

Lewis calls for better support of young families so they can thrive. She reflects on her experiences as a Black mother who got pregnant at age seventeen and found herself as a college student fighting for opportunities for herself and her child in a system that had little-to-no room or sympathy for people like her.

The lack of humane priorities in our lives, be that in college or at work, involves us all. Many other voices besides Lewis' are being raised questioning our assumptions. As we deal with the aftermath of the 2020–21 Covid pandemic, those voices are speaking with new urgency. For instance, in "We're Finally Starting to Revolt Against the Cult of Ambition" (*New York Times,* June 6, 2021), Kelli María Korducki, author of *Hard to Do: The Surprising, Feminist History of Breaking Up*, writes

> In a society that prizes individual achievement above most other things, ambition is often framed as an unambiguous virtue, akin to hard work or tenacity. But the pursuit of power and influence is, to some extent, a vote of confidence in the profit-driven myth of meritocracy that has betrayed millions of American women through the course of the pandemic and before it, to our disillusionment and despair. It is a cruel irony that ambition is what's often sold to women as an inextricable ingredient in our eventual liberation. From the career-branded Barbie dolls of my 1990s girlhood to the "lean in" ethos of Facebook executive Sheryl Sandberg to the so-called "girlboss" era of the last decade, an ethos of careerism has been intrinsic to the mainstream cultural conception of women's "empowerment." The . . . best thing . . . is to refuse to

capitulate to employers' demands at the expense of one's personal well-being. Saying "no" is not a mark of belligerence, but a requirement for surviving modern life.

## I'm hopeful love can win

While my unearned privilege combined with post-evangelical PTSD still shapes (deforms?) my thinking, I hope this book connects with you even if you have experienced a life very different from mine. I dare to hope this because of what I believe transcends everyone's differences: the vulnerability we all experience when held hostage by love.

As you will read in the chapters to follow, I believe that evolution is on the side of love. So I am hopeful love can win. I'm hopeful because my own lifetime experiences prove that even damaged goods like me can be at least partially healed and changed. I'm hopeful love can win because a series of national racial crises exposed our failings, and people who had previously stood on the sidelines stepped up to fight for fairness. I'm hopeful love can win because the desire for change in 2020 and in 2021 had a power that was made manifest as crowds flooded through American cities and small towns to protest the murder of George Floyd. I'm hopeful love can win because after the storming of the Capitol by a mob of White supremacists, Christian nationalists, militia members, and Trump cult fanatic evangelicals, even a few Republican leaders stepped up at great personal risk to condemn the riot. I'm hopeful love can win because public policy experts and economists have pointed out in the last several years the folly of excluding domestic work from economic metrics such as the GDP, given the data showing that unpaid women's work constitutes a huge slice of economic activity in every country. I'm hopeful love can win because Black marchers have noticed a change: many more White Americans are showing up for the cause of racial justice. Similarly, many men have woken up to the discrimination and harassment women face and have become feminists, demanding justice for all. And (as we shall see) many men are also figuring out that they have benefited from feminism. I'm hopeful love can win because American life has been dramatically upended by Covid, and when things are turned upside down, sometimes people change. I'm hopeful love can win because in its first one hundred days the Biden Administration initiated sweeping legislation designed to help families and children (on a scale never seen before in American history) and made family life a priority. I'm hopeful love can win because people like Nicole Lynn Lewis have stepped forward to lead. In *Pregnant Girl* Lewis notes that "Our results will disprove the pervasive myth that teen parents aren't capable of becoming college graduates. While half of parenting students across the country leave school without a degree, 90 percent of Generation Hope Scholars stay in college from year to year and 70 percent maintain a GPA of 2.5 or higher each semester, with some earning perfect 4.0s."

## But hopeful or not—we still have a problem: work/life imbalance

Hopeful trends notwithstanding, we have a problem. It can be summed up like this: our work lives are out of balance with living life itself because our society is anti-woman, anti-child, and anti-family. It is so anti-family that people like Nicole Lynn Lewis have had to step up to try to help young parents when the entire country should have already been helping.

The only winners have been corporations' shareholders and billionaires. Period. So the rest of this book is about why and how we can change this reality and claw our lives back from our wealthy masters. It is a how-to on giving love the best chance to win and defeat greed. It is a how-to on forging good personal and romantic relationships that can last, and raising happy fulfilled children, *in spite of* what we face in our love-*less* and brutalized consumerist culture.

## America redesigned on the basis of love

Let's fast-forward to some conclusions you might expect to find as a recap near the end of a book. I'm putting this list here because I want to lay my cards on the table up front regarding the social, political, spiritual, and lifestyle changes I hope this book will help bring about. And I'll do my best to back up the reasons for this list's demands in the rest of the book.

In the changed and better America, I hope you'll join me in fighting for the following:

- There would be no barriers to our careers when we leave work, care for our children, and then return to work.
- Care for preschool-age children would be top-notch, child-centered, free, and rooted in the hands-on experiences of nature, creative play, conversational skills, social skills, and making art and music—no matter the parent's zip code or skin color or gender or sexual orientation.
- Teen and other young parents (single or pair-bonded) would get total support to continue their educations and lives and suffer no downside for being parents while also completing school.

- Healthcare would be free and available to all.
- We'd lead the world with the highest minimum wage, constantly adjusted for inflation; in other words, we'd have no more working poor parents struggling to just survive.
- Our Social Security system would recognize support for parenting as the number-one national priority so parents who stayed home to care for small children would receive full benefits in retirement for those years, even if they had no job outside the home and so didn't pay into the system with payroll deductions.
- Gay, nonbinary, transgender—all forms of parenthood would be encouraged and supported.
- Relationship success rather than career success would be regarded as the highest human achievement.
- Parents in all professions would have socially desirable options regarding who goes to work and who stays home with young children, trading roles until their kids were in school.
- Bringing preschool children to work would be an everyday thing because many workplace nurseries would be the norm.
- The flexibility to work from home would be an option for many more people.
- Comfortable, safe places to pump breast milk—lactation rooms—would be as commonplace as restrooms in all buildings.
- Sex education would begin in kindergarten, prioritize relationship training, civility, and consent.

- In other words, we would adjust our society, education, family life, and political and economic lives to comply with the most basic evolutionary prime directive of all: *the survival of the friendliest.*

## How can those who are childless by choice or happenstance find family connection?

Is my argument for giving families real choices and supporting them an implicit put-down of people who've made different choices than to have children? *No.* Childlessness is fine. My son Francis (turning fifty as I write this) has had no children by choice, is a lifelong teacher, a person with a vocation wherein many hundreds of students he's taught with single-minded dedication have been incalculably enriched. "Francis's kids" do everything from winning computer-coding/robotic international competitions to finding that my—"Feed them first, then they can learn"—son will cook lunch for them when they need extra math tutoring.

A no-children version of caregiving—say, a vocation like teaching or animal rescue or scientific research, running for office, serving in the government, making art, or doing service to others in other ways—is an equally generous, loving form of engagement, also offering a community- and care-based life of joy. And it seems to me that (for instance) a ballet dancer who chooses not to have children because her body is her well-honed, perpetually trained instrument is not missing out but simply finding other good ways to declare the intrinsic worth of beauty, life, and love.

## Moreover, for some people their personal history mitigates against making having a child a choice

As my friend, writer, and movie producer Tiffany Kimmel

wrote to me in the notes she generously provided for this book, "A lot of people—self-included—want to make sure they are healed enough from past trauma to be present and good and stable for their offspring because they don't want to repeat the past. Or they need additional support. And I think the more we know, the slower we become [in making the choice to have a child]. We have to have two minds. The one that acknowledges the limits to what we can know in advance . . . and the other mind that says, 'I will rise to this challenge.'"

Tiffany makes an important point. Coming from a family with attachment or other disorders adds a special kind of complexity to the dynamic of having or not having children. Add in economic insecurity or chronic pain issues, and you've got a unique cocktail that makes choosing to start a family seem almost or actually impossible. Then there's intergenerational trauma and birth horror stories that may play an enormous part in someone's journey and their very reasonable fears. That said, in this book I'll be making the point that it is a pity so many of the people who *do* want children and who have worked through some of their qualms are nevertheless forced to wait so long to have children—even when they want them. I also think that we need to acknowledge that some people don't want to have children for good reasons and that is a valid choice during a time of climate emergency and overpopulation. (We'll look at this more and why I still think, nevertheless, that families do more good than harm.) The point being many people have good reasons to avoid starting a family, or even pair-bonding.

**I think the key is this**

Having children is more about love than any kind of "traditional" pair-bonding. If you can have a successful pair-bond, great. But if you take another path such as single motherhood, that's fine, too. However, maybe we all need a society and culture that helps us raise our kids *and* gives us time and support and real choices. The problem is, we need a ton of structural change before that is ever going to happen.

We need to form a better way of doing family that gives women (especially) *real choices*. Right now, we give women and parents few if any tangible choices. For example, we say to single women: Have an abortion or have the kid that you cannot afford and bankrupt and ruin your life. What kind of choice is that?

In short, we need more empathy for those making hard choices. And we need to fight for cultural, legal, and financial and tax law changes that offer parents real choices.

## My arguments in favor of having meaningful choices about family are not a put-down of choosing parenthood "late" or no parenthood at all

Genie and I paid a steep price for having our children crazily young. Sure fertility wasn't an issue, but being a very young parent is just as much a misadventure as waiting so long fertility does become an issue. A very young parent's children suffer from their parent's youth. Older first-time parents sometimes bring more wisdom, kindness, and experience to parenthood than Genie and I did as teens. So if you have a child when you're older, good for you. But here's the point: we're in a country that, judging by our social policy and the lack of a safety net, hates kids no matter when you have them. We need to change that.

## To change America into a pro-family culture we should emulate the total acceptance modeled in the LGBTQ and nonbinary communities

How to turn America into a pro-family, pro-love, and pro-relationships country that also has room for other people who do not have or want kids? I think that we have a good practical model for the revolution I'm calling for here, dedicated to embracing love above career, connection ahead of money, and community before greed: the total acceptance, other-oriented sexuality, and deep love modeled in the LGBTQ and nonbinary communities. LGBTQ members made the right to be defined by what we humans most essentially are—love addicts—into a powerful political, social, and moral movement about decency, freedom, and justice. Now it's past time for all of us to expand on the LGBTQ community's fight for an open, inclusive, and more humane culture. *Who* each of us is rather than *what* we *do* for a living is the only thing that really matters.

# CHAPTER 1

# Motherhood Is Going to Suck

**My granddaughter comforts me as Mom dies
and the circle of life spins on**

    Lucy, the day we were talking to my mother, she was dying. You were four. Mom was ninety-eight and staring earnestly into the laptop screen her nurse had set up so we could talk via Skype. On that February afternoon in 2013, my mother was three thousand miles away in Switzerland. She died a few days after this conversation. Lucy, you and I were sitting in my home in Massachusetts surrounded by piles of manuscripts, including a four-foot stack of twenty-three drafts of a new book I was working on. My paintings were stacked in deep piles, leaning against the walls and taking up the remaining space on every surface. The ubiquitous smell of turpentine and linseed oil was in the air. Mom had always loved that smell. When I was a kid, she'd walk into my room, breathe deeply, and say, "I just *love* the smell of painting!" You innocently whispered, "Does she have her perfume on?"

    "Your great-grandmother always wears perfume. So I bet she does," I answered.

Mom was beautiful, with her silver hair in a ponytail and wearing a red headband with matching shawl. But appearances can be deceiving. Trapped in a body she'd lost control of, it took all of her formidable willpower to acknowledge our love. She had a feeding tube in her nose and was slipping in and out of consciousness. Five minutes after we hung up, she wouldn't remember the conversation.

I kept reminding Mom of who we were, speaking rather slowly and loudly: "This is your son, Frank, and I have my granddaughter, Lucy, on my lap. Can you see her, Mom? This is John's daughter. John was our Marine. Remember praying for his safe return from Afghanistan? God answered your prayers, Mom. Say hi to your great-granddaughter, Mom."

When I asked if she knew we loved her, Mom acknowledged us with a slight nod and whispered, "Yes."

Through our glass doors on that dreary afternoon, the Merrimack River and Bay reflected the dark gray of the lowering clouds and was littered with car-sized slabs of ice that made tinkling sounds like breaking glass as they crashed into one another on the outgoing tide. The lock screen on my computer was a photo of Mom in her wood-paneled bedroom. For the last ten years, she'd been living here across the street from my sister's chalet. The room was decorated with dozens of paintings I'd made for my parents when I was in my early twenties. This was before I'd been stupid enough to quit painting in order to do what seemed like more important things, such as working as the sidekick to my evangelist father.

While looking at my mother and my artworks behind her, I felt as if I was watching outtakes from a movie about an alternative life. It was unsettling and made me wonder what I could have done if I'd stuck with art. On the other hand, Lucy, if anything had gone differently, I wouldn't have been sitting with you. And since you and my four* other grandchildren are the best part of my life, I'd have welcomed ten times as many mistakes and missteps, sins and regrets to stay on the path that brought us together that day.

Your great-grandmother died on the Saturday before Easter, March 30, 2013. The last time I saw her face as I peered into my laptop screen, my niece Hannah was with her body. A few months before, I'd flown to Switzerland to "be with Mom when she dies," as I told Genie. Then she didn't die. I flew home. Then she did die. I asked Hannah to stroke Mom's hair for me. I asked her to kiss Mom for me.

Hannah was hugely pregnant and would give birth two weeks later to her third child and yet another of Mom's many great-grandchildren. Mom looked much the same as when I'd talked to her the day before with you, Lucy, only then I could see her chest moving ever so slightly as she breathed. Now Mom was completely still. She lay curled up like a sleeping child in her bed, moments after death, looking more like herself now that the tube in her nose was gone. She was still clutching the teddy bear she had held in her gnarled hands to keep her arthritic fingers more comfortable. Hannah said, "We love you, Noni," while gently stroking Mom's hair and using the name all Mom's grandchildren used for her.

As I looked at Mom through tears, the memories flooded: Mom in the garden at dawn weeding and watering her flowers and vegetables . . . Mom typing up a storm while writing her thousands of letters and a dozen books . . . Mom so pleased that her good friend Betty Ford invited her to swim laps with her in the White House pool . . . Mom thrilled she'd met B.B. King when she was ninety-one, wearing her backstage pass ever after as

---

* This note was written before our fifth grandchild, Nora, was born.

if it was a piece of jewelry . . . Mom never making a sarcastic remark about her children or anyone else and the lifelong self-confidence that gave me . . . Mom cleaning up my vomit after I took drugs as a teen and then fixing me poached eggs on toast the next morning as if I was three again.

Lucy, you look eerily like your great-grandmother's child-hood pictures. Everyone says so. You are a truly beautiful child with exquisite features, high cheekbones, a lovely little nose, large wide-set intense brown eyes, a graceful frame, a radiant smile. As Mom would have put it—in the romantic Victorian manner she used for expressing such things—"You're stunningly lovely, Lucy, but with an inner beauty, too, my dear, which is far more important than mere outward beauty."

My mother might also have noted that you are incredibly friendly, saying hi to strangers and asking their names, speaking with a vocabulary that many American adults find amusingly precocious and somewhat disconcerting. You use words they'd think are exotic in our willfully dumbed-down society where even political leaders drop their Gs to avoid sounding elitist. But you don't yet know that in America we pride ourselves on all appearing to be equally inarticulate. So it's not often you hear a four-year-old say, "Well actually, it would be nice if we could dine together this evening," without a hint of irony or pretense. Then again, as Mom would've put it, you are having the "right books" read out loud to you.

I'm so lucky that I see you every day. Your dad, John, came back from three wartime deployments in the Marine Corps, went to the University of Chicago, married Becky halfway through school, graduated with honors and a degree in modern Euro-pean history, and then moved in with us and had you. You lived in our house until you were two years old. It was during that time that you and I bonded. Then you moved across the street, but by then we'd become sort of like twins or as Mom would have said, "Joined soul to soul." A few years later when Becky went back to work, your grandmother Genie and I became you and your brother Jack's, and soon after that your sister Nora's, lucky nannies.

Even though you and Mom never met in this life except via a computer screen and were more like ships passing in the night than great-grandmother and great-granddaughter, you were growing up loving what Mom had loved: words, art, music, gardening, cooking, and playacting. So Mom was communicating with you every time I read to you or listened to music with you or when we painted and gardened together.

Since she couldn't speak much while we talked to her via our computer, I read out loud to you and Mom from a book she'd written called, Mei Fuh—Memories from China. You loved the book and knew it almost by heart. As usual, we had to skip the "sad part." You never let me read the story where Adjipah, the gardener, ate Mom's goldfish when she was five. Mei Fuh was the last of many books Mom authored and her one and only children's book. It tells the story of how Mom was born to missionary parents in 1914 and about growing up in a missionary compound until she moved back to America at age six.

You asked Mom if she was "still upset about Adjipah eating your fish?" Mom tried to smile, but with her teeth out and the tube taped to her nose, her lower face no longer obeyed her wishes. The smile was crooked and faint, a mere echo of her former radiant self. So while we talked, I opened an album of pictures and whispered, "See how beautiful your great-grandmother really is? Look!" You nodded and said loudly to the screen, "You're beautiful, Noni!" Mom heard you and moved slightly, managing the hint of a crumpled smile. Then you said in an awed whisper, "She heard me! She nodded! She smiled!" I placed my hand on the laptop screen and showed you that when the lower part of her face was hidden, from the bridge of her nose to her eyes and silver hair, Mom still looked like herself as she appeared in the pictures in the album.

From time to time I'd ask, "Mom, do you remember that?" about some detail of her childhood, and she'd open her eyes a bit wider to signal that she did remember. Any mention of her early years got the biggest response. The neural pathways were shutting down, but the last remaining memories seemed to be the ones of her life at your age, Lucy.

The little girl who had once been Mom was peering at us through a thicket of memory loss. I reminded her of the five-week trip she took back to China with Genie when Mom was in her eighties. In 1990, they'd traveled to Mom's birthplace in Wenzhou, on the coast of southern China. Amazingly, given the Communist remake of China and the destruction of so much that was ancient, Genie and Mom found the old mission compound. In China the elderly are respected and revered. Mom was welcomed by the strangers living in her old home, and they let her wander through it with Genie. Genie said that Mom remembered everything, from the dusty courtyard where she had played to the thick gate with the little barred window she used to look through while wishing that she could go into the street and join the passing throng during processions and festivals.

I knew that this call might be the last time we'd talk. So I thanked Mom for her love and the joy-filled creativity she'd shared with me. Reading Mom her book also reminded me of the many hours she'd spent reading so many books to me out loud. She was a glorious reader.

Lucy, after about half an hour of sitting on my lap watching Mom drift in and out of sleep as I read to her, you went to my easel and painted. A few minutes later, you cheerfully called out to the screen, "This is a painting for you, Noni! I'll give it to you in heaven since you're going to die before I see you." You said this very matter-of-factly, with no fear, as if you were mentioning that you'd soon be seeing your great-grandmother someplace very ordinary. I don't think she heard you. But if she did, Mom would have liked what you said because my mother (unlike me these days) was nothing if not a believer in an actual place called heaven.

After the two hours or so we spent with Mom that day concluded, you were sitting up on a high stool in the kitchen while I was putting on your boots for the short walk back to your house.

"I'm so sad my mother is going to die," I said.

"You will be all right, Ba," you said.

"How?" I asked.

"You have me," you said and put your arms around me.

## It's ironic that it took a virus to pause our materialistic, consumerist way of life

Covid-19 was the ultimate confirmation of the irreplaceable need to have someone in one's life who puts their arms around you and says, "You have me." Schools and daycare centers shut, people lost jobs or started to work from home, public events were canceled—and parents and children suddenly found themselves living in a world where family connection and love were once again realized as the normal way of doing things and not something for which we had to carve out time from our overscheduled days. We weren't going out to eat. We weren't going to work. Family mealtimes were reinstated or perhaps discovered for the first time. People worked on puzzles together and bonded over the lost art of breadmaking. After-school sports, camps, and activities went away. Instead, families biked together and took walks in the evenings. For many parents it was the first time in years of balancing work life and home life where—unequivocally—home life won out, if only by grudging default. Many parents began to experience what Genie and I took for granted as self-employed people working from home who had been doing full-time grandchildcare for twelve years, before the pandemic hit.

The ironies multiplied. It wasn't just family togetherness that was forced on tens of millions of Americans. The virus did more in a matter of weeks to cut carbon emissions than all the talk about climate change had accomplished in half a century. Global greenhouse gas emissions plunged 8 percent in 2020, the largest drop ever recorded, as worldwide lockdowns to fight the coronavirus triggered an unprecedented decline in the use of fossil fuels. Even roadkill deaths dropped. Not since the day after 9/11 were the skies so clear and bare of jet trails. Birdsong could be heard in the airspace now free of the constant drone of engines. Flights were canceled by the tens of thousands. Roads were empty. China vastly reduced its pollution as factories powered by coal-fired plants temporarily closed. The resulting change in air quality was visible from space.

## The pandemic also illustrated our failings in sharp, horrible detail

As the historian Jill Lepore notes in "What's Wrong with the Way We Work" (*New Yorker*, January 2021):

> Americans are told to give their all—time, labor, and passion—to their jobs. But do their jobs give enough back? Americans work more hours than their counterparts in peer nations, including France and Germany, and many work more than fifty hours a week. Real wages declined for the rank and file in the nineteen-seventies, as did the percentage of

Americans who belong to unions, which may be a related development.

Lepore goes on to describe how one can argue that these "post-industrial developments" mark a return to a pre-industrial order: "The gig economy is a form of vassalage." She says that even workers who don't work for gig companies now work "like gig workers." That's because most jobs created between 2005 and 2015 were temporary jobs. That's because companies like Amazon fight any attempt to unionize while their owners and shareholders make obscene fortunes. Four in five hourly retail workers in the United States had no reliable schedule from one week to another. And their schedules are often set by algorithms that aim to maximize profits for investors by reducing breaks and pauses in service—the labor equivalent of the just-in-time manufacturing system that was developed in the 1970s in Japan, a country that coined a word for "death by overwork."

As the sociologist Jamie K. McCallum writes in *Worked Over: How Round-the-Clock Work Is Killing the American Dream*, Americans work too long and too hard, and some lack consistency in their hours and schedules. Work hours declined for a century through hard-fought labor-movement victories, but they've increased significantly since the seventies. Americans have fewer paid holidays than workers in other countries, and the United States is all but alone in having no guaranteed maternity leave and no legal right to sick leave or vacation time. Meanwhile, we're told to *love* work! We're led to believe that working hard will pay off. A well-established cottage industry has goaded us to find our meaning in it, as if work were a family, or a religion, or a body of knowledge given by God.

As anyone who ever tried to take even a month or two of childcare leave knows, extended child-related lapses in employment are at best frowned upon. They are interpreted as a lack of professional dedication. Leaving the workforce tends to be a one-way street, especially for women. Moreover, a year of Covid-19 lockdowns undid decades' worth of progress toward gender equity in America. President Biden did his best to right some of these wrongs in favor of empathy, compassion, women, and families, but that was just a start.

As Kim Brooks, author of *Small Animals: Parenthood in the Age of Fear*, wrote in the *New York Times*, in "Feminism Has Failed Women—If the Pandemic Undid Three Decades of Progress on Gender Equality, One Has to Wonder: How Real Was That Progress in the First Place?" (December 23, 2020):

> The pandemic made visible what's been hidden: what many mothers and child specialists . . . have long sensed but aren't supposed to say: *that whether the primary caretaker is a mother, a father, an extended family member or a close friend, newborns and infants do better in our homes.* We don't talk about this, we barely acknowledge it, because if we did, we'd have a moral obligation to provide financial support to make it possible for all babies. We'd have to acknowledge the social value of infant care and child rearing and empower parents to provide that care in the way they think is best for their children.
>
> We might even have to reconsider our idealization of the nuclear family, which we've now seen cannot really function without the support of broken institutions, to make way for the notion that raising children is a communal obligation, of benefit not just to an

individual woman or couple trying "to have it all," but
to society at large. (Italics added.)

Was a deity, perhaps, sending us a message with the pandemic, as a condemnation of our failures? Perhaps. But there
was certainly a "memo" of sorts delivered to us: while experts
noted that the lockdowns wouldn't last forever, many expressed
hope that they might reveal some of the benefits of switching
to cleaner energy, less travel, and more care for our planet and
for one another. From this new vantage point, many of us besides
Kim Brooks found ourselves reconsidering the notion of *genuine*
work-life balance and understanding, perhaps for the first time,
living with fulfillment.

Brooks writes that Covid was teaching some startling lessons,
for instance, that in the United States the survival rate of infants,
"the most dependent age group of all, has gone way up during the
pandemic. There are reports that premature births, one leading
cause of infant mortality, fell significantly in the early months of
lockdowns, when women in their final trimester of pregnancy
were able to do something many of them cannot afford to do in
normal times: Stay home from work."

**The twin events of 2020—a pandemic converging
with urgent demands for racial justice—presented
us with life-choice options to consider**

By 2021, many of us were both getting vaccinated and considering what the world would look like post pandemic. Is life really
about the survival of the fittest, as the most powerful in our society like to think of themselves? Is it normal that a few billionaires
own most of our nation's wealth and this same plutocratic class
(with hobbies like building private space programs) think they

are being generous if they slightly raise the minimum wage they pay stressed-out workers?

Now that we've seen blue skies and clear waters even in our largest cities, do we need to go back to trashing our planet? Do women and men really have to keep balancing family and career with no help? Could we finally admit that young kids do better when one or both parents are home with them without disregarding our fragile commitment to feminism? Can we find ways to really give women a *choice* as to when *they* want to have children at times *best for them* without women paying an outsized unhappiness price for their choices? Is there a way to make the super wealthy share their wealth? Do we need to go back to finding our meaning in careers and power over others rather than in our primary relationships? Many of us are asking questions like these. In "The Pandemic Has Reshaped American Fatherhood. Can It Last?" (*New York Times*, June 22, 2020), journalist Martin Gelin noted:

> During the quarantine, millions of men have spent significant time at home with their children for the first time. In my neighborhood, a stroller-dense part of Brooklyn, I have never seen more dads with babies on weekdays. The nearest avenue is closed off to car traffic, so the street is now filled with dads joyously teaching their daughters to ride bikes and scooters. Under the oak trees in Prospect Park, on an average weekday afternoon, exhausted fathers rest on blankets with one eye on the Zoom meeting on their laptops, while their kids fly kites around them.

Gelin describes how a study showed that 45 percent of American fathers were spending more time on childcare than they did before the pandemic. "The pandemic has reshaped the way fathers are involved with their families and children," Craig Garfield, a professor of pediatrics at Northwestern University, said when the study was presented. Author Trish Hall wrote in "What Does the Good Life Look Like Now?" (*New York Times,* April 18, 2020):

> We told ourselves that consuming services and experiences was somehow better than buying stuff, that flying halfway around the world to India and staying in luxury hotels was the peak of sophistication while moving into a McMansion was a signifier of crass consumerism. But the different kinds of consumption are just social markers, of class and political leanings and education. If I emerge alive from the pandemic—with asthma, I'm not confident—I plan to spend less and rely on myself more. I won't need so much money. Which is fortunate because I will have a lot less. Savings that were supposed to get me through retirement will be gravely dented.

## A cosmic lens through which to see that our way of life was off the rails

Survey after survey, editorial after editorial, poll after poll told the same story: hand in hand with our degradation of the natural world, our acceptance of racial injustice, and amoral business-as-usual values, we'd also degraded our personal and family relationships. We were putting work and making money ahead of bonding, putting success, as defined in material and job-description terms, ahead of the experience of sharing love. And we were getting perilously used to lying. We lied and said women could choose when to have a child when we all knew that really it was corporate (and university and college) America deciding. The "choice" they offered was: You live your life on *our* terms and with *our* consumerist values. We will destroy your chances for career success unless you play ball. Go to university, then spend your life in debt. Have a baby, then watch your job prospects suffer. And if you show up in university or high school with a child or pregnant, we will treat you like an outcast.

We lied about the environment, too. We talked about ecology but actually measured progress strictly in terms of economic growth with no recognition of the limits of the Earth to sustain this so-called growth. So in reality, much of what we were doing that was labeled *success* had already backfired long before the pandemic. Global warming. Increasingly catastrophic weather events. Rising seas. Farming land turned to desert. President Obama's era of hope was replaced by Trump's American carnage and divisive rhetoric. And loneliness was surging. Officially women were equal to men. In truth since the entire system was weighted to male domination of work stripped of support for parents, we'd built a system that was a combination of the worst of both work *and* family. In other words, our American libertarian individualistic selfishness—the American Dream—had proved to be as squalid as it is environmentally and spiritually unsustainable. We told people, "You can do anything!"—then made damn sure in fact, they could not.

As Lewis, writes in *Pregnant Girl*

> [T]he fact that I had a child was an inconvenience that wouldn't be accommodated. During freshman year, [in college] when Nerissa had pneumonia, my theater professor told me that I would have to bring her to class if I didn't want to fail. I bundled her up that morning, packed her into the car, drove to Williamsburg,

walked with her across campus in the frigid cold, and made sure I was there at the start of class. The professor barely acknowledged Nerissa as she sat on my knee, whining now and then. After that, the professor treated me differently, more harshly. I mentally took note that my parenting status might affect my grades, not because I couldn't do the work but because some professors would simply hold it against me. This fear will understandably be shared by so many parenting college students I will meet over the years, contributing to their invisibility.

## A plan on how to get unstuck, free, confident, and creative in our "ordinary" lives

At the heart of the malaise already in place before Covid-19 hit was the Very Big Lie: that education and profession define us, that making money and gaining power over others equals success. This lie destroys our chance to be happy because (as we shall see) humans evolved to be social animals who derive joy from our connection to others. In other words, we evolved not to first crave a seat in some boardroom (let alone a place in college) but a seat in a place we call home in a community we care about with people we love and trust.

As my friend Johanna (José) Zeilstra, CEO of Gender Fair (an advocacy organization asking companies to do more and do better when it comes to equality and diversity), put it in an email to me:

The pandemic/racial tension has taught us valuable lessons— mostly good:

**What's in:**
1. Family dinners
2. Pets

3. Finding enjoyment in simple pleasures—locally
4. Flexible work arrangements/work-life balance/remote
5. Care about community/elderly
6. Healthcare for all
7. Importance of teachers and healthcare workers
8. Stakeholder capitalism—purpose-driven organizations
9. CEOs as upstanders
10. Global connectivity
11. Correcting racial injustice

**What's out:**
1. Consumerism
2. FOMO (fear of missing out)
3. Long commutes/face-to-face work arrangements
4. Work/career focus
5. Individualism
6. Shareholder capitalism
7. CEOs as silent/neutral bystanders
8. Nationalism
9. Ignoring racial injustice

## Evidence that we're not in sync with our evolutionary roots is not hard to find

Almost every day before *and* after the pandemic, many of us found ourselves reading yet another opinion piece underlining the fact that our utilitarian values are out of sync with our need to connect, love, and be loved. For instance, in the 2018 survey "Young Women Are Convinced Motherhood Is Going to Suck—and They're Right" (E. J. Dickson, *Bustle*, March 30, 2018) conducted by Bustle Trends Group, respondents indicated in regard to work-life balance "that having it all is a joke."

The survey respondents no longer saw the point of even trying to balance love, relationships, and work. Interviewees reported feeling such anxiety over the prospect of balancing love with their careers that they weren't sure if they wanted to start families. In the survey of 332 women, many said that they were extremely concerned about the effect that having children would have on their professional lives. "As a woman, having a child is guaranteed to impact your career," one respondent said. Others were more pessimistic: "I think if I decide to start a family it will negatively impact my career," one woman wrote. Another wrote, "We aren't having children, so I won't have to deal with the issues working parents face about maternity/paternity leave, childcare costs, discrimination against childminders in the workforce, etc." One respondent summed up many others' fears, writing, "I do not plan to have children. I think that will advantage me throughout my career."

## We live in an anti-family, anti pair-bonding country

No one should feel pressured to have children as if this were somehow required in order to have a full life. It's not. But we tell younger people who *do* want a family someday to do big, important things *first*. And those big, important things seem to always focus on career, money, and consumption, which breed greed and result in tacit planetary destruction in the name of growth—not relationships and community. And these big important things somehow always also seem to side with us delaying starting families until we've made the fertility industry dealing with (as it were) our moldering fertility clocks gathering dust into a multibillion dollar industry.

In this context career ambition exacts a terrible cost. If nothing has value in and of itself, then life is lived as if everything must be measured in money and status. That poses an emotional risk because evolution favored the human genes that encouraged love, nurturing, and community rather than greed. For obvious reasons, the genes that didn't encourage love, nurturing, and community mostly didn't survive. So when we structure our society to effectively deny ourselves the evolutionary fact of the need for relationships, family, and connection—things that are of intrinsic value to humans (in other words, priceless)—it had better be for better reasons than some fucking job!

## Pitting ourselves against evolutionary reality

I am more than familiar with the result of pitting ideology against science, truth, and reality. That's one of the reasons so many people like me raised in fundamentalist-type religions find themselves, as I did, damaged and damaging those closest to them. What we were raised to believe *runs counter to the way evolution actually engineered us.* In other words, putting anything ahead of what really makes us happiest is to live a costly lie. As we shall see, evolution's rule for success is this: cooperate, be friendly, help others, and survive.

Looking at my own broken self and my past, I happen to know that living a lie costs dearly. It costs kindness and compromise. It strips us of agency. One spends one's life trying to pound circles through squares. Reality says one thing, and your beliefs say another. You take this discrepancy out on others. Or, just maybe, you change and try to conform your reality to actual reality. Then maybe all those others outside your circle begin to look like family members deserving of love.

Maybe you admit that what you did was wrong and try to change and make amends. And maybe you are in for a big surprise: you are now looking through the correct end of the telescope and everything suddenly seems closer and friendlier and not so unreachably far away. Maybe even the people you thought of as "the other" become touchable. Your ironclad caste system fades away, and you admit we are all one human family.

## On fertility and involuntary childlessness

Speaking of the price we pay for living according to a lie, Zeynep Gurtin, a lecturer in women's health at University College London, writes about one aspect of the struggle to conform to the religion of career. In "More Women Over Forty Are Getting Pregnant. But Is That Really About Their Choices?" (*The Guardian*, April 18, 2019), she explains that:

> Many women who become mothers after forty tell me that rather than deliberately delaying motherhood they were simply trying to fulfil the necessary [work] conditions. . . . Women's susceptibility to age-related fertility decline and increased reproductive risks as they get older make these particularly pertinent considerations for the over-forties. The absence of such information obscures the reality that many in this age group face serious difficulties in conceiving and may suffer complications in carrying their much-wanted babies, and *that many others will—very sadly—remain involuntarily childless.* (Italics added.)

## Tamara Jenkins: our indoctrination vis-à-vis our work-life *imbalance*

One of America's most brilliant movie directors, Tamara Jenkins, made an era-defining movie that also implicitly asks the "Do I live by the rules of the Church of Corporate Greed forever or is there another way?" question—*Private Life*. The movie confronts the incongruity we've backed ourselves into with our careers-versus-life doctrines of the kind Gurtin addressed in her article on fertility-related heartache forced on many women.

*Private Life* stars Kathryn Hahn and Paul Giamatti. They play Rachel and Richard, a forty-something New York couple trying to conceive. The movie explores the roulette-like nature of IVF, along with the intense and unreliable relationships formed online with potential surrogate mothers. When we meet Jenkins's characters as this wildly funny and jarring movie begins, their sex lives are divorced from intimacy. The husband has been reduced to a sperm mine, the wife to an egg bank. As they push into their forties, they are feeling ambivalent about their careers, too.

*Private Life* was drawn from Jenkins's experiences of trying to balance career in the church of greed and her desire for a family, undergoing egg donation, looking into international adoption options, and fertility clinic red tape that became a fraught daily experience for her. Back in 2007, before making the movie, Jenkins was flying around the world promoting her second film, *The Savages*. Oscar nominations had followed. Professionally, life was perfect. Privately—not so much. Jenkins (then forty-five) and her husband, the screenwriter Jim Taylor, were trying to start a family.

In a *Guardian* interview, "'Having a child is a distraction from your own mortality': Kathryn Hahn and Tamara Jenkins on their IVF film" (November 15, 2018), Jenkins explained the fertility dilemma she'd found herself in:

> I had thousands of reasons, like my own shitty family, my terrible relationship with my mother. I never had any dreams of weddings and babies. I was so butch.

Then, cut to me being married and desperate to have a baby. You don't really know who you are until things that you take for granted are not available to you. And nobody's saying: "Well, it's probably not her eggs and it cost her $87,000 and years of heartbreak." It's fucked up. It's not the full story. And no one should have to publicly share all this. But when people say: "Oh my God, we were just so lucky," you're like, "No, you weren't lucky—you spent a lot of money." Which is fine, but it's very confusing.

## Sussman: lifetime messaging directs us toward work

In "The End of Babies" by Anna Louie Sussman, a journalist who writes on gender, reproduction, and economics and who wrote this article in partnership with the Pulitzer Center on Crisis Reporting (*New York Times*, November 16, 2019), we read:

> In the United States, the gap between how many children people want and how many they have has widened to a 40-year high. . . . *Our increasingly winner-take-all economies require that children get intensive parenting and costly educations, creating rising anxiety around what sort of life a would-be parent might provide. A lifetime of messaging directs us toward other pursuits instead: education, work, travel.* (Italics added.)

## Jabour: "Do I want a child?"

Some of us are asking ourselves questions along these lines: *Do I hate my job? Do I want a child? Am I not, actually, all that special after all?* Those are the questions that the opinion editor at the *Guardian Australia*, Bridie Jabour, posed in a piece about people her age: "The Millennials at 31: Welcome to the Age of Misery" (December 30, 2019). Jabour writes:

> Every thirty-one-year-old I know is miserable. . . . They are beginning to look around at the shape of their lives and realize, well, this is the shape of their lives. . . . Maybe we won't be famous. Maybe this job is the "career" we thought was waiting for us around the corner. Is a big love coming? Are our parents really going to die? We already know a few that have. . . . [T]he day after turning 31 is all about waking up sweating and asking "should I have a baby?" The next question is sometimes "and who with?" . . . *People who have spent years striving and hustling are suddenly questioning it all. If they are not happy being defined by their job, then what do they want to be defined by?* (Italics added.)

## Our true legacy is the "epigenetic" footprint we leave

Sometimes real-life experiences send us a different message that focuses our attention. One such focusing lesson came home to me as I wrote my oldest grandson Ben's and my name in the fresh white plaster on the wall he and I were building. Ben is my daughter Jessica's child and my oldest grandson. He was nineteen at the time and on a three-month visit with us a few years back. We'd been working together each day for over a month building a new addition on our home. I scratched: "Ben and Grandpa, 2016." And Ben said, "That's good," as we completed the job.

I know that whatever else he changes when I'm gone (if our family still has the old house when I'm dead), that wall won't be touched—if Ben has anything to do with it. That scribbled tribute to our working together represents more than sentiment: it represents the findings of the latest science of *epigenetics* (a term I'll explain in a moment). And those findings tell us that in reality it is how we treat people that is our true legacy, not job title, money, or fame. It turns out that taking time to do something with my grandson was more important to the future of the world (as it were) than most of the "big important things" I was trying to do.

It turns out that our children's and grandchildren's experiences not only shape them but will shape their children, too. That's what *epigenetics* means. It's the study of *heritable* changes that do not involve alterations in the DNA sequence. This means that what we *do with and to children* changes their children's way of experiencing the world. In other words raising a child or caring for a grandchild is quite literally an intergenerational endeavor that will never end. It is the only thing we do that will last. Our careers will end. Our names will be forgotten, but our parenting will never end. And when I say parenting, I mean the actions we take that shape others, be they our actual children or not. In that sense we are all parents.

Consider the subject of the May 2013 issue of *Discover* magazine. There's an article by Dan Hurley: "Grandma's Experiences Leave a Mark on Your Genes." It speaks of this never-ending cycle at the heart of the very fabric of our lives I was unconsciously enacting as a sort of religious ritual as I scrawled Ben's and my name in plaster:

> Darwin and Freud walk into a bar. Two alcoholic mice —a mother and her son—sit on two bar stools, lapping gin from two thimbles.
>
> The mother mouse looks up and says, "Hey, geniuses, tell me how my son got into this sorry state."
>
> "Bad inheritance," says Darwin.
>
> "Bad mothering," says Freud.

Hurley writes that for over a hundred years, those two views —nature or nurture, biology or psychology—offered opposing explanations for how behaviors develop and persist, not only within a single individual but across generations. Then, in 1992, two young scientists following in Freud's and Darwin's footsteps actually did walk into a bar. And by the time they walked out a few beers later, they had begun to forge a revolutionary new synthesis of how life experiences could directly affect your genes.

## The molecular residue that holds fast to our genetic scaffolding

That bar was in Madrid, where the Cajal Institute (Spain's oldest academic center for the study of neurobiology) was holding an international meeting. One attendee, Moshe Szyf, a molecular biologist and geneticist at McGill University in Montreal, had never studied psychology or neurology, but he had been talked into attending by a colleague. Likewise, Michael Meaney, a McGill neurobiologist, had been persuaded to attend by the same colleague, who thought Meaney's research into animal models of maternal neglect might benefit from Szyf's perspective.

Meaney and Szyf spoke about a new line of research in genetics called epigenetics. The word *epigenetics* was created to describe how environmental and external factors influence the expression of genes. The field of epigenetics is growing and with it the understanding that both the environment *and* individual lifestyle directly interact with the genome to influence developmental change.

In one study, neuroscientist Eric Nestler, of the Icahn School of Medicine at Mount Sinai in New York City, exposed male mice to ten days of bullying by more aggressive mice. At the end of the experiment, the bullied mice were socially withdrawn. To test whether such effects could be transmitted to the next generation, Nestler took another group of bullied mice and bred them with females, but kept them from ever meeting their children. Despite having *no contact* with their depressed fathers, the offspring grew up to be hypersensitive to stress. "It was not a subtle effect; the offspring were dramatically more susceptible to developing signs of depression," said Nestler.

*In other words, our experiences, and those of our forebears, are never erased, even if they have been forgotten.* They are as indelible as names written in plaster. Experiences such as sharing art together or building together become a part of us, a molecular residue that holds fast to our genetic scaffolding. And this transcends parenthood. It is about everybody and all our relationships with others.

We can change the future by ignoring and hurting our children or by helping them. The same is true of our relationships with those we work with. When children experience unconditional love, or when employees do, or when fellow workers do, or our friends do, they will also shape their descendants. Bullying marks us, but so does love. It's our choice as to what we pass on —sorrow, fear, and loneliness, or love and joy. As we shall see in the rest of this book, passing on love and joy is the evolutionary purpose of families, friendships, work relationships, and even casual acquaintances, and (maybe) even life itself.

CHAPTER 2

# Big-Brained Babies
# Are Why We Crave
# Love, Connection,
# and Community

## Hélène Grimaud, Lucy, wolves, and love

Lucy, we grabbed a box of tangerines and trooped up to the attic, kicked off our shoes, and sprawled on the floor to watch Hélène Grimaud playing the piano. You (age five) and I watched her playing Sergei Rachmaninoff's Piano Concerto no. 2 in C Minor, op. 18, on YouTube. You were completely absorbed. I congratulated myself for helping you to grow your musical neural pathways as you added yet another brilliant woman to your role model repertoire. In that moment, you and I were unwittingly confirming the most essential human truth of all—our capacity to use our brains as malleable organs over which we can exert some control. We also discovered something surprising about Grimaud: she had wolves! We had watched a documentary about the pianist's life that included scenes of her cavorting in the snow with her pack. That led to us reading about wolves and, thereafter, they intruded into our games. We created a make-believe world where pillows became carcasses. We took turns being the Alpha and the Omega in the pack hierarchy and growled, snarled, and howled over our "kills." Sometimes we hunted elk and other times we were the elk being hunted. Sometimes we settled for roadkill and a pile of blocks became carrion. We crawled into our den, with our pups—an assortment of dolls and several stuffed animals—you defended while I went out to find more meat to leave for you and the babies at our cave entrance.

We bantered about wolf packs' social structures on and off for weeks:

"Grimaud plays the piano like a wolf," I said.

"Is she the Alpha female?" you asked.

"Yes, she's the Alpha female, and the orchestra is her pack."

"Who's the Omega that waits patiently to eat until last?" you asked.

"The lonely piccolo player," I said.

"Are there wolves in this?" you asked as you snuggled into a mound of pillows while Grimaud walked onstage to thunderous applause.

"No, it's all music," I said, "but seeing and listening to Grimaud playing is just as exciting as watching wolves. Wait until you see how her hands hit the keys!"

Grimaud's wolves never tore into a roadkill deer carcass with fiercer joy than she threw herself into playing that music. Grimaud also created long, almost uncomfortable silences between some passages as if the notes had an inner life of their own and needed coaxing out into the open. Grimaud's tender cajoling of the music "shy notes" (as you once called the quiet parts) changed in a heartbeat into cascading crescendos played at such shattering speed it seemed impossible that the stunning wall of sound engulfing us was pouring from such a slight figure.

At those moments you'd sit bolt upright. I'd watch you watching; you were so attentive and so beautiful, literally stopping your breath for a few moments, only exhaling after a particularly passionate attack on the keyboard. Then you'd take a deep breath and lean forward as if bracing against a gale. Your eyes were very bright. Lucy, seeing you watching her playing and feeling the music with you was one of the high points of my lifetime. You were so vividly alive! You made me feel so alive! Thank you!

In some ways, watching a video of Grimaud playing was even better than a live performance. You and I could see her face close-up from an angle no concertgoer gets. Grimaud's face was the face of a mystic in thrall to a celestial vision.

"Why are her eyes closed?" you asked. "How can she see the keys?"

"She knows where they are by touch. Blind people can play the piano, too, you know."

"Why does she look up and not look at what she's doing?" you asked.

"She has synesthesia."

"What's that?"

"She 'sees' notes as colors. Many musical geniuses have had synesthesia. Duke Ellington said, 'I hear a note by one of the fellows in the band and it's one color. I hear the same note played by someone else and it's a different color.'"

After I read that Duke Ellington quote to you, Lucy, you'd keep saying "I see blue!" or "I see red!" when you listened to his music. Your favorite was Duke Ellington's "Diminuendo and Crescendo in Blue." I told you that he (in my opinion) is the greatest composer since Bach and America's most indisputable musical genius.

Speaking of epigenetics, everything my mother was in the core of her being came alive for you, Lucy, in those moments when we listened to music together. All the concerts Mom scrimped and saved to take her children to, all the books she'd read aloud, all the time she'd spent encouraging me to paint, all the stories she'd told me about herself as a child that remind me so much of you, Lucy. Mom's love of music, her playing records by her idols Vladimir Horowitz and Glenn Gould, tied so directly to what we did together watching Grimaud.

Besides Grimaud, I "introduced" you to women like Evgenia Obraztsova, the Russian ballerina who danced as prima ballerina with the Mariinsky and Bolshoi Ballets. Obraztsova, like Grimaud, became a favorite of yours. And watching her led you to *The Nutcracker,* and that led to your and my all-time favorite ballet production: Prokofiev's *Romeo and Juliet,* choreographed by Rudolf Nureyev.

The *Romeo and Juliet* we watched is the stunning Paris Opera Ballet production. When we'd watch your favorite scene, the grand ball where the incredibly stirring theme of the Montagues and the Capulets kicks in with all those somber low notes, you stood up and marched around. And then when Tybalt comes out and spots Romeo at the ball, when Juliet is dancing with him, the sense of impending doom, the threat-laden music was almost more than we could bear, and you jumped onto me and I held you while we survived "the scary part."

The great thing about ballet, as an introduction to a classic piece of drama, was that, unlike the play, the scary parts were less scary for you at a young age. Music and dance, not words, told the story and drew you in. After we'd watched the ballet and talked about the story, you knew the plot of the play, and one of your games became playing Capulets and Montagues. You also decided that we needed to "go to Paris as soon as possible!" since your favorite ballet production (of the moment) was staged there.

You also assumed that I knew how to dance! I was your dance partner since you started using the upstairs bathroom as our stage and the shower stall as backstage, and the towel rack as "my dance studio practice bar." Given that I'm a polio survivor with an atrophied left leg, believe me, it hasn't been often that I've starred in ballets!

From the time you were four, you pretend-danced the role of Juliet or of Clara in *The Nutcracker* or starred in your after-bath productions of *Swan Lake* as Odette and Odile. I was Lord Montague or Prince Siegfried or Von Rothbart, the evil sorcerer who—as directed by you, Lucy—was "not as mean as the one in the usual ballet." Or I was the Nutcracker Prince, or "Clara's bad little brother grabbing away her nutcracker doll," or Clara's uncle who gives her the doll, or any assortment of stagehands. I also filled in as the audience and the provider of snacks during intermissions.

## As we evolved, our brains increased in size

Before we undertake any major redesign of our political and social life, we need to answer these questions: Why did Lucy and I want to dance ballets in our bathroom? Why did I get such satisfaction out of passing on my parents' love of art and music (a somewhat unlikely yet blessed love of art given their fundamentalist evangelical views) to Lucy? Why does childhood last so long that Lucy and I found ourselves with the time to listen to so much music? Why were some people surprised that childcare wasn't such a bad thing to be plunged into full time when they were forced to stay home (assuming they had the financial means and did the kind of work that allowed this) by the 2020 pandemic? Why am I happier and less of a jerk since denying everything I was raised to believe was true about male dominance being what God wants? Why are women in my view better suited to leadership roles than males? Here's the answer: big-brained babies.

## The child-centric, pelvic-size accommodating, aggressive, male-involving scenario

As I mentioned in my introduction, our babies' brains got so big that they couldn't complete their growth in utero. Unlike most mammals, humans had to birth babies with huge heads and still survive. To make our unlikely child-centric, pelvic-size accommodating, male-involving, dancing-in-bathrooms scenario work, communities and tribes had to get along well enough for long enough not to kill one another off—while doing all that long-term parenting. So evolution gifted us with the survival mechanism of strong feelings of pleasure that we experience when we connect with others. In other words, evolution knew not only that the giving birth is tough-to-fatal for human females but that motivating the successful raising of humans was going to need a powerful community-wide, gender-neutral inducement.

Parents as well as grandparents would have to be motivated to not abandon their young because baby care is hard and seemingly endless. Just ask any young parents at 3:00 AM with a crying baby who has deprived them of sleep for four months. So evolution gave us a drug-like high from experiencing parental connection, with its very own hormone: *oxytocin.*

## Oxytocin: the love hormone

Oxytocin induces labor and is released in high doses during childbirth as well as during breastfeeding. Once the baby starts suckling, the mother's body secretes the hormone, triggering the letdown of milk as part of the lactation process. Perhaps this is one reason why that 3:00 AM feeding goes from an experience of muddled sleepy resentment, a "Why did we have this horrible *thing*?" to a moment of (to invent several new words) *oxytenderness*, even *oxyjoy.*

Thanks to oxytocin, sacrificing for the humans we love most—our pair-bonded partners, lovers, children, adopted children, grandchildren, and other members of our communities—feels rewarding in ways that (speaking for myself) go beyond anything else. The *oxyjoy* we feel makes all our struggles seem worth it.

## Feldman: fatherhood/motherhood/parenthood

Ruth Feldman is a psychologist and brain scientist at the Gonda Multidisciplinary Brain Research Center at Bar-Ilan University and adjunct professor at the Child Study Center at Yale University School of Medicine. She has published a series of studies describing the hormonal activity (what I call oxyjoy) in new fathers that enhances the feeling of connection to newborn infants. Most research before Feldman's sought to measure the bond between mothers and newborns. In contrast, the study led by Feldman researchers studied the levels of oxytocin and *prolactin* (a hormone produced in the pituitary gland, named so because of its role in lactation) produced in fathers when interacting with their infants.

Feldman's study measured the level of these hormones in the blood and saliva of fathers in the second and sixth months of the newborns' lives. Forty-three fathers were documented as they played with their infants. As reported in "New Dads Secrete Hormone That Tightens Baby Bonds, Israeli Study Shows" (*Haaretz*, August 17, 2010), the researchers tracked the connection between the fathers and babies in terms of fathers' attention to the children, their demonstration of affection, and physical contact, including hugs and kisses. The higher the level of oxytocin, the more likely the fathers were to establish a strong social connection with their baby.

## Abraham et al.: hormones and parenting behavior

In "Father's Brain Is Sensitive to Childcare Experiences" (a study by Eyal Abraham, Talma Hendler, Irit Shapira-Lichter, Yaniv Kanat-Maymon, Orna Zagoory-Sharon, and Ruth Feldman) published in the *Proceedings of the National Academy of Sciences* (PNAS July 8, 2014), oxytocin and parenting behavior were measured in "primary-caregiving mothers, secondary-caregiving fathers, and in primary-caregiving gay fathers raising infants without maternal involvement." As noted in the study, "Primary-caregiving fathers exhibited high amygdala activation similar to mothers, alongside high superior temporal sulcus (STS) activation." The abstract of the study summarizes the findings on caregivers this way:

> [L]ittle [was] known about the brain basis of human fatherhood, its comparability with the maternal brain, and its sensitivity to caregiving experiences. We measured parental brain response to infant stimuli using functional MRI, oxytocin, and parenting behavior in three groups of parents. . . . Findings underscore the common neural basis of maternal and paternal care, chart brain–hormone–behavior pathways that support parenthood, *and specify mechanisms of brain malleability with caregiving experiences in human fathers.* (Italics added.)

Mother Nature is sending us a message about our survival. She generously gave us a maternal *and* paternal care hormone pathway to love, and we are squandering it. And now our greed-enabling rape of the Earth is unfolding in ways that even mitigate against fertility and our species' survival. If that's not a pretty direct message from Nature, what could be?

## Fertility: greed's death wish

Whatever our path to parenthood, or none, all those big fancy jobs and GDP growth through worship in the church of greed has made it harder to be the happy caring people we want to be. How is this working out? Not well. Those big fancy careers are hurting us biologically by producing the consequences of pollution. Talk about our religions being out of sync with reality: The religion of greed can't even reproduce and breed. It is undermining our very ability to survive.

Shanna Swan, a foremost expert on fertility at the Icahn School of Medicine at Mount Sinai in New York, makes a sobering point in her book *Count Down*. Swan predicts that a large share of the world's human population will not be able to even reproduce on their own by 2050. Her 2017 study found that sperm counts declined by more than 50 percent between 1973 and 2011, at a rate of a little over 1 percent a year. The CDC has estimated that 9 percent of men were infertile in 2018. Swan's study suggests that rate will rise to 41 percent by 2050. Swan and other experts say that "everywhere chemicals" called phthalates, used in countless products, are driving the trend along with the pesticides used by mass industrial, Earth-destroying, soil-depleting agriculture.

One thing that might be important to mention here is that, not only is fertility declining, but also the poison we keep pumping into the air and water causes birth defects. And those "everywhere chemicals" are there because the religion of greed put fancy "important" careers serving shareholders at the heart of our economy instead of prioritizing what's actually good for us—if, that is, we want to survive.

**Eisler and Fry: origins of our care-rewarding neurochemistry**

We face a future not only of career-life imbalance and a growing chasm between reality and our religion of greed but a time when even having a child becomes hard to impossible unless we drastically change our social, environmental, political, and spiritual ways. Bluntly: we have to redefine what we mean by the word *success* or perish in a physical sense and also in an emotional sense.

**What's reality's message?**

What is evolution telling us? Answer: If we're deprived of love, we wither. If we get "born again" into the religion of greed, we kill ourselves. This is a point that Kim Brooks made indirectly in her essay about the impact on women and families of the Covid pandemic. She noted that even infant mortality rates dropped when babies were home with their families during the pandemic because parents were with them more. According to "Covid-19 Lockdowns May Have Saved Kids' Lives" (*Bloomberg News*, September 17, 2020), "Twenty-two of the twenty-nine countries with weekly data for 2020 in the Human Mortality Database maintained by scholars at the Max Planck Institute for Demographic Research in Germany and the University of California at Berkeley have seen deaths in the fourteen-and-under age group decline this year." And in the *New York Times* (July 19, 2020), "During Coronavirus Lockdowns, Some Doctors Wondered: Where Are the Preemies?" by Elizabeth Preston, she reported that hospitals saw startling dips in premature births and that "researchers found that during the lockdown, the rate of babies born before twenty-eight weeks had dropped by a startling 90 percent."

What changed? Mothers were at home more while carrying their baby to term. Parents were at home more with their children. It seems children are affected before and after birth by proximity to those who love them most. Duh!

Family, it seems, is a "thing," and so, it seems, is love. To pretend otherwise is destructive. That brings up the question: why love? In their book, *Nurturing Our Humanity: How Domination and Partnership Shape Our Brains, Lives, and Future*, Riane Eisler (adjunct professor at California Institute for Integral Studies) and Douglas P. Fry (professor and chair of the Department of Peace and Conflict Studies at the University of North Carolina) explore the evolutionary origins of our "oxytenderness." They delve into the biological motivation to experience family-balanced love that Feldman and others have documented in male parents that is almost indistinguishable from female's experiences.

## Why love?

Eisler and Fry write: "Once the capacity for loving appeared on the evolutionary scene, love became a feature in relationships beyond those directly connected with reproduction. . . . [L]ove seems to be a motivational drive in itself." Or put it this way: dancing with five-year-olds to Bach and Duke Ellington needs no justification. Nor should parents have to justify their desire to care for very young children at home for a few years before returning to work outside the home.

Some things have intrinsic value when it comes to our happiness, and nature confirms these values. Parenthood and the development of our big brains are inextricably interwoven with why love matters to us all, and parenthood is rewarded with pleasure. That's why so many men feel they are missing out when work separates them from their children. That's why falling sperm counts are a big deal emotionally besides the question of our species' survival. That is why researchers were surprised to learn that when the pandemic sent parents' home, there were fewer premature births and fewer children died. These discoveries weren't a good fit with the corporate religion of greed, so the research got buried except for a few cursory mentions in the media. These were inconvenient facts to corporate fundamentalists, in the same way as the sort of evangelicals who raised me didn't really want to discover that gay people are born gay and don't choose that lifestyle.

### Fatherhood: shifting roles after the pandemic

Somewhat prophetically, the pre-Covid pandemic studies on fatherhood seemed to predict the results of a 2020 mid-pandemic study, which showed that 45 percent of American fathers were spending more time on childcare than they did before the pandemic—and liking it. What the pre-Covid-19 researchers into fatherhood would not have found surprising was how many fathers seemed to be enjoying the experience of actually being fathers and caregivers.

Researchers Daniel L. Carlson (University of Utah), Richard Petts (Ball State University), and Joanna R. Pepin (University of Texas-Austin) surveyed 1,060 US parents in mixed-gender marriages in late April 2020. They wanted to see how divisions of housework and childcare changed after the beginning of the pandemic and stay-at-home orders were issued as schools, childcare centers, and nonessential businesses were shuttered. The study found that 43 percent of fathers reported pitching in more with care of older children, and 42 percent reported an overall increase in housework time.

"The pandemic has reshaped the way fathers are involved with their families and children," Craig Garfield, a professor of pediatrics at Northwestern University, said when the study was presented. This trend in enhanced fatherhood might end, but what if it's the beginning of a more significant shift?

The journalist Martin Gelin, writing in "The Pandemic Has Reshaped American Fatherhood. Can It Last?" (*New York Times*, June 21, 2020), notes:

> In Sweden, where I grew up, it's typical for fathers to spend several months at home after the birth of a new child. This time kick-starts a virtuous cycle: Several studies in Sweden and elsewhere have shown that spending a short amount of time on parental leave significantly changes fathers' long-term attitudes toward domestic work. Once at home, men realize how hard the work is—they discover the challenges, demands and joys of parental responsibility. And that makes it more likely they will keep doing housework even after their parental leave is over. Could the pandemic get this cycle going?

As to Gelin's statement "Once at home, men realize how hard the work is—they discover the challenges, demands and joys of parental responsibility," there are precedents for parental roles shifting. A paper released by the National Bureau of Economic Research in April 2020 compared the pandemic to World War II, which led to significant changes in American family dynamics and social norms as millions of women joined the labor force for the first time. The comparison "suggests that temporary changes to the division of labor between the sexes have long-run effects." That millions of American fathers found themselves taking more responsibility for childcare, the authors write, "may erode social norms that currently lead to a lopsided distribution of the division of labor" in the home.

## No guarantee of mandated paid parental leave

My son John and his wife, Becky, were one of those mothers and fathers forced by the pandemic to work from home. They found themselves spending more time with their children. But not everyone had two healthy and willing youngish grandparents across the street to help out as John and Becky did, which made working from home a happy experience. And, Covid aside, the United States is currently the only industrialized country with no guarantee of paid parental leave, for fathers or mothers, and no state-funded childcare. That's because we've convinced ourselves that somehow the religion of greed's GDP is a bigger deal and more important to our happiness than, say, listening to Hélène Grimaud and Duke Ellington while dancing with five-year-olds. We think making more money is more important than staying home with a young child or protecting our pregnancies by more rest and home-based self-care.

For all the right-wing evangelical talk about family values, when it comes time to increase the minimum wage, pay parents for stay-at-home childcare, build better schools, or make laws to protect parents' jobs when they want to return to work, the right wing screams, "Socialism!" and ends the discussion. In fact, the fake family-values right wing I was part of is actively and practically *pro*-abortion while also trying to prohibit access. That's because the right wing has created a world in which actually having a child is discouraged at every turn. Again, this is misogyny, not pro-family, let alone pro-life.

The dirty little secret evangelicals and the religion of greed's high priests in corporate America share is this: both of these brutal fundamentalist religions ask more of women than of anyone else. Both of these religions oppress women to keep men in charge. Both of these religions are based on antifertility lies. And both ignore the truth of how evolution shaped us to love first, cooperate, and share.

Journalist and author Rainesford Stauffer writes in her book *An Ordinary Age: Finding Your Way in a World That Expects Exceptional* that

> It became obvious, if it wasn't already, that so much of our hyper-focus on being exceptional, individualistic, and extraordinary was built on a foundation of lies: that all this would save us; that it would all be enough someday. Extraordinary as a standard of living is inherently inequitable, a standard given to all but attainable for only a few. It's easy to focus on being exceptional, for example, when you aren't worried about paying rent or finding a job. When you have healthcare. When you have a support system. When you aren't staring down racism, bigotry, and prejudice—all of which mean additional standards of extraordinariness just to get by; when you have to do quadruple the work to go half as far and have even less margin for error.

At last there is some pushback and questioning of the misogynistic religion of greed. But we have yet to even begin to reform our society to become a fact-based culture that actually encourages choice as to how we wish to live our lives. For example, the Family and Medical Leave Act of 1993 offered only a measly guarantee of twelve weeks of unpaid leave. By comparison, most well-off countries offer six to twelve months of *paid* parental leave. And many governments pay for and encourage one or more parents to stay home until their child reaches school age.

We Americans are without excuses. There are examples out there of how we could actually change to become real family-values people. I'm talking about offering all of us choices that are better than the "choice" to abort or go broke, stay at work or love your baby, accept our religion of greed or become a second-class citizen shunned because you wanted to have a baby as a single mom or you were "too young" or "too old."

If we cared about providing real choices, single motherhood as it presently stands in America would not lead (as all studies show) to risking impoverishment. And no one would be forced to wait to have a child if they wanted one as a single person. There would be cultural, social, *and financial support.* There would be no "working poor" single mothers. Any woman that wanted to have a baby could have one and not fear she'd suffer financially. She wouldn't have to work at her career as she also watched her fertility ebb away. And if she needed fertility treatments and help, these would be free. In other words we'd have social services and a safety net for her comparable to Iceland's.

### Iceland promotes actual family values

Single parents in Iceland find themselves cared for. They have actual choices. If the parents of a child are not married or in a cohabiting partnership when a birth takes place, then the mother will have custody, unless the parents have agreed on a joint custody. The parent that has custody gets child support payments.

Maternity/paternity pay is made to *any parent* single or otherwise living in Iceland who is supporting a child or children below the age of eighteen. Single parents including students can apply for and get subsidies for daycare and nursery-school fees. Most local authorities only require single parents to submit proof of residency.

College and high school single-parent students submit a certificate from their school or college confirming that they are in a full-time study program. Then they are paid *full parent support.* Single parents of any age can apply for housing benefits and financial assistance as well from the local municipal family and social services. This is on top of the basic child support payments. And these housing benefits are used to lower costs for lower-income tenants (like many single parents who are still students before they get jobs) and to explicitly "reduce the differences between individual citizens on the housing market," as it is stated in the government's legislation. When calculating housing benefits, the reference point is rent, income, and assets minus liabilities and support for children.

The objective of social services in local Icelandic communities is to "ensure the financial security of the residents" as it is stated in the government's legislation. People who want to be parents, or find themselves pregnant, be they single or pair-bonded or women who just want to have a baby alone without pair-bonding, *have actual choices.* And those choices are made possible by real family values. These values are designed to *help* women, not to keep them subservient to men or slaves to the interests of corporations and their religion of greed.

## Conversely, in America we aren't "pro-choice" or "pro-life"—we're just pro-greed

Bringing America up to the Icelandic standard of an authentic choice to be parents would improve conditions for all families.

But, as Gelin writes, "If corporate norms remain conservative, changes to public policy are not enough." We'd need a change of religions, too. We'd need to abandon the fundamentalism of greed. Gelin notes that "Japan offers twelve months of parental leave, but only six percent of fathers use it." That's because the corporate mentality of jobs first (the religion of greed and work) has penetrated Japan so completely that men define their self-worth by their job status. That being the case, all the social programs to help men live fuller lives come to nothing.

A similar dynamic plays out in American businesses, where according to a 2018 Deloitte survey, one in three American men worry that taking paternity leave could hurt their careers. But perhaps the unexpected fulfillment more fathers found in the pandemic-forced time of family togetherness could result in significant pressure for policy changes and, more importantly, changes in the way men see their roles. That happened to me in the grandfather role.

### Covid-19 long summer vacation

All through what I'll forever think of as the 2020 Covid-19 long summer vacation, Lucy (age twelve) painted in my art studio while I read to her. Other days, I was teaching her to cook. Every day Lucy was joined by her brother Jack (age ten) and their little sister Nora (age six), playing, reading, painting, listening to music, swimming in the river, and hanging out. Genie and I cared for all three.

The Covid-19 lockdowns and social distancing turned our house into Summer Camp Schaeffer. It was one of the best times we've ever had. I taught Nora to snorkel while taking the children swimming in the Merrimack River. Nora also helped me cook, build, garden, and, best of all, play for hours every day. And our

Covid sheltering together took my relationship with Jack a step out of the ordinary. I found myself teaching him carpentry and masonry every day. (Hold the emails; my granddaughters also build things with me all the time.) That said, during the first Covid lockdown I was Jack Schaeffer's first employer. It was a paid apprenticeship of sorts where he earned twenty dollars a week beginning in March 2020 until the end of September to work with me on three building projects: the entire renovation and reconstruction of a two-story barn, the construction of a granite patio/vegetable garden enclosure, and a large French-style village fountain made of thousands of pounds of granite to celebrate my wife Genie's and my fiftieth anniversary. (I do masonry and carpentry, in case that isn't clear.) It was hardly kid stuff to simply pass the time. We worked five days a week for three to five hours a day, sometimes more. This was rain or shine, Swiss peasant-style, Calvinist, hard-assed work!

We'd start at eight in the morning each day—until, that is, Jack, learning that I was beginning work earlier, began to show up at 7:30, then at 7, then at 6:45. He took the job seriously and wanted to show responsibility.

Jack was a quick and brave learner. Brave because power tools are scary, and his Ba (as I'm called) is sometimes scary, too; Ba shouts when tired. Jack learned to use drills and table saws. He also tamed me. I quit bossing him around so much after a month or so because he was just too damn indispensable and good-tempered. I mean this. I have too much respect for people who work well with their hands, and not too much respect for people who don't, to lie about someone's work ethic or lack thereof.

After a few weeks Jack brought me every tool I'd call for, each kind of wood—a four by four, pressure-treated, a two by four, whatever. He retained information. He knew my toolbox. He knew where stuff was. Jack worked in hot, buggy weather without complaining.

Jack learned a lot, and I liked teaching him. And I discovered that Jack is an empathy machine who never spoke an unkind word back to grumpy old damaged me. Jack forgives. Best of all, Jack was (mostly) *happy*, so I was (mostly) *happy, too*!

I was not alone in my newfound single-mindedness. In "The Pandemic Has Caused Parents to Slow Down. Here's How to Preserve That Pace" (*Washington Post*, April 6, 2021) , Christine Koh writes:

> One of the biggest pain points I hear about from parents involves time. Time feels scarce, and schedules become bloated with activities and appointments that feel obligatory, annoying or unwanted. The pandemic served up the ultimate reset, recalibrating us all to a new, empty baseline. At first, that line was deeply unsettling; the losses represented missed milestones and a lack of control. Yet, as time passed, many people reveled in the slower pace. . . . For many parents, remote schooling meant looser schedules and room to experiment; embrace the routines that retain calm and foster independence. "I never realized how [stressful] our weekday morning routine was until we had to stop doing it," says LaShawn Wiltz, a mother of an 11-year-old and an Atlanta writer and photographer whose work focuses on capturing everyday moments. "This past year, instead of rushing, there was time to talk a little, laugh more, and there has been no yelling, 'We're going to be late!' I want to keep this slow . . . routine. . . . "

Speaking of being happy, Nora (then age six) was playing Snow White. We got to the part where she'd eaten the poisoned apple and was now waiting for the prince to wake her. I was the prince and rode through the forest. I found Snow White on the living room couch.

Nora (as did Lucy before her) will break the so-called fourth wall (a performance convention in which an invisible, imagined wall separates the audience from the performer) and whisper me directorial suggestions. Then jump back into character.

*I, shaking Snow White by the shoulder*: Wake up.

*Nora stays asleep.*

*I kiss her on the forehead.*

*Nora is still asleep.*

*I kiss her on the tip of the nose.*

Nora *(in her off-stage whisper hissing)*: Kiss me on the lips.

*I pretend to miss her lips and kiss her on the cheeks.*

Nora *(keeping one eye shut and squinting at me with the other half-opened eye, now in a furious, louder whisper)*: The *lips!*

*I kiss her shoulder.*

Nora *(glaring through her one open eye and speaking in a very loud whisper, while grinding her teeth, and then through a flexing and clenched jaw, slowly and very deliberately)*: You are the *stupidest* prince EVER! KISS ... ME ... ON ... THE ... LIPS, ... IDIOT!

## Pascoe: the centrality of relationships

Many missed directorial cues aside, the fact that Genie, Jack, Lucy, Nora, and I were happy working and playing together is no surprise. That there is growing pressure to reconfigure work to meet our most basic emotional needs isn't surprising, either, because we now know love is a scientific thing. Sara Pascoe knows this.

Pascoe is one of the world's great comedians. She's also science obsessed and first unpacked her what's-love-all-about theme in her 2018 BBC Radio 4 comedy series *The Modern Monkey*. And Pascoe's amusing, informative book *Animal: The Autobiography of a Female Body* reexamines anthropology and presents it as wickedly clever science-based comedy based on what I call *oxyjoy*.

In her book and radio comedy, Pascoe explores our social world though theories of evolutionary psychology. She sets us up by asking: How does our monkey past influence our modern lives? Why are we still hijacked by our primitive emotions even though we know what's happening to us? Pascoe mines the humor inherent in this conflict between our older selves and newer selves—what she calls our Old Brain and New Brain.

Our newer brain stops to ponder. It's the "Hey! Wait a minute, what the hell's going on?" part of us. It's the "Wait a minute, do I really believe men should be in charge? Do I really want to be a professional male bully for the rest of my life?" part of our brains. Our older brain does the unthinking instinct stuff. But our older and newer brains don't always get along. Sometimes, strong content is activated by our older brain, which triggers emotions in our newer brain, and we start feeling threatened, sad, guilty, lonely, and unhappy. And because we're a social species, emotional threats—say, feeling as if we've missed out on love or a chance to have a child or had a child and then slapped her—are experienced just as intensely as physical pain.

## Humans don't do loneliness well

Some mammals do loneliness just fine. We don't. Let's compare ourselves to the foxes I watch running around in my yard every springtime. At one month of age, the cubs emerge from the den near my grandchildren's swing set to explore their surroundings and start eating solid food (including stuff they grab off my compost heap). Three months later, the cubs are fully grown. The family breaks up. The youngsters disperse.

Fox solitude is bliss. Not so for us. We need others, and we need them a lot. And we need them for life. We most often express this need through family. When trouble hits, we turn to our families for comfort and support. When we are cut off from connection with others (as happened to many in the days and weeks of self-isolation in the spring of 2020), we suffer. It's why there were tears in my eyes when Nora, Jack, Lucy, Genie, and I were—at last after a year of not touching one another, and doing only outdoor activities—able to hug and kiss one another again. This was a few weeks after the happy moment we all savored when Genie and I got our second vaccine shot in early March 2021. "I'm missing at least a thousand hugs!" I said holding on to the children like a drowning man clinging to an upturned dinghy.

## It's about the love, stupid!

In *Animal,* Sara Pascoe explains why we suffer if deprived of love and, conversely, why we feel whole when we are loved. She sums up something similar to what Eisler and Fry call love's "motivational drive in itself" amusingly (capitalization in the original) like this:

> The parents who wanted to be together with their partners were the evolutionary victors. And it's a huge set of emotions and compulsions. It's not a muted "Oh, I should probably help out, that's the right thing to do" but a bellowed "I WILL DIE WITHOUT THIS PERSON THEY ARE BETTER THAN ANYTHING ELSE THAT HAS EVER

EXISTED I CAN WATCH THEM GOING TO THE TOILET AND STILL WANT TO KISS THEM OH GOD OH GOD MY BODY IS NOT BIG ENOUGH TO WITHSTAND THE FORCE OF MY FEELINGS."

## Small: love is indeed a "thing"

Cornell University primate behaviorist Meredith Small also explores the love thing and wryly notes in "Sex and the Evolution of Love" (*Live Science*, February 14, 2008) that:

I am such a loser. According to evolutionary psychologists, women are supposed to look for mates who are good providers. . . . But I've chosen an artist, someone with no real income, no access to affordable health care and no financial future. But then he's a loser too, at least in the evolutionary sense. He's supposed to look for a young, attractive woman who could have lots of babies and pass along his genes. Instead, he got me, someone 15 years older and so past her reproductive prime that we'd be on the cover of the *National Enquirer* if I ever became pregnant. . . . [L]ove, not natural selection, is often guiding mate choice, and *love is the wild card in the game of reproductive success.* (Italics added.)

## Another set of priorities—and then love

I discovered Small's "love wildcard" serendipitously. As a teen, I never would have dreamed my happiest years would come as I close in on my seventies while doing yet another round of childcare —this time for the three youngest of my five grandchildren. My younger self believed that aging was bad and that anything that might have tied me down or limited my choices would be a big mistake. My younger self was a bully. God (I thought) had imbued us with a natural order, and I was a male and therefore in charge.

Luckily for me, evolutionary biology, in the form of hormones, intruded on my idea of what a good male-dominated Christian life should look like.

Fall 1969: a frosty night of bright stars. I hear the door open, and I poke my head around the corner of our communal dining area filled with L'Abri students. Regina Ann Walsh has come to save me and our unborn and as yet unknown children and grandchildren and all their descendants from God's wrath. She is standing tall and lovely under our old chalet's Venetian wrought-iron and glass lantern. High cheekbones, full lips, and almond-shaped, almost Asian hazel eyes, slightly slanted at the corners, some sort of apparition of unattainable perfection. Genie's eyes are framed by her long auburn hair falling to her waist, points of pelvic bone defining her hips, belly tight under those second-skin slacks, high glossy boots up to her knees, generous breasts, and that gorgeous face defining a moment that remains, for me, holy. With a smile, Genie acknowledges me. I hastily set an extra place at our table. Later Genie mentions that she wants to hear the just-released new Beatles album, *Abbey Road*. I happen to have the album downstairs in my studio. Genie—a genuine San Francisco hippie princess who (I soon learned) *had watched the Stones in concert live and the Beatles live THREE TIMES EACH!*—was visiting our wacky Christian commune as an accidental tourist while traveling in Europe as a high school graduation present.

She was eighteen, and I was seventeen. Genie knew nothing about evangelicals. She was going to stay one night. Genie didn't know it at the time, but her very presence was to present me with a choice: remain a White male evangelical bully or become a human. As the years went by, that choice broke up all my certainties. I—like some frightened animal crawling out of a den after hibernation—started to look around, blinking in the unaccustomed light. What I saw was not what I'd been brought up to expect. Genie's light was blinding. And Genie wasn't up for domination. I chose Genie's light again and again over the dark gloom cast by my religion. This choice was not instant. It played out over many years. And because Genie loved me, she stuck around, and she saved me.

Genie not only demanded respect for herself but also demanded that I treat our children better than I did at the start of our teen parenthood journey. Genie was like a mother tiger defending her young. She threatened divorce if I ever slapped Jessica again. This was after I slapped Jessica even after promising not to do so. Genie screamed at me, too, after I spanked my sons. She threatened to leave and take everyone with her. I was shocked. Compared to my upbringing, I was (in my bent mind) going easy on everyone. In Genie's world my version of "loving discipline" was that I was acting like a monstrous crank. She was right.

Genie fought for decency and won. It was a long battle. Never has anyone been so grateful for being conquered so thoroughly by someone as I am today for Genie defeating me! The fact that our children's childhoods consisted of mostly good days is only because of the force of Genie's love and character in defending us all. She gradually converted me to a new religion: the blinding, humbling light of love.

## We become teen parents

We had sex for the first time after Genie had been at L'Abri a week or two. And then, about a year later, we got pregnant after having had unprotected sex one time too many. Note: when hippie free love encounters evangelical no-condom horny boys, this doesn't work very well. "I'll pull out!" is not a strategy.

Marriage—"a picture of Christ and His bride, the Church" (no kidding)—was the only remedy to an unexpected and, at first, unwelcome pregnancy. Abortion was illegal in Switzerland and in America at that time. We decided to keep the baby, and Genie eventually sincerely converted (for a while) to our brand of born-again faith. The Alps were beautiful. L'Abri was a free place to crash. Genie fell for me. My parents were nice. And my parents went along with our let's-get-married idea as God's will. Genie had gone to Europe for what was supposed to be a monthlong trip. She came back to the States ten years later with two children and pregnant with our third, having (from her parents' sensible view) joined a cult.

It was a few years after we were married that I directed my dad's documentaries. Then I became a rabid antichoice activist and his nepotistic sidekick. Why? How this could happen to someone married to the sensible person Genie was and is was because of my attachment to Jessica. You see, when abortion was legalized by *Roe v. Wade* in 1973, mine was an emotional reaction carried over from my anger at the people who had said Genie and I should have aborted our teen pregnancy. This was what some of Genie's and my friends suggested. Some of our abort-the-unwanted-baby friends were even evangelical workers at L'Abri.

*Little known and well-hidden fact, so please listen up: Many evangelicals at that time were pro-choice. Only later and because of our film series did most evangelicals switch to being antichoice.*

So Dad's and my "pro-life" stand in the early 1970s wasn't just against liberals but was (at first) directed at changing many evangelicals' minds and their leaders' minds from pro-choice to antiabortion. As for me, in my head I was defending baby Jessica and Genie's and my decision to have her. This was personal.

## My version of "pro-life" was horribly unfair

By the time Roe was handed down, I was in love with my toddler Jessica. I was a failing father in many ways but not for lack of love. In my mind, when standing up against abortion rights, I was somehow retroactively protecting Jessica. I soon found myself shilling for the antiabortion movement that the pro-life juggernaut would become as it linked arms with far-right misogynists. *BUT* . . . my pro-life position was very unfair. You see, Genie and I had deep reservoirs of support when we had our child. We were not alone. We had an apartment to live in for free, a loving family, and kind parents. We were given money. We might as well have been kids living in a modern, accepting, social safety net country such as Iceland. All our medical expenses were paid by my parents. We had unlimited access to babysitters and experienced help from a multitude of older mothers and fathers raising children in our community. From that entitled privileged perch, my anti-choice activism smacks of out-of-touch moralistic selfishness.

My friend Johanna (José) Zeilstra (CEO, Gender Fair) responded to an email from me asking "the abortion question." Her statement reflects the way I feel about this these days: "I do believe if there was more sex education, birth control, post-birth care and community support, as we see in other parts of the world, we would have fewer abortions. The problem with the 'right' is that they think the 'left' is pro-abortion/baby-killers. This is a term often used to incite division and is false. No one is pro-abortion.  I am both pro-life and pro-choice. It's a difficult decision left to the woman (and perhaps partner/doctor) but never an easy choice, especially if she doesn't have family nearby and financial support to be a single mom. My dad always said that 'every child should be a wanted child.'"

## Myrna Perez Sheldon and "the theology of abortion"

It was only many years later that I began to understand my emotional reaction and how unfair it had been. By 1990 I was out of the antiabortion movement and on the other side, pro-choice to the core. Nevertheless it has only been more recently in the last few years while working on this book that I began to understand the issues surrounding abortion in a deeper, more nuanced way. I've been helped by one person in particular to better understand what's at stake.

I first met Myrna Perez Sheldon in 2016 when she'd traveled from Harvard University to Rice University in Houston to interview me for a Harvard magazine she had founded and edited that deals with the intersection of science and spirituality. I happened to be speaking at Rice to a group of comparative religion graduate students gathered from the University of Chicago, Princeton, and Yale, who were using my memoir *Crazy for God* as a textbook.

These days Myrna teaches two subjects as assistant professor of Gender and American Religion, jointly appointed in two departments, Classics and World Religions and Women's, Gender, and Sexuality Studies at Ohio University. Lacking academic credentials, I found the idea of being interviewed by her intimidating. Yet during a pre-interview coffee, Myrna didn't talk much about her career achievements. Instead, she spoke about her mom's influence on her life.

Myrna and I have since become close friends. We talk often and she tells me about her hopes to pass on what her mother gave her—a sense of wonder—to her two young children. She even says she's learned something useful watching Genie and I interact with each other and our grandchildren. We swap baby pictures: her children, our grandchildren. One of my paintings hangs in her children's bedroom.

Myrna has made some interesting choices and turned down several chances to take jobs at prestigious Ivy League universities in order to be closer to her family. Some of her colleagues thought she was nuts to do that. Ironically, they also say they envy her. Myrna decided to put community, family, and love ahead of career status. As a mother of two, she wants grandparent involvement in her parenting efforts. She's made career prestige and pay sacrifices to get this. She told me, "I wanted to do what your kids did and be near my mom and have a family with a support system." This was by way of explaining her move from Cambridge, Massachusetts, to Ohio—a move that mystified some of her colleagues.

Myrna tells me about swapping childcare roles with her tech-innovator husband, Seth, and how Seth and she accommodate each other's careers by making family togetherness their priority. Which brings me to this: the best articulation of the abortion question that I've read. It came from Myrna in her essay "A Feminist Theology of Abortion." (This essay is to be a chapter in a book Myrna is contributing to.) I'm quoting what Myrna writes at length here with her permission. And as I said, to me this seems like the best take on some aspects of this issue I've encountered.

> The U.S. Supreme Court's opinion in the landmark 1973 case *Roe v. Wade* consistently assumes that any doctor providing an abortion is a man. Throughout the text of the bench opinion, physicians in the abstract are referred to as "he" and "him." For instance, in

addressing a potential hypothetical decision to perform an abortion in the early stages of pregnancy, the Court refers to the reasoning of "a physician and his pregnant patient." Throughout the opinion, the decision-making authority for an abortion flows more readily between the expertise of the (male) physician and the State than it does to the pregnant woman.

I have argued that abortion has both a history and the potential to be a tool of eugenics and that an abortion ethic cannot rest on a clear separation between woman and fetus or mother and child. A theology of abortion is, therefore, an argument for a radical trust in women that cannot guarantee either that abortion policies have no eugenic motivations, or that the termination of a pregnancy is not the end of a life or of a person. *It is an ethics of risk and a feminist embrace of that risk.*

A feminist theology of abortion is an openness to the ways in which our view of human life, suffering, and personhood have materially transformed through the history of technology. It suggests that our views of what is valuable, what is livable ... have changed and may yet again in the future. It is an ethic of imperfection, humility, and an acknowledgment that we may do something truly wrong. . . .

Trust is not jurisprudence. It is not a commandment. Trust happens beyond any proof that can be given; but it can also be violated beyond repair. The call to radically trust women is not an exhortation that women be viewed as essentially good moral actors. It is a reorientation of the affective posture of lawmaking and public health policy which is currently threaded through with the persistent belief that women are not to be trusted. That they are unaware of their own best interest and their decisions must be guarded against lest they bring harm to themselves, their children, or the nation at large.

When I imagine a feminist theology of abortion, I picture a set of open hands. Hands that might do the bloody work of obstetrics. Hands that might tenderly hold a newborn. Hands that might be held up in protest. But most of all hands that remain open, not grasping at control or certainty or authority. This feminist posture does not rest in the confidence of its own righteousness. Nor does it relax into an assurance of the purity of its intent. It sees work that must be done, lives that must be cared for, and communities that must be protected. *And it is willing to be wrong, in order to take the risk of trusting women entirely. Without reservation.* (Italics added.)

## Daycare for my grandchildren inspired me to become more community minded

At the other end of life's spectrum from pair-bonding, loving babies, and parenthood, and/or struggling to change our culture to (damn it!) trust women is the issue of experiencing oxytenderness. That's why I feel like the luckiest man on earth. I have found a modicum of redemption.

My prostate is enlarged. I take blood pressure medication. I pee twice during the night. So I never seem entirely rested on any given morning. Sex with Genie is lovely, but I need to work a little harder (no pun intended) to keep my part (parts?) going. As an "older person," I'm getting increasingly invisible to other people. And Genie and I were in the at-risk cohort for Covid-19. Above all, the hollow sorrow I carry at having helped push so many people to hate rather than to love haunts me. However, as we became our grandchildren's Covid-era daycare, school, and summer camp in 2020, I never once asked myself why I am here in the metaphysical sense. I felt I'd fallen into a more natural state where all my evolutionary instincts were aligning with what I found most durably satisfying and actually true. If caring for my grandchildren was what getting older was all about, then that was fine with me. I never ask myself if life is worth living when a grandchild hugs me. I can't take the past back, but I can try to get things right as this second chance to love unfolds. And I can try to share that love.

## Like everything else that's worth doing, being a hands-on grandparent is trying at times . . . but then there's community involvement

I end some days shouting at the kids. I have to say "I'm sorry" a lot. Sometimes, I exchange some pretty curt texts with my daughter-in-law, Becky, and my son John when we get our scheduling wires crossed. Sometimes, Genie and I fight because we're exhausted by the childcare we provide and then we dive into our Friday night drinks pretty hard. But there's still nothing we'd rather be doing. Childcare has even changed the way I (a bit of a reclusive writer-type) now "do" community involvement.

When our grandchildren were in school before the virus hit, I'd find myself comparing notes with a throng of parents, people half my age, while waiting around for the dismissal bell at our local public school. After they got back to school full-time by April 2021, I relished seeing the teachers and parents as I started picking them up again. We live off the bus route, so I do the pickups every day and then bring the kids back to our house.

What do the parents and I have in common? It is our children and our children's children that bind us together. Rich or poor, young or old—if anything awful were to happen to the children we love, the universe as we know it would end. We understand one another.

So these days I do not envy mammals whose children fend for themselves in a matter of days rather than decades. Being part of a parental community has reinforced my bonds to my neighborhood, town, and country. Besides, I can't get enough of experiences like this: to keep up with six-year-old Nora-of-the-many-costumes, I have to ask her who she "is" at any given moment. I did this the other day when she marched into our kitchen wearing a toy tiara. "Who are you now?" I asked.

"I'm an evil goblin goddess!" Nora pronounced, and then nonchalantly added, "But you can call me Jane."

Pre-coronavirus, when I took Nora ice skating, this happened one afternoon: "Ba, I'm hot. Can I take off my mittens?" Nora asked.

"No, if you fall, you'll hurt your hands, and it's cold," I said.

"Please!"

"No! *Look, everyone skating has gloves on!* No one else is even *thinking* about taking off their mittens!"

There was a pause. Then Nora fixed me with her most penetrating gaze and in a casual conversational tone asked, "How do you know they're not *all* thinking about taking off their mittens?"

If playing with an "evil goblin goddess" who trusts and loves me unconditionally (and wins mitten discussions with precocious flashes of wit) isn't a good definition of the purpose of life, what possibly could be?

## Alexandra Torres does it her way

Human beings are creative. So we react to social decay in ourselves or in others by creating new opportunities to shape the future. Alexandra Torres, a friend of mine in the millennial age bracket, made choices to buck the greed creed in her own way. Alexandra recently completed her PhD in cancer biology. Before that, she studied at Harvard and majored in evolutionary biology. Since completing her PhD, Alexandra spent a year working for a small tech company developing education software for mental health professionals. This position allowed her to gain experience in building and growing a small business. She also started a family before any of her friends did. This did not make her life perfect. This entailed sacrifices and some regrets. In an email to me (in the context of her very kindly reviewing this book's manuscript, and used here by permission), Alexandra noted that she is nevertheless . . .

> So thankful I'm a thirty-year-old who is feeling incredibly fulfilled. On the flip side, I do feel inadequate about not having a bustling, impressive career. That is the yearning I have, hoping that will one day come. But I'm learning you can't have it all. Wish we could though. But I would always rather err on the side of providing a fulfilling childhood for my kids than being an absent career-driven parent (the worst of all worlds). All very conflicting. I am career-driven. And yet, it was so important for me and my husband, when we got married seven years ago, to start our family sooner rather than later. Many PhD students wait until after they complete their studies (average biology PhD is five to six years) to start a family. We thought that was too long of a wait, and made the crazy decision to begin having kids during my PhD because it was that important to us. So few other students make that choice. Culturally, having kids while pursuing a science

PhD is generally not highly regarded (I was lucky and had a supportive boss). Having kids impacted my progress in completing my studies (it took me six and a half years to graduate rather than sooner than that). And yet, I do not regret making that decision. I am still torn at times, wishing I was further along in my career. But my husband and I have made an effort to be present for our boys and make sure their young lives are fulfilling. The career progression will come in due time, and I have learned to be patient in that regard, meanwhile, I am happy with the balance I have found.

Fewer of us seem to have the balance in our lives or the honesty to admit regret. The regret comes from the fact that the way our culture operates in its greed religion leaves us with no really great choices. Alexandra regrets not having a career for now but is even happier she has her children. In "I've Picked My Job Over My Kids" (*New York Times*, June 30, 2019), law professor Lara Bazelon laments over another sort of regret.

I am a lawyer, a law professor and a writer. I am also a divorced mother of two young children. I'm often asked some version of: "How do you excel at work and be the best mother you can be?" Every working mother gets this question, which presupposes that a "work-life balance" is achievable. It's not. The term traps women in an endless cycle of shame and self-recrimination. Like many women, I often prioritize my job. . . . I have missed: my daughter's seventh birthday, my son's tenth birthday party, two family vacations. . . . Sometimes my choices make me sad.

Bazelon is not self-pitying. Like my friend Alexandra, her attitude is brave. She ends her essay with this positive thought: "I hope my kids get it. I think they do. I love them beyond all reason, and their existence gives my life profound meaning. And I have the same feelings about my job." But what is disheartening to me about Bazelon's opinion piece and thousands like it isn't the writer's attitude of trying to make the best of her tough work/life situation. What's disappointing is so many people's surrender to the anti-family, anti-parenting status quo. We get a personal story about how someone is coping with the way our culture does jobs and family but not a demand, let alone a program, for change. Few seem ready to challenge *the entire set of priorities* that seem to never prioritize love. It is as if we have accepted some sort of careerist theology as a belief system or career cult unquestioningly. It is as if we are obeying commandments, handed down by an anti-family corporate deity, like these that follow.

## Four corporate "commandments"

Delay starting romantic relationships—let alone having children—in favor of training for, and then establishing, and then endlessly striving for, a career.

Don't get tied down too soon by relationships that might slow your pursuit of career.

Earning more money is *always a good thing*, no matter how many of life's most rewarding experiences you must forgo.

Careers are essential—family is a luxury.

## Carter: Stonewall and the gay community's revolution

It seems to me that these commandments represent an injustice perpetrated in favor of shareholders against ordinary people. If merely outlining personal mechanisms for coping with this kind of injustice had been the gay community's tactic for the last fifty years, gay men and women would still be in the closet, in jail, or dead. No one in the LGBTQ community would be allowed to marry, let alone have children. But the LGBTQ community did not settle for writing opinion pieces about their struggles. Instead, they stood up and fought for justice and for change. For instance, in *Stonewall: The Riots That Sparked the Gay Revolution* by David Carter, we read about a twenty-six-year-old musician in the Stonewall riots in New York City's Greenwich Village asking, "How many times can one turn the other cheek?" by way of explaining why he was rioting. "Whose streets are these? These are our streets," another protester shouted during the protests. Another man yelled, "And you cops are not from this area! This is our area! It's gay people's streets!"

Change can only happen when you and me stand up and demand it. It's time to raise hell until we shape a better, more humane society that caters to who we actually are—evolving primates who discovered our ultimate joy in being loved and loving in return. We need a stay-at-home mom and also a career lawyer both accommodated! It isn't either-or. This is about giving moral and social support real choices. This is about facilitating love, however we approach the career-family quandary. This is about admitting that maybe we are just biological machines, but those machines paradoxically look for—and need—spiritual meaning. Deal with it!

## Iliza Shlesinger and the evolutionary wild card of love

We evolved to hope for more than career success. We also evolved to strive for more than just family. One person who has been making this point (and raising her own brand of hell) is Iliza Shlesinger. I use her here as an example of people fighting for the right to love above all else. Pascoe (as I've noted) is also doing this in her science-informed comedy routines and writing and finding a receptive global audience. So is Iliza Shlesinger, described by *Elle* magazine as "a comedian wrapped in a social critic."

Shlesinger is a stand-up comic who has been riffing on the centrality of relationships to our lives from a perspective informed by evolutionary psychology. Shlesinger is an incredibly talented actor, able to transform her face and body from young woman to old crone, from anorexic silhouette to catty "party goblin"— an example of true dedication as a physical performer. Without prosthetic makeup or costumes, using only body movement and crazy voice tics to highlight her gags, Shlesinger delivers deadly accurate relationship and pair-bonding humor (and implicit sex advice, too) with her Netflix specials, *Elder Millennial, Confirmed Kills*, and *Iliza unVeiled*.

Shlesinger delves into evolutionary history as she examines our relationship quandaries and contradictions, while riotously riffing on pair-bonding as the bedrock of our deepest aspirations and our most humiliating (and sometimes guilt-inducing) follies. For Shlesinger's elder millennial generation, ideas of sexual liberation had already devolved to chaos before they were born in the 1980s. We'd already moved from the reasonable 1960s observation, "Young people shouldn't have to wait for marriage to have sex," to the nightmarish early twenty-first century decree, "Something's wrong with you if you're not having casual sex with strangers," to the bizarre dead end of today's "Who has time for relationships anyway?" Thus Shlesinger's comedy is replete with rueful references to her generation's alcohol-fueled (anesthetized?) post–sexual revolution, career-is-everything mores to her fraught dating habits—that is, before she got engaged at age thirty-five and then married in 2018.

In *Confirmed Kills*, Shlesinger says:

> What upsets me is that women spend so much time and energy flogging themselves mentally for being single, and changing and trying different methods and looking for guys. And men don't have to do that. They have the luxury of relaxing because they don't have eggs. There are no articles in GQ like, "You're single. Now what?" There's none of that.

"A big part of my job is being honest about the good, the bad, the ugly that we're feeling in any stage of life," Shlesinger said in a *Billboard* interview (November 19, 2019). And she is unembarrassed by gender differences as they affect pair-bonding. In *unVeiled*, Shlesinger offers this somewhat politically incorrect view:

> Men are visual creatures . . . which means, girls, they have to be physically attracted to you for at least a second to get engaged and then want to get to know, like, your amazing personality. . . . That's what it is. It does not go the other way. No man's ever been like, "I want to set you up with a girl." And that guy's been, "All right, tell me about her remarkable charity work first." No. They're attracted to you. And then they move in. Okay? He saw you and then the rest of it was yours, okay? . . . You want a man that is wired that way for as annoying as it can be . . . A man would have to be so broken by society to be like, "I don't care what she looks like, just don't let her spit in my food."

Shlesinger's overarching relationship messaging seems to me to be: *we all need somebody* and don't pretend otherwise. We need them for more than casual sex. The need for relationships, she implies, goes for females and males as well as nonbinary people. This is true in spite of the fact that many of us still repeat the cliché that relationships are a female thing and that males just want sex. That's not true. Just ask Jerry Seinfeld.

In season six of *Comedians in Cars Getting Coffee*, Seinfeld tells one of his interviewees that if he had to do it all over again, he would have married earlier and "had lots more kids." Speaking of the pleasure he discovered in his marriage and children, Seinfeld (rarely given to such personal public expressions) turns uncharacteristically serious and says of his family life, "There's nothing better."

## Food and sex, pair-bonding and love

Shlesinger bears witness to the fact that our society doesn't make it easy to find love. Love is low on the social/economic GDP calculation of greed worship priorities. Shlesinger's observation about men, "They have the luxury of relaxing [about finding love] because they don't have eggs," would not be a truism if we were in tune with our evolutionary history. Instead, we're indoctrinated by both secular and religious evolution-denying cults. In a saner world, our society would be geared to balancing relationships and family *with* career —not the other way around. We would offer real choices backed up by spending tax money. We'd recognize that having a child means women must cope with bio-terror. We'd take to heart the deep truths about pregnancy and having children revealed in the remarkable film *Pieces of a Woman*.

## *Pieces of a Woman*

The movie starts with an extended twenty-three-minute scene, which was shot in one stunning take, where Martha (played by

Vanessa Kirby) gives birth, and then catastrophically loses the baby during a home birth gone wrong. The scene is tough to witness and brilliantly portrayed by Kirby. When Kirby received the script, she said, "It felt like a total journey of female courage" (*Variety*, January 8, 2021), explaining that the film "gives a voice to a subject that is so often silenced and so rarely spoken about."

According to a BBC Radio 4 "Woman's Hour" interview I listened to in March 2021, in preparation for her role, Kirby spent time with many women who had been through losing a wanted baby at many different stages, whether early in pregnancy or just after they're born. She also watched a woman give birth, which she says changed her life forever. (Maybe it wasn't coincidental that Shlesinger played a small part in the movie—Martha's sister, Anita.)

### Bleeding in the "Rape Room"

To me the film captured the daunting physical challenges women face and reminded me of watching helplessly when Genie was confronted with the betrayal her body foisted on her. To me the movie confirmed Myrna's point that we have only one choice about the "choice issue," no matter how fraught it is: trust women or not. I trust women. Period. I even have shared a little of what women go through.

I'd watched my three children being born. I'd seen a doctor cut Genie to make the passage wider when Jessica—our firstborn— was tearing her mother's flesh as she made her way into the world. I'd seen a scary forceps delivery of our son John (a ten-plus-pound baby) after he got stuck and nearly killed Genie after thirty-six hours of labor. A couple of years later, after a year when Genie's increasingly long periods became one long trial, it was as if something inside her had broken loose. Even bath towels couldn't soak up all the blood. I'd been squatting on the bathroom floor at her feet in the middle of the night, watching her bleed dreadful clots that looked like slices of raw liver. At her request I was zeroing in on the clots because one possibility she considered was that, long periods or not, Genie was having a miscarriage. So I studied those clots looking for little hands or feet, wildly imagining a small face staring back at me.

Was that a tiny foot?

This was nuts, but it was three in the morning, and MY WIFE might be dying!

Then we were in the hospital.

Then the bleeding slowed. Genie was waxy pale, waiting to be examined by a gynecologist. There was a smear of blood on her cheek that I washed off with a paper towel. I was gingerly perching on a stainless-steel stool close to a short table with stirrups. I was holding her hand while our first meeting as teens replayed in my brain like a loop of film. Next to me was a plastic bag hand-labeled "Rape Kit." Genie looked so beautiful. My heart was breaking. It was easy to imagine her dead.

We'd been stowed in a gynecology examination cubicle reserved for female emergencies like ours—and, apparently, for gathering evidence from rape victims. I surreptitiously studied that clear plastic bag. There was a fine-tooth comb for combing through a woman's pubic hair to snag a rapist's pubic hairs. There was a test tube with a Q-tip-type swab in it to absorb fluids from the next rape victim. There was a sharp plastic stick, something like an overgrown toothpick, used to scrape under the victim's fingernails to retrieve blood or tissue from the rapist, if the victim had scratched her attacker. Next to the rape kit was a Polaroid camera with a handwritten label taped to it that read "Evidence Camera. Do *NOT* Remove from Rape Room."

The night duty nurses kept us waiting for the doctor, a bleary-eyed, none-too-gentle male gynecologist (and a stranger to us since Genie's doctor was several towns away and we'd made a beeline to the nearest emergency room) who smelled faintly of liquor. We'd waited for over two hours—plenty of time to study everything in the rape room twenty times over while Genie grew colder and colder. I asked for another blanket and eventually was given one that was as thin and useless as tissue paper.

We'd found ourselves a long way from the level of care, not to mention compassion, Genie received a year later at the Mayo Clinic. There Genie finally got the sort of care women should always find available. And by then, I finally had at least a small notion of the price evolution asks women to pay for the simple fact of procreation. *The idea that anyone but women themselves have any business deciding how to navigate the biological and social challenges women face (and sometimes must extricate themselves from) is just plain evil. The idea that there might be some better way to legislate issues related to reproduction than to simply trust women is stupid.*

## Carstensen: a major redesign of life

It seems to me that besides facing procreation, women's ability to be happy as parents has been attacked by our capitalist system that makes sure they have no good choices unless they are rich. Fortunately, plenty of people are calling for change with women leading the charge. In "We Need a Major Redesign of

Life" (*Washington Post*, November 30, 2019), Laura L. Carstensen, a professor of psychology and the director of the Stanford Center on Longevity, calls for the sort of sweeping changes we need. She writes:

> It's time to get serious about a major redesign of life. Thirty years were added to average life expectancy in the twentieth century, and rather than imagine the scores of ways we could use these years to improve quality of life, we tacked them all on at the end. Only old age got longer. . . . [So] it would be a mistake to replace the old rigid model of life—education first, then family and work, and finally retirement—with a new model just as rigid. *Instead, there should be many different routes, interweaving leisure, work, education and family throughout life, taking people from birth to death with places to stop, rest, change courses and repeat steps along the way. Old age alone wouldn't last longer; rather, youth and middle age would expand.* (Italics added.)

Work-related complaints are multiplying. Here's one: "Women Did Everything Right. Then Work Got 'Greedy'" (*New York Times*, April 26, 2019). It explores the pitfalls confronting even some of the most "successful" of us. "The returns to working long, inflexible hours have greatly increased. This is particularly true in managerial jobs and what social scientists call *the greedy professions*, like finance, law and consulting—an unintentional side effect of the nation's embrace of a winner-take-all economy."

The *Times* article documents how overwork—time in the office or more recently post-Covid-19 from home online—has become increasingly common in any job in which someone's manager stays late or sends emails on weekends and expects employees to answer. "Certain changes," the *Times* notes, "would lighten parents' demands at home, like universal public preschool, longer school days, free after-school care and shorter school breaks. But the ultimate solution, researchers say, is not to make it possible for mothers to work crazy hours, too."

Journalist and author Rainesford Stauffer notes in *An Ordinary Age: Finding Your Way in a World That Expects Exceptional* that

> If you're a young adult today (or even just know a young adult today), it's a challenge not to feel as though finding yourself has been turned into a competitive sport. . . . Omnipresent illustrations of best lives, bodies, and selves constantly play out on Instagram, and the churn of perfectionism has radically amped up expectations that turn "perfect" into a theoretically meetable standard. There are new timelines for entering young adulthood, and what it means to be a fulfilled young person is being rethought in real time. But the myth of a best self, and a best life, following certain patterns and meeting certain benchmarks, remains.
>
> As I moved through my early twenties into my mid-to-late-twenties, I found myself yearning for simple things that rarely made the list of dream jobs, big moves, and adventures that have been marketed as cornerstones of young adulthood. I thought about the steadiness of a partner and community when I was supposed to feel confident and proud to go it alone. A sense of self that wasn't tethered to what I achieved or who I pleased.

## Brooks: more is demanded of parents

Kim Brooks, author of *Small Animals: Parenthood in the Age of Fear,* whom we met earlier, describes our pre-coronavirus world of career striving imbalance in "We Have Ruined Childhood—for Youngsters These Days, an Hour of Free Play Is Like a Drop of Water in the Desert. Of Course They're Miserable" (*New York Times* August 17, 2019):

> No longer able to rely on communal structures for childcare or allow children time alone, parents who need to work are forced to warehouse their youngsters for long stretches of time. School days are longer and more regimented. Kindergarten, which used to be focused on play, is now an academic training ground for the first grade. Young children are assigned homework even though numerous studies have found it harmful. STEM, standardized testing and active-shooter drills have largely replaced recess, leisurely lunches, art and music.

## Solomon and Julian: "What's it like to be in love?"

It's not just parents that are having trouble balancing careers and family; younger people have been finding it's difficult in our work-first climate to even get relationships going. For example, in "Why Are Young People Having So Little Sex?" (*The Atlantic,* December 2018), Kate Julian, the magazine's senior editor, writes a masterful overview of our "state of the union" when it comes to sex and relationships (or the lack thereof) in the context of preparing for careers. She introduces her essay this way:

> Marriage 101, one of the most popular undergraduate classes at Northwestern University, was launched in 2001 by William M. Pinsof, a founding father of couples therapy, and Arthur Nielsen, a psychiatry professor. . . . The class was meant to be a sort of preemptive

strike against unhappy marriages. Under Alexandra Solomon, the psychology professor who took over the course six years ago, it has become, secondarily, a strike against what she sees as *the romantic and sexual stunting of a generation.* (Italics added.)

Julian describes how, insofar as Solomon's students find themselves choosing between casual sex and no sex, they're doing so because an obvious third option—*bonding and emotionally fulfilling relationship sex*—strikes them as "unattainable" and even "potentially irresponsible." Solomon says that many of her students have absorbed the idea that love is "secondary to academic and professional success"—or at any rate "is best delayed until those other things have been secured."

Alexandra added this in her notes to me about her struggle between enjoying her kids yet wishing she could also have had a career sooner. She seems to back up Solomon's point. Alexandra writes: "When I was first dating my future husband, it took time and effort. Instead of spending the evening in the lab, I went out on a date. I felt guilty for leaving the lab 'early' at 6 PM and for leaving the lab at all. Later, when my lab PI (boss) at the time knew I was engaged, he (jokingly but clearly serious at the same time) told me to not have kids (while I was in his lab) until I finished graduate school. I will never forget his bluntness. For other professional reasons I soon thereafter left his lab to join a new lab, but this was also always in the back of my mind."

Solomon has described our anti-relationship culture's bias for work my friend Alexandra encountered. Solomon says it's both a cause and an effect of social stunting. Or, as one of her students put it to her: "We hook up because we have no social skills. We have no social skills because we hook up."

"Over and over," Solomon says, "my undergraduates tell me they try hard not to fall in love during college, imagining that would mess up their plans." One young woman told Solomon, "You're supposed to have done so much before you can get into a relationship." Another said that when she was in high school, her parents discouraged relationships because they might "diminish her focus." Even today, in graduate school, she said she was finding the attitude hard to shake. "Now I need to finish school, I need to get a practice going, I need to do this and this, and then I'll think about love. But by thirty, you're like, what is love? What's it like to be in love?"

# CHAPTER 3

# Feminism— Evolution's Gift to *Men* (as Well as to Women)

Certain experiences changed my life for the better. Being sent to Great Walstead School (GW), a boarding school for boys in Lindfield, Sussex, England, was one such experience. Up to then I'd been homeschooled by my parents, who wanted to protect me from "worldly influences." My parents always feared their children would be seduced away from Christian beliefs and into worldly ways, such as smoking, drinking, dancing, sex, and, worst of all, *bad theology*. GW was my first shot at a less stressful life. I was no longer trying to save the world but just trying to learn to read a little better. I was sent there at age ten because (very late) my distracted parents ("distracted" by paying more attention to the Lord's Work than to their children, traveling on speaking trips that got longer and longer) decided that homeschooling wasn't working. The word *dyslexia* wasn't part of anyone's vocabulary back then. A wealthy donor in the UK said he'd pay my school fees. And the school was nominally (and rather sanely "low church Anglican") Christian—so that was all right. There was chapel twice a day.

Gordon Parke was the wonderfully kind and creative head-master. His wife, Eunice Parke, was both a teacher and his eagle-eyed coleader. She (like her husband) gave "her" boys opportunities that I only came to fully appreciate years later. Without Eunice Parke, I'd never have believed that it was possible for me to function in the wider world outside my parents' mission. Without Eunice Parke I would not be a writer, reader, and lifelong student. Without Eunice Parke, I would not have had the confidence to try new things, change my mind, and change my life. One of the only things I know for certain I've ever done that was 100 percent right was to fly to England some fifteen years ago or so to expressly thank Eunice and Gordon in person when they were getting on in years. It was a joyful reunion.

## Great Walstead School became my liberating home away from home

GW's grounds covered 294 acres of fields, woods, ponds, a small river, playing fields, and lawns nestled in a gently hilly landscape midway between London and Brighton. When Mom and I arrived on my first day by taxi from the Hayward's Heath station, we passed the school's small farm and its half-timbered Elizabethan farmhouse and drove up to the door of the brick Victorian mansion that had been converted into the school in the early 1900s. Mom and I took a quick tour, along with several other new boys and their parents, while following one of the Sixth Form (senior) boys. Mom left me crying and hiding in a rhododendron thicket. I was scared and homesick.

Four years later when I left the school (everyone had to graduate at thirteen), I was crying again, this time at the thought of leaving. The next boys' school I went to, St. David's in Wales (a private high school or "public school" in English parlance), was a miserable place by comparison. I lasted there two years, and then, at age fifteen, I ran away. All I took with me was the then-new Beatles' album *Sgt. Pepper's Lonely Hearts Club Band*.

Most boys came to GW at age five. (Sorry but the idea of parenthood in the British upper classes really is revolting.) I arrived late by comparison and never did catch up academically. I did catch up socially, however, because polio or not I was good at soccer. And after getting over the homesickness, I was very happy.

A few months into my first term at GW, Mrs. Parke stopped me in the narrow, musty-smelling back hall that led down to our dining area. She was wearing a white apron over a gray, knee-length skirt and briskly drying her hands on a dishtowel. Eunice Parke was thin, trim, and birdlike, including a sharp beaky nose. Her eyes were dark brown, bright, and sparkling. She fixed me with the most direct look I'd ever experienced that left me rooted to the spot. Maybe it was the disconcertingly steady way she met my eyes, but diminutive or not, Mrs. Parke exuded a no-nonsense, cast-iron will, and I felt a twinge of fear.

"Schaeffer!" she barked, after she popped her head out of the staff sitting room door that I'd been walking past.

"Yes, Mrs. Parke," I said, nervously wondering what I'd done now, and also wondering how on earth she knew I was passing.

"Why haven't you tried out for 'Pinafore' yet?"

"I can't do that sort of thing, Mrs. Parke."

"And jolly well why not?"

"I can't learn words," I blurted.

"Reading and spelling have nothing to do with opera, Schaeffer. How do you know you're no good at opera?"

"But, Mrs. Parke, I'm no good at learning."

"A play isn't 'learning,' it's acting. All you have to do is pretend."

"But . . ."

"Can you remember music?"

"What do you mean?"

"I mean if I sing this, da, da, ta—tah! What is it?"

"Beethoven's Fifth."

"Brilliant! You see?! You *can* remember anything as well as anyone else once it's set to music, so you jolly well come to the rehearsal today."

"But . . ."

"I shall read the words out loud to you, and then we'll sing them together. It will be rather jolly!"

"Yes, Mrs. Parke."

It always was "Yes, Mrs. Parke." So a few days later I found myself rehearsing madly for the role of Dick Deadeye in my warbled, uncertain, tuneless soprano. Mrs. Parke was thumping away on an old upright piano with one hand and directing me with the other.

Eunice Parke changed my life. She was a teacher who led through stern, no-nonsense caring. She had the charisma and authority chops to be a prime minister.

## Strong women leaders are better equipped to guide us out of any crisis

According to "What the Pandemic Reveals About the Male Ego," by columnist Nicholas Kristof (*New York Times,* June 13,

2020), death rates from the coronavirus for twenty-one countries around the world, thirteen led by men and eight by women,
showed the male-led countries suffered far worse in the first
wave. He quotes former national security adviser under President Barack Obama, Susan Rice: "I don't think it's a coincidence
that some of the best-run places have been run by women: New
Zealand, Germany, Taiwan. And where we've seen things go most
badly wrong—the U.S., Brazil, Russia, the UK—it's a lot of male
ego and bluster."

It's not that the leaders who best managed the virus were all
women. But those who bungled the response worst were all men,
and mostly a particular type: authoritarian, vainglorious, and
blustering. The words *child minding* and *caring*, let alone *empathy* and *parenting* and especially *love* do not came to mind when
considering the male leadership qualities of thugs like India's
Narendra Modi, Vladimir Putin in Russia, Donald Trump in the
US, Jair Bolsonaro in Brazil, and Ayatollah Ali Khamenei in Iran.
Put it this way: if they'd been teachers at GW, they would have
ignored boys who couldn't read and/or beaten us into submission.
When Modi, Trump, Bolsonaro, and others of their strutting
ilk applied their nationalist, strong-man, populist, anti-science
tactics to protecting their people from the virus, they effectively
murdered hundreds of thousands.

The female leaders guiding their people through the crisis
well were not necessarily coming from a place of simple nurturing:
all evidence points to these women leaders' actions and strategies
as being science- and data-driven. The co-founder and chief medical officer of BioNTech has credited its speed at producing a via-
ble vaccine to the fact that its workforce was more than 50 percent

female. Speaking on International Women's Day, Özlem Türeci said the fact that women are so underrepresented in decision-making roles in medicine is "destroying value" for stakeholders. The Pfizer/BioNTech vaccine was the first to be approved in the UK, and Türeci said it was the company's balanced workforce that "made the impossible possible" in creating a vaccine in just eleven months. They made difficult decisions about public-health risks versus economic fallout from shutdowns based on empirical evidence in much the same way that the leading female characters in the Netflix series *Away* do. It's a mission-to-Mars drama I happen to admire for the way it portrays women leaders, motherhood, career, and religion intermixing and balancing—or not balancing into real struggle. Hilary Swank and Vivian Wu play science-guided women leaders who *also* struggle with family issues to which there are no simple answers.

It was the absence of male hubris and macho bullshit populism that seems to have made the women who saved so many lives the best leaders during the Covid-19 pandemic. Which brings me to this point: feminism is not bound by biological determinism. It is a natural evolutionary step *but also a deliberate step that needs to be chosen.*

### For obvious reasons, I approach feminism from a male point of view

I bring the perspective of personal gratitude to the women who shaped my life: Eunice Parke; my mother; Jane Smith and Betty Carlson (you'll meet them in a moment); my lifetime partner, lover, and friend, Genie; my friend and daughter, Jessica; my friend and confidants and granddaughters: Amanda, Lucy, and Nora; my childcare co-conspirator daughter-in-law, Becky; my granddaughter-in-law Claire, who married Ben early in 2021 and *also* read this book and gave me notes while she was still in college; and of course the incredible women like Myrna who helped me so tirelessly with ideas and corrections for this book.

That list doesn't even include the many female associates I have worked *with* and *for*—the editors, agents, actresses, camera people, news anchors, interviewers, TV news-show bookers, my friend and agent, Jennifer; not to mention my longtime primary-care doctor of the last twenty-three years, Lela; and many other women besides who shaped, guarded, and improved my life and, in some cases, such as my beloved friend, children's book illustrator and artist Holly Meade, still improve my life as they exert their influence over me posthumously. Nor does it include the women like scientist Alexandra Torres, political activist and movie maker Laura Murphy (someone who as I tell her is the "little sister I never had"), and artist Kristin Breiseth (KB)—who read various drafts of this book, contributed invaluable notes and suggestions, and helped shape it.

Shorthand: in women I trust for very good reasons.

## My first introduction to feminism was via my evangelical mother, Edith, who said she believed in wives "submitting" to husbands—but mostly didn't

Mom taught by example by standing up to my father's bullying. She shaped their ministry in a way that made it far more hers than his. Thus, I grew up seeing female leadership as my mother handled my perpetually moody and sometimes physically abusive father and yet did exactly what she set out to do in everything from child-raising to writing her many books to the vacations we took to how our family spent our "treat money": season classical concert tickets.

In the lead *New York Times* obituary tribute to my mother, "Edith Schaeffer, Definer of Christian Family Values, Dies at 98" (April 6, 2013), the *Times* noted that:

> Mrs. Schaeffer wrote more than two dozen books, including *Hidden Art* (1971) and *What Is a Family?* (1975), describing her vision of women's domestic role in the battle with secular humanism and declining morality, as fundamentalist Christians defined the prevailing threats to humanity in the postwar world. That role, she said, was to make one's home a work of art, she wrote in *What Is a Family?*: "There needs to be a homemaker exercising some measure of skill, imagination, creativity, desire to fulfill needs and give pleasure to others in the family." . . . *[I]in some ways [Edith Schaeffer] was the model of a sort of evangelical feminism.* (Italics added.)

Mom's evangelical feminism stuck. More than that, in my childhood (besides my mother and Eunice Parke) another powerful woman opened doors for me from the time I was five. I didn't know at the time that Jane Smith was a lesbian in a long-term (if more or less closeted) relationship. Of course, I have no knowledge about how sexually active she was, but years later I realized that Jane and Betty Carlson were an item.

"Two lovely single Christian ladies who live together" was the way Mom described them back in 1959. That's when they moved in together in a chalet they bought across the street from ours that then became part of my parents' ministry of L'Abri.

## Jane and Betty

Mom and Dad were not fools, and so I'm sure they knew that Jane and Betty were more than "spinsters" sharing a house. My parents were also (for their day) tolerant evangelicals, at least when it came to how they treated homosexuals (as they called gay people then) and/or ignored what were perceived as their weaknesses.

My parents' ministry at L'Abri swept up many unique and interesting people from Betty Ford to Timothy Leary and the actress Glynis Johns, countless Beats (1950s) and hippies (1960s), and a steady stream of evangelicals (1970s to the present day) seeking spiritual renewal. Some stayed for a day or two, others for the better part of a lifetime. Many just crashed for a few days seeking a free bed while hitching across Europe. Mom was often on her hands and knees scrubbing the floors, rising at four in the morning to pray and then to type up the dictation she'd taken from Dad as his sometime secretary the day before, or spending hours talking to and counseling the guests. She spent half of each day in our kitchen producing meals for twenty, thirty, or fifty freeloaders.

Mom always paid as much personal attention to whomever she was with, from a hotel chambermaid to some new guest, to the President of the United States, when, in later years, she became an evangelical star and was a guest in the Ford White House, sleeping in the presidential family apartment, and over the years carrying on a lengthy personal correspondence with Betty Ford.

## My parents' compassion was sincere and consistent

Unlike today's American far-right, post-Trump, cult evangelicals, Mom and Dad never let Christian belief make them into bigots, at least not before we launched into right-wing leadership roles ourselves as crusading pro-lifers. In fact, when people ask me why I fled the evangelical movement, I tell them that what started the process of my exit was me comparing the fraudulent big-time Christian leaders I got to know in the 1970s and 1980s to my sincere parents. For a start, Dad wasn't a thief. L'Abri wasn't a criminal operation as is every single big American ministry I ever came to know. By contrast, I believe Pat Robertson, Jerry Falwell, Dr. Dobson (and later Ralph Reed, Franklin Graham, and company) were and are con artists. They were and are malignant, two-faced narcissists. As I moved in evangelical leadership circles, I soon came to know that the leaders were cruel. In contrast, my parents were wrong about many things, but they put what they earned (after they hit bestseller pay dirt) back into their ministry.

My exodus from evangelical nepotistic stardom really began when I realized that L'Abri and Francis and Edith Schaeffer were the decent *exception* to the fraudulent rule when it came to American Christianity. Then, of course, once I began to no longer accept the theological truth package (about what we were supposed to believe about the Bible), the mythology of Christianity itself began to unravel for me.

That said, Dad knew better than to do what he did working with those he knew were fakes, frauds, and thieves. *But he got as greedy as I did for access to power and influence.* So for a time, Dad and I worked with openly homophobic fakes, thieves, and bigots such as Jerry Falwell and Pat Robertson, for the "good of the cause."

Our collaboration with these evangelical bullies ("whited sepulchers" to use the biblical term) was shameful. Given the way Dad had run his own ministry, we knew better. By the time we were leading the antiabortion crusade, we'd slipped into outright misogyny. Just knowing the great women who raised me like

Mom, Mrs. Parke, and Jane and Betty, I should have known better. So should have Dad. We not only were betraying an idea of what Jesus's love was supposed to be about, we betrayed the women in our lives, too. The fact that some pro-life evangelical women were also betraying other women was no excuse. Many of them had been conditioned from birth to submit to male authority as "God's will."

## Back to Jane and Betty . . .

After meeting each other at L'Abri when they were in their thirties, Jane and Betty lived together for the better part of sixty years—the rest of their lives. I spent hundreds of hours of my childhood with Jane and Betty. When I'd cut across the main road that led past our chalet up to the ski resort of Villars from the Rhône Valley far below, I'd be looking down on Chalet Le Chesalet's lichen-splotched tile roof. There was a stone retaining wall right behind the chalet that I would climb down rather than walk by the path.

Jane had been an opera singer until she "accepted Jesus," stopped singing worldly music, and stayed on to become a worker at L'Abri and then a leader in the ministry. She still practiced every day and sometimes, when I was on the way down the wall, I heard her singing scales up and down and up and down to higher and higher notes and then sliding all the way to the bottom notes and starting over.

Jane grew up in Roanoke, Virginia, where her father was the president of a railroad. Mom said her father had once rented Carnegie Hall for Jane to sing in "so she could have a New York debut." Jane offered us many concerts, bought a Dutch Flentrop organ for our chapel, formed a musical ensemble, sang in the chapel, and even toured with her ensemble performing classical Christian music—mostly Johann Sebastian Bach and George Frideric Handel. And Jane drank wine with her meals! We Schaeffers were "real Christians don't drink" teetotalers. So Jane seemed like a revolutionary to me. She wasn't bothered by our evangelical taboos, even after she got "saved." Jane was doing her own thing, as they say, with or without anyone's permission.

While my parents opened their home to guests as part of their communal living outreach, Jane never had guests stay with her. She limited her ministry to serving meals twice a week to some of our guests, individual counseling, and giving a monthly lecture on whatever was interesting her just then, from art history to J. S. Bach's theology. Sometimes other L'Abri workers complained to my parents that Jane didn't share the workload of having students in her house. Other times they'd complain about the content of her lectures, wherein Jane included what some regarded as heretical ideas, not to mention lots of naked images illustrating her art series. (Pieter Bruegel the Elder was her favorite.) Despite their displeasure, no one ever dared to bring up complaints to her face, let alone ask her why she and Betty shared a bedroom. Jane was formidable, loud, and—easily and operatically—enraged.

I would get a huge welcome from Jane and Betty at least once a day throughout my childhood. Betty was a writer who had once penned a column for a newspaper in Rockford, Illinois—a pursuit she gave up to "serve the Lord." Post-salvation, she only wrote Christian articles for evangelical magazines and, in later years, several inspirational books. Betty had a short butch haircut and, although diminutive, pale, and quiet, the direct manner of a woman who knew who she was and was comfortable in her own skin.

Jane and Betty had very different personalities. Jane was flamboyant and filled rooms. Betty was incredibly kind and sympathetic and hovered in corners. She used to invite everyone to her birthday—and give all her guests presents. Any time I had a problem, Betty would be the person in whom I'd confide. She was always there to be a sounding board, and she would make empathetic little growling and clucking noises interspersed with many an "Oh, dear, *aw*, what a shame...."

When Jane would say something unusually outrageous, even for her—anyone who disagreed with her talk on the symbolic meaning found in the art of the Hebrew tabernacle and Solomon's temple thereby proved they were not Christians because "Only idiots would disagree with me, and I don't care if they *are* L'Abri workers, and *you know who I mean!*"—Betty would offer a quiet "Jane, you don't mean that." And Jane would yell, "Yes, I do!" and flush a deep scarlet.

## Viva l'Italia!

Betty drove their car on trips to Italy. Jane's job was to read out loud to her. When they returned they would sit me down and tell me about the art they had seen, the food they had eaten, and the books they had read. Then they would show me the art books they had bought. The way they talked about Italy was as if they had been to heaven.

I didn't need convincing that Italy was the place any sane or lucky person would go when they die, if they had a choice. So it stands to reason that my favorite time of the year was our Schaeffer family two-week holiday in Portofino, a ten-hour train trip away. In those days, it was an inexpensive vacation that my mother nevertheless scrimped and saved all year to pay for. (It's no coincidence that *Portofino* became the title of my first novel.)

Almost every time I visited, Jane played me parts of Bellini's opera *Norma*. She showed me glossy black-and-white photographs of herself in costume, holding a spear in the part, as well as many other photos of herself in other roles.

"Why don't you sing anymore?" I asked.

"I sing in church every Sunday!"

"You know what I mean."

"I gave it up for the Lord! The world of opera is a wicked place! You have *no idea* about the TEMPTATIONS I faced!"

"Was it terrible?"

"NO! It was marvelous! *That* was the problem! I *loved* those temptations!"

I spent hours looking through Jane's scrapbooks of photos and opera programs, trying to imagine what those temptations had been that had made her leave such a wonderful life. I drummed up the courage to ask one day, and Jane snapped, "Never you mind, honey, never you mind!" and glared at me.

Another time I said, "Will you *please* sing some opera for me?" Jane answered, "No, honey, I won't. My voice is too big for this little chalet living room! Why, if I was to sing in here at full volume so close to you, it would probably kill you!"

One time, when I was nine, we were listening to opera and Jane said, "Now we're coming to the 'Casta Diva,' the greatest aria Bellini ever wrote. And in this recording Joan Sutherland is singing the role. Maria Callas was more famous, but Joan's voice is far, far better, honey! So don't ever believe anyone who says Maria Callas could sing!"

"I won't, Jane."

"Hush! Just listen!"

I wrote to Jane many years later when she was very old and back in Virginia, caring for Betty, who had Alzheimer's. I wrote to tell Jane what she and Betty meant to me. I thanked her for being one of the people who shaped my life and made it so much richer than it would have been. Jane wrote back and enclosed a fistful of yellowing clippings. They were of some opinion pieces I'd written for the *Washington Post* and dozens of reviews of my first novels. Jane had been watching over me even though we hadn't been in touch for years. Jane said she was proud of me! I'd changed my ideas and my politics. I was no longer "a Christian" by my parents' definition of the word, but the art, love, and dedication to the intrinsic worth of beauty had stuck. So in Jane's "Book of Life" (recording the "saved") I was still listed as one of the "elect"!

When I'm with my grandchildren caring for them, they are meeting Jane. And since I make art, still love "the right music," and Nora sings along with the operas she watches, I know in Jane's eyes I'd still be counted as a "real Christian"—maybe almost an honorary Italian, maybe even still "saved," though I'm now an evangelical outcast and describe myself as an atheist who believes in God.

The fact that I still go to church, a local Greek Orthodox church, and still crave liturgy and spirituality—all the while *not* being a "believer," as my parents would have defined the required certainties I've abandoned—is a testimony to Jane's ideas of the merger of beauty and spirituality. To Jane, loving God and, in turn, feeling loved were one and the same. Spirituality to her then and to me now me was and is the sense that some things have intrinsic worth. They are beyond price or even definition, they just *are*. And it is these things that make life worth living and give me hope that, just maybe, human life has some meaning beyond the sum of our parts.

## Feminism is a push for justice, primarily for women

Perhaps some men like me became feminists because they were nurtured by strong compassionate women. Maybe we also just get sick of ourselves! Maybe one woman puts her foot down. Maybe the love of children changes us. Maybe all of that happens to us. But coming to respect women, be they eighty or six years of age, isn't a definition of feminism. So how to define the word *feminism* more generally rather than from one man's fond personal point of view? The American author Rebecca Solnit defines feminism well, I think, in "Younger Feminists Have Shifted My Understanding" (*Guardian*, February 29, 2020):

> Feminism is part of an immense endeavor on all seven continents (and sometimes a space station or two) to change how we imagine gender, rights, equality, consent, voice; to create a conversation that invites participation for those who have felt excluded, silenced. It's a conversation about race, gender, sexual orientation, trans rights, disability rights, religious freedom, neurodiversity, and so much more, and about how these things can intersect in a single person or interaction. Anyone in this conversation learns from others to look harder, see farther, ask new questions, use new terms that admit new possibilities.

Rebecca Solnit also wrote a great book called *Men Explain Things to Me* and an excellent memoir: *Recollections of My Nonexistence*. I think she beautifully explores female erasure, trauma's effects on women and their bodies, and modern gender dynamics. And I love Solnit's definition of feminism but would add this: it seems to me that feminism is also *evolution's best gift to males*.

I use the word *gift* because feminism is about accelerating human connection and cooperation and thus increasing the odds of our individual and species' survival and happiness. That's because feminism is rooted in the evolution of cooperation as our primary survival tactic: cooperation, not domination. Thus (to me), feminism is about women's rights, but it is also how we may all unite to transform our crowded, interconnected, and interdependent lives on our fragile planet into a community that better safeguards everyone's future *and* fosters joy.

## Why feminism? Buchanan and Powell explain

As we evolved into communities that depended on one another, empathy and egalitarianism also evolved. Feminism was thus inevitable as an evolutionary step. This is one of the subjects of *The Evolution of Moral Progress: A Biocultural Theory*, by Allen Buchanan (James B. Duke Professor of philosophy at Duke University) and Russell Powell (assistant professor of philosophy at Boston University). Buchanan and Powell argue that we can extend our understanding of our moral identity to encompass the kind of new moral obligations feminism represents. This new moral obligation calls for humanistic solutions to conflict and how we share what we have with one another. They write:

> Morality first developed as an adaptation in the distant past for coping with certain basic problems that all human societies faced at that time. More specifically, there was [evolutionary] selection for norm-following that helped groups to cope with conflicts of interest, to achieve the coordination needed for successful foraging and other subsistence activities within the group, and to compete successfully with other groups when there were conflicts over the appropriation of resources.

This capacity (driven by our need for problem-solving and pattern seeking) eventually created what we would recognize today as the institutions we use to order our lives—everything from governments to churches. These social institutions (religious, tribal, political, and otherwise) evolved to enforce what we'd come to understand were our best survival tactics: how to get along with those around us.

During our evolutionary past, small groups of humans began to have increasingly more contact with other tribes and eventually larger societal groups. We compared ourselves, both individually and collectively, to others. As groups of humans came in contact with one another, we started to compare social structures, too. This led to thinking about what worked or did not work best to give us a shot at survival—maybe even a bit of enjoyment of what comes along with that.

Ideas evolved about fairness (humans looked for situations in which they were treated well or cared for well), and right and wrong (recognition of rules and attitudes that protected us from arbitrary harm by others). Buchanan and Powell talk about the origins of this process as making "moral judgments." They say that we found that morality "is not only dynamic and open-ended . . . it has also become increasingly self-reflective, with morality itself an object for [contemplation]. . . . For many humans, morality is no longer simply 'how we do things' or 'what God commands,' but about process for how we organize ourselves best for survival."

According to Buchanan and Powell there are four interconnected core components of partnership systems seeking feminist-style justice:

1. **Support.** The first component is a democratic egalitarian structure manifested in social practices, values, and
   institutions.
2. **Equity.** The second component is equal partnership
   between women and men and nonbinary people.
3. **Caring.** The third core component is the rejection of
   abuse and violence.
4. **Well-being.** The fourth component consists of beliefs
   about human nature that support mutually respectful
   relations.

If this view is correct, it suggests that feminist moral systems, and the institutions they inspire, are natural evolutionary developments. Once again evolution is pointing us to how to survive. The message is clear: listen to and follow the female voice within your species—or die. This, in turn, gives us hope that with a full-fledged biocultural, feminist egalitarian theory of moral progress in hand, we will be able to increase the odds that the arc of the moral universe will, indeed, bend steadily toward justice and perhaps even joy.

## Plank, Holter, Reeves, and Stuckler: the status of women is the most accurate predictor of men's well-being

Speaking of making life beautiful for everyone, when it comes to extending men's life spans and increasing men's well-being, feminism is any person's best defender. Besides coronavirus survival rates, the communities in which feminism has had the most influence are also the most successful without exception.

Because feminism encourages the idea of mutually respectful relations between all people, *the status of feminism in a society is the most powerful predictor of a society's quality of life.* This is documented in "Women, Men, and the 2015 Global Quality of Life," a study based on statistics from eighty-nine nations conducted by the Center for Partnership Studies. This study's findings were replicated in the 2000 World Values Survey, the largest international survey investigating how attitudes about women correlate with economic development. This study shows that the nations with the lowest gender gaps between males and females in wage earning, child-rearing, and labor-sharing expectations, such as Iceland, Norway, Sweden, Switzerland, Taiwan, and Finland, score regularly at the top of the World Economic Forum's global competitiveness reports. These countries are freer of the rampant social pathologies that are afflicting men in less egalitarian cultures.

In the *Washington Post*'s "Why the Patriarchy Is Killing Men" (September 15, 2019), Liz Plank, senior producer and correspondent at Vox.com and the author of *For the Love of Men: A Vision for Mindful Masculinity*, writes, "It turns out that when women do well, men do, too." Plank points out that no rational man should be afraid of feminism, yet many are because "Giving up a small slice of privilege in exchange for a longer (and happier) life seems like a pretty sweet deal to me. But guys, if you don't believe me, just ask Icelandic men. They have time—3.8 more years, to be exact."

Plank writes about the fact that Iceland is ranked by the World Economic Forum as number one in gender equality and that, consequently, in Iceland men enjoy the highest life expectancy in Europe. If longevity is one of the strongest signs of all-around well-being, then Icelandic men are doing well in arguably the most women-friendly, egalitarian society in the world. Men in

Iceland live almost as long as women do. And in Iceland there are lots of single moms. The social projects I described earlier work. This is what authentic pro-life and pro-family looks like. Women have real choices. Single moms are no big deal because families are frequently nontraditional and support services are effective as we've seen. So fertility is less of an issue, too. Many more women who want children can have children younger than in the States and still succeed at their careers. With all the social services, not having a partner doesn't destroy parents' lives.

## Men saved by feminism

Norwegian sociologist and men's studies professor Oystein Holter has researched the correlation between the state of gender equality and male well-being as measured by mental health, fertility, and suicide statistics. Holter found that men in purposefully gender-equal countries are less likely to get divorced, be depressed, or die as a result of violence. These findings undercut one of the stupider complaints of the right-wing American so-called men's rights movement: that men die younger than women do, so somehow they are owed special privileges by women.

A study by sociologists Aaron Reeves and David Stuckler found that in countries with high levels of gender equality, "the relationship between rising unemployment rates and suicide in men disappeared altogether." In a comprehensive study, "Suicidality, Economic Shocks, and Egalitarian Gender Norms" (February 2016, U.S. National Library of Medicine, National Institutes of Health), the authors report that comprehensive research shows:

> Men who lose jobs in countries with greater gender equality will have lower risks of suicides than those in countries with lesser gender equality. This hypothesis

is consistent with previous evidence that while both men and women have better mental health in gender egalitarian societies, *men also appear to benefit more than women*. . . . In the context of suicide specifically, this may be because negative mental health consequences of job loss may be greater for men in societies where gender norms are less egalitarian and where traditional conceptions of masculinity predominate. (Italics added.)

Conversely, it's from the ranks of the most anti-feminist (and least childminding male archetypes) American males that many of the most alarming statistics related to loneliness, suicide, and drug overdoses have come. This population was also greatly at risk from Covid-19 as smokers or ex-smokers, perennially overweight, older, uneducated, and having gone years without proper healthcare. (Later it was in the ranks of these right wing and often evangelical males that many refused the vaccine as well.) It was also this cohort that was overrepresented in the sad, rather pathetic rabble that stormed the American Capitol on January 6, 2021.

As Buchanan and Powell note:

Poorly educated White men [were and are] disproportionately represented among Trump supporters. This demographic not only is sympathetic to authoritarianism but also is among the most vulnerable to the recent economic downturn (the so-called Great Recession that began in 2008), exhibits poor health outcomes, and is now being forced to come to terms with the challenges that gains in racial and gender equality pose to the traditional privileged status of White men.

Columnist David Brooks discusses the male-harming

breakdown of family stability in "The Rise of the Haphazard Self" (*New York Times*, May 13, 2019). Brooks, despite his conservatism, blames unbridled capitalism. He points out, "A society is [only] healthy when its culture counterbalances its economics. That is to say, when you have a capitalist economic system that emphasizes competition, dynamism, and individual self-interest, you need a culture that celebrates cooperation, stability, and committed relationships. We don't have that. We have a culture that takes the disruptive and dehumanizing aspects of capitalism and makes them worse."

## Edin: the "haphazard self" and the ceaseless hustle

Kathryn Edin, a sociologist and professor at Princeton University, along with several other scholars, did a study tracing the accelerating disintegration of social connections between American working-class males and their families. In "The Tenuous Attachments of Working-Class Men" (*Journal of Economic Perspectives* 33, no. 2, Spring 2019), they sum up their study thus:

> [W]e explore how working-class men describe their attachments to work, family, and religion. We draw upon in-depth, life history interviews conducted in four metropolitan areas with racially and ethnically diverse groups. . . . We interviewed roughly even numbers of Black and White men. . . . We discuss the extent to which this *autonomous and generative self is also a haphazard self, which may be aligned with counterproductive behaviors*. (Italics added.)

According to *Reuters Health News* (January 19, 2020), "People with no more than a high school education may be less likely to die by suicide when minimum wages rise, a U.S. study suggests." The lack of good wages plays a part in their self-destructiveness.

The men the researchers interviewed in the Tenuous Attachments study told them that the economy doesn't allow them to provide for their families and that this has created a culture of "ceaseless hustle." The men typically had to hold three or four jobs in different occupations. The men's private lives were as unattached, unstable, and distracted as their work lives. They expressed the desire to be good fathers but had little commitment to the mothers of their children. Can you blame them? The message of American capitalism is loud and clear to males and everyone else: *"You are on your own, buddy!"*

"Nearly all the men we spoke to viewed the father-child tie as central while the partner relationship was more peripheral," the researchers reported. The men's best intentions aside, since the same men weren't committed to being partners as well as fathers, and since there is no social welfare in America that supports parenthood, their actual involvement with their children was minimal. This, the researchers concluded, "strongly suggest[s] that the autonomous generative self that many men described is also a haphazard self." I'd put it this way: many men may be described as those in which the instinct to nurture and mother has been crushed by our career-oriented culture where we measure everyone's success in terms of job titles, power, fame, and money.

"I've spent two years talking with boys across America— more than 100 of them between the ages of sixteen and twenty-one—about masculinity, sex, and love: about the forces, seen and unseen, that shape them as men," writes Peggy Orenstein in her book *Boys & Sex*. In her research, Orenstein found that when asked to describe the attributes of "the ideal guy," those same boys appeared to be harking back to 1955. "Dominance. Aggression.

Rugged good looks (with an emphasis on height). Sexual prowess. Stoicism. Athleticism. Wealth. And while a 2018 national survey of more than 1,000 ten- to nineteen-year-olds commissioned by Plan International USA and conducted by the polling firm Perry Undem found that young women believed there were many ways to be a girl—they could shine in math, sports, music, leadership—young men described just one narrow route to successful masculinity. One-third said they felt compelled to suppress their feelings, to 'suck it up' or 'be a man' when they were sad or scared, and more than 40 percent said that when they were angry, society expected them to be combative."

Orenstein notes that, according to Andrew Smiler, a psychologist who has studied the history of Western masculinity, the ideal late nineteenth-century man was compassionate, a caretaker, but such qualities lost favor as paid labor moved from homes to factories during industrialization. In fact, the Boy Scouts, whose creed urges its members to be loyal, friendly, courteous, and kind, was founded in 1910 in part to counter that dehumanizing trend.

**Manosphere**

In "To Learn About the Far Right, Start with the 'Manosphere'" by Helen Lewis (*The Atlantic*, August 7, 2019), a London-based staff writer at the *The Atlantic* and the author of *Difficult Women: A History of Feminism in 11 Fights*, we read:

> The manosphere stretches from the kind of lukewarm anti-feminism that would pass virtually unremarked in a newspaper column through to glorifications of extreme misogyny. Although the manosphere's leading figures have appeared at far-right events, and vice versa, the links between the two are more about an exchange of

ideas. . . . These ideas circulate through YouTube videos, anonymous message boards such as 8Chan, Facebook. groups, and Twitter accounts. The online ecosystem allows dense, rambling conspiracist tracts to be chopped up and recirculated in more palatable forms.

What's the perceived source of this bitterness directed toward women? As Lewis reports: "The 'family wage'—where a man earns enough to support a wife and children—has disappeared; working women have greater economic freedom, instead of being dependent on men; and women control their fertility and their bank accounts so do not have to be subservient to men." Yet the more a man identifies with such politically and religiously powerful lies, these same lies goad him to resentment and self-pity, which turns to deep anger. Why the anger? Maybe because studies of active fathers involved with their children prove that men are actually wired to love and care, not to be macho goofs. Maybe because, as happened to me, if you buy the lie that you as a male should be in charge, the burden of trying to enforce this bullshit becomes intolerable. You can become a brute, become suicidal—or change.

### Enter a hero in his own mind

When the essential male nature as nurturing protector is squandered, men lash out. Maybe that erasure of males' essential nature as nurturing beings is why when I listened to a podcast interview with Jordan Peterson, a Canadian philosopher who has been embraced by a lot of men's rights groups, I reacted negatively. It was like an alcoholic being offered a drink again. It seemed he was a vehemently anti-feminist and as a Christian he echoed (as cleverly as he could but still unmistakably) the fundamentalist crap I was raised on. He was telling other men that when they want to put a woman in her place, this is what nature (and/or God) intended. In a deeper way, Jordan comes off as a toxically anti-nurturing male. He seemed to be dog-whistling to a lot of disenfranchised boys or angry men who have a hard time keeping up the front of authority over others, with rhetoric about the so-called hero's journey (a common narrative archetype, involving a hero who goes on an adventure, learns lessons, wins a victory with that newfound knowledge, and then returns home transformed).

Besides providing the foundational myths of so many fascist movements in history, the hero's journey is used to sell us lots of shit today and make certain types of males feel good about shitty behavior. Ultimately it leaves many men feeling unfulfilled because it preaches to them that *if* they just did all the right things in the correct order, *then* they could be complete. And when one of these completed "winners" decides he's the hero in his own mind and story—look out everyone! Wallowing in malignant narcissism will be seen by this "hero" as his right. To wit, a decade before Donald Trump became the Republican nominee for president, he shared candid views on women that were caught on tape. "I'm automatically attracted to beautiful women—I just start kissing them, it's like a magnet. Just kiss. I don't even wait. *And when you're a star, they let you do it. You can do anything,*" he said in the 2005 conversation. "Grab 'em by the pussy."

## Misogyny conditioning is no fluke

The manosphere is actually a nightmare for men. It decries feminist influence, mocks women in the military, glorifies abuse in the name of God-given male authority and entitlement, and longs to return to what some men view as a traditional relationship with society: male domination combined with career success.

I was steeped in this. Only men could be pastors! Only men could preach! I was in charge of my home! I was in charge of my children! But being branded as the provider (who must lead and dominate to be a success in order to fulfill one's male destiny) is a road to resentment and anger, not to mention to a shorter, stressed-out, less-prosperous life span.

It seems to me that the countries in most perpetual wars are often characterized by misogyny. The perpetual war status that has characterized Afghanistan for centuries isn't conceivable outside the context of male chauvinism enabled by fundamentalist Islam, which is disturbingly comparable to male chauvinism in America enabled by fundamentalist Christianity.

Conversely, when men's workload and responsibility are shared by a partner, when the joy that comes as the reward of childcare is experienced and shared, when expressing oneself openly to a trusting and sympathetic mate is a daily fact of life, when the guilt felt from being a domineering bully is replaced by the relaxed equality of friendship, a great burden rolls off men's backs. At least it did with me.

**It took me years to emerge from the self-defeating and joy-strangling, self-loathing, and anti-evolutionary "survival of the fittest" misogynist theological conditioning**

When I left the evangelical fold, I changed my mind. But it took far longer to change my domineering qualities. I'm still battling them, but it has gotten better. Genie, as I've said, was my tutor. Her method combined gentle persuasion, reason, love, forgiveness, furious screaming, and threats of divorce, good sex, and no sex, and door slamming. Her project became my project, too: a behavior modification and healing process I chose to be initiated into. I chose it because I love Genie. But the changes would not have lasted unless they made me much, much happier. To lay down the burden of male supremacy is such a relief!

I always tell Genie she's strong. Genie always answers, "Not strong, just stubborn. I didn't want to give up on us. I knew we could do better if given a chance." Genie never did give up on us. The end result was that by the time the coronavirus changed our lives, I found that I was happy—in fact, insanely happy—at being stuck at home with my wife and three youngest grandchildren, teaching the children to cook, do carpentry, paint pictures, build granite walls, watch operas, hang out and play for hours, and swim. I owe Genie my life—quite literally. And I'd like to pause here and say this to her: thank you for letting me see everything you are.

## Coleman: the lethality of male-centric mythology

Research on 2,431 young adults by Daniel Coleman of Fordham University found that men who identified with rigid beliefs of the kind I used to hold—that a man "must provide at any cost, be invulnerable or be self-sufficient"—are more likely (as I once did) to have suicidal thoughts. They are more likely to (as I once did) exhibit signs of depression. Coleman concludes that idealizing "high traditional masculinity" is a risk factor, especially for men who aren't able to fulfill that ideal because of life circumstances such as illness, disability, lack of education, or the loss of a job.

Some of the men worse off in terms of well-being are those in cohorts most associated with the traditional manly roles. Suicide rates by gun have skyrocketed within our heavily armed conservative American male population, including in our armed services and the police. The men who are angriest are often not winners, even by the degraded standards of corporate America. Nearly 60 percent of the people facing charges related to the Capitol riot showed signs of prior money troubles, including bankruptcies, notices of eviction or foreclosure, bad debts, or unpaid taxes over the past two decades, according to a *Washington Post* analysis of public records for 125 defendants with sufficient information to detail their financial histories.

In 2019, four times the number of male police officers died by suicide than were killed in the line of duty. In the light of the level of police brutality that the demonstrations of 2020 highlighted, it is no wonder that many officers find themselves with suicidal thoughts. Being a thug takes a toll. These are demonstrably brutalized men (and some women, too) over-armed, under-trained, and all too ready to kill, suffering from PTSD and even ready to murder Black people in one racial attack after another. Put it this way: That White guy in the big pickup tailgating you and then roaring past with his "Don't tread on me" sticker isn't a happy person. Those with the most guns often live in the most fear. How do you ever feel safe when the greatest risk you face is yourself? American manhood as understood by a large right wing White cohort is a sad mess. These folks are more to be pitied than anything else. They, too, have been stripped of real agency and choices.

The manly man culture of stigma for showing any weakness (let alone indulging in the pleasures of childminding) backfires spectacularly. The most extremely rigid societies, such as the male-centric culture of Afghanistan and ever more disgusting Saudi Arabia, have become cultures of death—by "honor" killings of women by family members, by jihadist suicide vest, and by endless war. In "Manly Honor and the Gendered Male

in Afghanistan" (Middle East Institute, April 23, 2012), Sippi
Azarbaijani-Moghaddam writes:

> In recent research on gender equity within a national
> project, we have tried to look at gender relations at
> the community level from a male perspective. Findings
> are preliminary but indicate that there is tremendous
> social pressure on men, especially younger men, to
> adhere to stereotypes of masculinity; for example,
> disallowing womenfolk to emerge from the confines
> of the house and enter the public domain. . . . Jokes,
> slights, and name calling which indicate that the male
> in question has lax morals or lacks the masculinity to
> control his womenfolk form a critical, insidious, and at
> times painful part of socialization.

In America we, too, face "tremendous social pressure on men,
especially younger men, to adhere to stereotypes of masculinity." That doesn't even cover the bullying of gay men and nonbinary people by men indoctrinated with evangelical and other
religious and/or cultural ideas about what real men are supposed
to be and become. Many of our most toxically masculine—insecure, least childminding, least educated males—are part of a
death cult that is also a homophobic bullying cult. Some are the
police officers who are brutal or excuse those who are. Others are
into male-dominated, risk-taking, environmentally destructive
so-called extreme sports as a meaning-seeking lifestyle choice.
Many of the angry men that invaded our Capitol came dressed in
military gear. The entire White-supremacist, American terrorist,
militia movement is made up of paranoid, conspiracy-addled
people playing army and trying to be manly while looking like
insecure teens playing with their daddy's guns.

## The answer to America's lost men: the feminist movement

As the coronavirus story broke, predictably gun sales sky-rocketed. More guns is the only answer to any perceived threat that many a disconnected male (and a few females, too) can come up with these days. In the parlance of the Afghan/Islamist and American death cults, no place is safe without a gun! Real men carry guns! Your home is likely to be invaded! Your family will be brutally molested or killed or raped or dishonored unless you are armed with an assault weapon with a high-capacity magazine and armor-piercing bullets! Honor must be defended! But when the family is recalibrated into a community of shared roles and nurturing values, the compulsion for men or women to strut to our destruction as domineering armed suicidal sociopaths is lessened. Fewer of us males commit suicide, too.

Like men, educated women benefiting from feminism's struggle for equality are also better off. For a start, they have smaller families. This takes pressure off men as well as off women. And the children born into smaller families headed by loving, nurturing, equal partners have a better chance to thrive and survive than children at any other point in human history. These families also have a better chance at not traumatizing their children, especially if one or more parents stay home (or work from home) to care for preschool-age children. And nothing we do to help others or to make the world a better place is more important than fighting for the right to education for girls. Put it this way: If you want to imagine a face that goes with the words "the most marginalized persecuted people on our planet," the face is that of a young girl. That face represents tens of millions of people. Whatever happens to her *is* the destiny of our species. So goes women's rights, so goes the species. So goes women's rights, so goes the well-being of us all. And it seems to me that all other justice issues, race issues, economic issues, and happiness issues come down to this: How do we treat women?

It is hard to imagine a society that sees and treats women as fully equal to men also nurturing some cult of hate related to race or sexuality. Again: So goes women's rights, so goes the well-being of us all.

## Caregiving: men's work

In this context, my pro-feminist statement here is not some theoretical defense of nebulous women's rights. It reflects my gratitude for an altogether better (and arguably longer) life, as a father, grandfather—and childminding parent always sustained and often led by women. The groundwork for that life and the foundation to my openness to "conversion" by Genie (as my favorite and most stubborn therapist) was built by Jane, Betty, Eunice, and my mother. Above all I no longer define myself by job titles or gender but by the joy and quality of life I find in my deepest relationships.

Caregiving for my children and now for my grandchildren— "women's work," as stupid, post-industrial, "gender-appropriate," male supremacist tradition would have it—gave my life a sense of meaning and purpose far beyond any domineering, striving role. It has given me meaning and purpose as I edge into a time of life that sets me up as more of an observer preserving memories than an active participant in the larger world. But feelings of depression, uselessness, and the looming unforgiving passage of time are healed as Nora's hand reaches for mine when we walk together. When her school shut and we were isolated together every day,

Nora's six-year-old version of the redemptive feminist message was crystal clear: YOU ARE NEEDED! YOU ARE LOVED!

# CHAPTER 4

# A Loneliness Epidemic

## Ba, show me *The Triumph of Death*

Lucy, when you were five, we were playing on the big out-cropping of granite in the middle of the marsh. Nestled in the grass, I spotted a ball the surging high tide had brought us. I walked over the marsh to get it for you while trying not to fall into one of the many water-filled ditches. The ball was printed with a bunch of cheesy cartoon TV characters. I brought you the ball and said, "We'll have to do something about this because *this* is really bad art and of course you know what happens if you look at bad art."

"What happens, Ba?" you asked.

"Your head explodes," I said, and looked at the ball and shouted, "BANG!"

That's when we invented the Ba's head explodes game. I carried you and the ball across the marsh and up over the granite ledge and then down the path to our home. Then we—or rather you—spray-painted over the "bad art." On the way out of the marsh we happened across a seagull carcass that had been torn to pieces by a fox. There wasn't much left but scattered feathers and a beak.

"See," I said, "he must've looked at the pictures on this ball and his brain exploded!"

You laughed, and of course you knew that this whole business of brains exploding was a joke, but it was one you enjoyed and kept playing along with any time you saw something you didn't think was good.

You wanted me to bring what was left of the gull's head home for your nature collection, which I did. We added it to the shells, rocks, dead bugs, driftwood, and your greatest treasure of all: the possum skeleton.

Each time we took those bones out we talked about the "Day the vultures arrived," as you put it. You were truly stunned one summer evening when you were three and you looked out the window to see seven huge turkey buzzards sitting in a row on top of the swing set. They were so big that from the back they looked like a row of black sheep or dogs somehow perched on the bar; anything but birds. They were taking polite turns swooping down to where a dead possum was lying in putrid glory. Day after day, those vultures came back until they'd meticulously picked the carcass clean.

Then we collected the bones, bleached them, and added them to your box. And this got you into all things skeletal, from books about dinosaur bones of all kinds, to the drumsticks of some chicken you ate, to the bones of the dead in Italian frescoes pulling themselves out of the ground on resurrection day. I had a video of one priceless incident in particular. You were gnawing on the remnants of a chunk of meat on a T-bone. Your mouth was full. With juice on your chin you mumbled, "Ba, show me *The Triumph of Death*!" You wanted to look at Bruegel's painting in the old book Jane Smith gave me when I was six or seven, when she characteristically said, "Anyone who doesn't like Bruegel is probably dead, honey!" Jane's favorite was Pieter Bruegel the Elder's *The Dutch Proverbs* (1559).

"Jane, are those naked bottoms sticking out of that window?" I asked.

"Yes, honey and look, they're pooping into the river! Don't tell your mother I showed you!"

Lucy, like Jane, you loved Bruegel's "pooping" Dutch Proverb bottoms and also his skeleton armies marching forth in the Apocalypse. I pulled the book from the stack of art books we kept on the kitchen table for you and Jack. Jack (age four) loved Goya's pictures, the odder, the better, like *La Maja Desnuda* (The Naked Maja) and its twin *La Maja Vestida* (The Clothed Maja). We'd flip the pages back and forth: Clothed! Naked! Clothed! Naked!

A few years later, Nora's favorites were the Greek mythology illustrations in her book of the John Singer Sargent paintings she bought with her own fifth birthday money at the Museum of Fine Arts, Boston (MFA). They are on the ceiling above the grand staircases at the MFA. Nora especially loved the ones of *Hercules and the Hydra* and *Orestes Pursued by the Furies*. Each time we went to the museum, all three of you kids would lie on the floor looking up as bemused visitors glanced down and probably wondered if they should tell somebody about the three kids lying in a row on the floor and worst of all, some unmade bed of a crazy old guy lying next to them, staring at the ceiling.

You nonchalantly chewed while pointing out this or that skeleton with the bone and what it was doing to the terrified sixteenth-century peasants with which Bruegel populated his painting. And no lunch was complete for either you or Jack and these days Nora's obligatory look at Goya's *The Colossus* (also known as *The Giant*). "Look, Ba! They're all running away!" Nora always says, pointing to the fleeing masses and their cattle. That painting inspired Nora to build sandcastle villages over which she'd preside as a "*nice* colossus," ruling and "defending my villagers."

Lucy, you had no problems with nudity in art, let alone skeleton armies of the dead, and—between mouthfuls of meat ripped "like wolves eating Ba!" from the bone—made a precocious comparison between Maja's perky young breasts and the tired aging breasts in Michelangelo's *Night* that you liked to study. You made your first art history/breast analysis remarking: "Night's breasts look much more older, Ba, because she had her babies already and they got full of milk. Maja's breasts look lots newer." I was amazed. Before me was a six-year-old art historian!

## Letterman, Clooney, and Stern: profiles in changing masculinity

Kids are many things but not trivial. My grandchildren ask frankly about things grown-ups don't. "Ba, when did you get old?" Jack asked out of the blue one afternoon when he was nine. He was staring at my face as if noticing for the first time the sun spots and wrinkles, white eyebrows, and all the rest of the mortality one-way signposts written on my face. "Last Thursday at three fifteen in the afternoon," I answered.

I laughed at Jack's surprised expression and then explained that sixty-seven isn't old. Then I admitted it was sort of old. This exchange was a reminder that childcare keeps me realistically connected to life's passage in ways nothing else does. And I'm not the only person to notice this. Talk-show host David Letterman has taken the quality of pair-bonding, childcare, relationships, and parenthood rather more seriously than he once did. Maybe it's because he's a father.

Letterman has used his latest show, *My Next Guest Needs No Introduction*, to confess that he's somewhat unexpectedly found joy, meaning, and heartache in caring for his son, Harry.

Letterman has made his show a forum for similar confessions. Letterman's guests have included the once notorious shock-radio host Howard Stern, and the "I'll never marry" movie star George Clooney, who's now married and extolling marriage as a great thing and who loves mothering his twins.

When Letterman interviewed Howard Stern in 2018, they talked about how they both believe their more youthful career-worshipping quest for success was toxic. They talked about how making long-term relationships work changed their lives for the better. Letterman, at age seventy-one, and Stern, at sixty-four, discussed their spiritual, social, and sexual journeys in ways that would have been unthinkable for them not too long ago.

Stern and Letterman provided a virtual master class on how it's possible to be rich, entitled, and famous as well as miserable, thanks to having self-destructive behaviors born from misplaced life priorities and skewed ideas about masculinity "I don't know how my first wife could have been married to me because I was all in on my career," Stern said. "That's not a way to be in a relationship. . . . It's very hard to think of even your children's well-being."

Letterman cited a similar dynamic during his decades as a late-night host. "I went through a version of the same thing where all I cared about was being on television, to the exclusion of everything else that I now realize is actually life." According to Letterman, enlightenment only came about after his son was born in 2003, a decade into his tenure hosting CBS's *Late Show*. This was also after he had publicly repented for cheating on his wife.

I've found there are lots of people of all ages who are eager to find ways to buck today's shallow, materialistic, careerist, consumerist trend. But they receive little to no support. I think they just need someone to tell them they aren't crazy for feeling that our culture's negative attitudes about love, connection, commitment, and family are self-defeating. Maybe they just need somebody to say, "Everything could turn out okay—if you choose to love. Go for it!" or "Have that baby. So what if you're forty-five, go for it!" or some version thereof.

## Cass: the misguided priorities of our educational system

"We've created this idea that the meaning of life should be found in work," says Oren Cass, senior fellow at the Manhattan Institute, in "The Misguided Priorities of Our Educational System" (*New York Times*, December 10, 2018). "We tell young people that their work should be their passion. 'Don't give up until you find a job that you love!' we say. 'You should be changing the world!' we tell them. That is the message in commencement addresses, in pop culture, and frankly, in media. . . . "

"But our desks were never meant to be our altars," writes Derek Thompson, in "Workism Is Making Americans Miserable" (*The Atlantic*, February 24, 2019). "The modern labor force evolved to serve the needs of consumers and capitalists, not to satisfy tens of millions of people seeking transcendence at the office. It's hard to self-actualize on the job if you're a cashier— one of the most common occupations in the United States—and even the best white-collar roles have long periods of stasis, boredom, or busywork."

Thompson says that the mismatch between expectations and reality is a recipe for severe disappointment, if not outright misery, and it might explain why rates of depression and anxiety in the United States are substantially higher than they were in the 1980s, according to a 2014 study. That great big fancy job still sucks most of the time. The idea that we're all supposed to find something we love to do is plain silly. To wit, I recall being asked to speak at a Google event.

## Google's failed promise

I was rather taken aback by all the odd self-important layers of security I had to pass through, more like going to visit the National Security Agency headquarters (when my Marine son was posted there for a few months) than a mere tech company office in the Boston area. A sushi chef served me and the employees' lunch. I gave my "Talks at Google" talk about my (then new) book, *Why I Am an Atheist Who Believes in God.* I took questions. I must have done well enough since a few weeks later I was invited to do another talk at their Chicago office. But what struck me at both events was how, in spite of sushi chefs and plenty of toys strewn about—from skateboards to pinball machines—reminiscent of a teen playground, the youngish people working there seemed pretty dispirited. Fun is what the work was supposed to be so workers weren't called workers. They had other names. *Noogler*: if they were new to Google and so forth. No one seemed all that happy.

Maybe it was occurring to these workers that, even working for the vaunted tech giant instead of, say, being a cashier in a supermarket, it is still just a fucking job. Their questions to me tended to be about things we all face: family, relationships, finding meaning in life, spirituality, love, and loss. Sexy work in a place requiring security passes, where visitors aren't allowed to wander too far into the inner secret kingdom, nevertheless demanded too much of them. I said nice things about the company from the platform. I was sincere back then. Google helped me research many subjects. I thanked them. I was ego-stoked about the fuss this big important company was making about me. I was grateful. But . . . chatting in private with some of the Google people, I discovered that they seemed to be having problems getting their lives on track outside of work. One woman said to me, "You said all that nice stuff about the research doors Google is opening for you, but that's not how it is here. We're being consumed by opening those doors. Do you know that this company wants us to give it everything, but if we ask what about our lives and a bigger picture, we find it's really all about work?"

The older Googlers seemed disappointed, too. They might have been singing along with Peggy Lee's memorable "Is That All There Is?" So I wasn't surprised to read a few years later that Google wasn't quite as nice to workers as they once pretended to be. In "She Sued for Pregnancy Discrimination. Now She's Battling Google's Army of Lawyers" by Kari Paul (*Guardian*, April 9, 2021), we read that:

> When Chelsey Glasson found out she was pregnant with her second child in 2019, she did not anticipate the first three years of her new baby's life would be overshadowed by an epic legal battle against a trillion-dollar company. The 38-year-old sued Google, her former employer, in 2020 alleging she had been discriminated against while pregnant and witnessed others being treated similarly, and faced retaliation from her manager when she spoke up about it. Since then, Glasson says, battling to win her case has become nearly a full-time job, one that's pitted her against a company with a global army of lawyers at the ready. Despite being represented by attorneys in

Washington and partially backed by a not-for-profit group, the American Association of University Women, she finds herself putting in grueling hours preparing for her upcoming trial this year. She spends her nights, after her two kids are asleep, discovering documents and preparing for processes such as her recent deposition in March. The fight has affected her children's lives almost as much as her own, she says.

I'm far from the only person pointing out that we need to change the way we regard work. Charlie Warzel, writer-at-large for the *New York Times* opinion page, and Anne Helen Petersen, former senior writer at *BuzzFeed News,* are the authors of *Out of Office.* They write that the lessons of Covid-19 reveal that there is another work/life path forward. The authors argue that we are at an inflection point where workers and employers across America, and around the world, are finding new ways of working that make people happier and more productive. Their book aims to reshape our entire relationship with the office and outline a path toward a new kind of work-life balance that can improve our lives and strengthen our communities.

## The road to experiencing meaning in our lives: wonder

My friend Myrna Perez Sheldon, about whom I've been talking and quoting herein, added this note in the margin next to one of my reminiscences about my mother and the other women who opened so many doors for me:

I have lovely memories of doing science with my mom (she's a science teacher): we raised tadpoles, went to aquariums, and learned the names of trees and fishes and frogs. I didn't know the names of great composers or artists as a kid, but I knew how to use a microscope, the structure of a cell, and the names of the phyla in the animal kingdom. Perhaps you should include some of these examples here—particularly because I think that seeing the natural world as having intrinsic beauty and wonder is a deeply spiritual thing.

Myrna is right: seeing the natural world as having intrinsic beauty and as a source of experiencing wonder is indeed "a deeply spiritual thing." And maybe that's what those Google employees were missing.

It seems to me that our sense of wonder that Myrna swears by as a scientist is the only secure road to experiencing meaning in our lives. It is wonder that bridges the gap between knowing and feeling, heart and mind, science and spirituality, fear and hope, knowing and paradox. It is wonder that teaches us the humility to accept paradox, doubt, and uncertainty as the ultimate and truest kind of self-knowledge. It's the wonder that caring for a child inculcates in otherwise bruised and cynical grown-ups like me that makes the experience of parenthood uniquely healing. It's wonder that makes good teachers into great teachers who can change the world one student at a time.

## Code writing for robots—many paths to wonder

We can be childlike and a wonder-filled parent *and* a university professor like Myrna. We can be a parent who does manly things like building concrete walls (as I do), *as well* as a caregiver who dances ballets in a bathroom with six-year-old granddaughters. We can be like my son Francis and not have kids of our own but become a creative loving parent (as it were) to his nieces and nephews, and to the hundreds of students Francis has inspired to make wonder-filled discoveries. We can wait to have children until the cusp of infertility, have them anyway, and so immerse ourselves in the wonder and discovery of community that we make up for the fact there are now no grandparents around to help out because we waited so long. The wonder is the constant here—not how we get to experience wonder. And the wonder of real life is being crushed even by the sexiest of elite jobs because when work is seen as a defining end in itself, it is too small a goal. Stuff, titles, and prestige cannot compensate for spiritual impoverishment.

And spiritual fulfillment is open to everyone, be they a parent or not. The scope of what someone can do who has taken a very different life path than having children was borne home to me by an email my son Francis sent me recently. He was answering my question about the specifics of the computer/robot-creation/coding program he initiated for his high school students. Francis has taken his robotics computer coding teams to the state, national, and world championships. Over the last few years several of his students' robotics projects have scored highest in the world out of thousands of international teams competing. Francis is a hero to students and their parents alike for opening creative doors for "his" kids in wonder-inspiring ways so similar to what I had experienced Mrs. Parke doing for me.

Hey Dad,

You asked me to tell you about the latest stuff with my FTC robotics team at the Waring School. (FTC stands for FIRST Tech Challenge. It is one of the three FIRST robotics competitions. FIRST Lego League is for middle school. FIRST Tech Challenge is for small high schools, or at least small teams. FIRST Robotics is for big high school teams.) I love teaching physics, but this year, I would have to say that the big highlight has been my FTC team. As you know, I started this team with all the kids who were on my First Lego League team last year. It's so amazing to see the work they can do now that they are a bit older. The students "ping" me with DM's at all hours of the day asking what I think of their latest design ideas and programs. I get questions all night long and need to turn off my notifications to sleep.

I find their creativity inspiring. The most mind-blowing recent development has been the vision system and auto-targeting that they wrote. The robot now looks for the goal itself, using vision code the kids wrote, calculates its own distance and angle from the goal, and then rotates itself into the optimal firing position for the rings. The kids have been working on it for months. I got to see them come up with an idea and see it all the way through. One of the kids recently told me that his math class has just started studying the trig he had needed to teach himself to write the auto-aiming code. I was talking to his teacher later in the day and she mentioned that my FTC kids seem to "learn trig really quickly." I smiled to myself.

Love,

Francis

## Front yard med school

Francis's note jogged my memory about the fact that in addition to sharing art and music with me, my door-opening mother Edith also cooked, swam, and gardened with me. Francis got me thinking about and remembering so many specifics about the family, friends, and teachers who opened doors for me. Mom let me do things that were dangerous: climb, build, and wander for hours away from home in the mountains. By age seven, I'd walk into the mountains and disappear for the day; help herd cows; help slaughter and gut pigs, goats, rabbits, sheep, and chickens; work alongside the local stone mason pouring concrete and building walls—whatever. In other words in this sense Francis is a parent because he is a door-opener. And opening doors is what sharing real wealth that lasts is about. It is spirituality in action. It is love in action.

When sometimes people ask how I learned to build well enough to construct a new wing on my son's house, or build a staircase and granite wall with Jack, or build a twenty-foot high, ceramic-lined stone chimney for my barn's wood stove (it draws well!), or butcher a deer, the answer is simple: My mother let me explore, experiment, and take risks. *She opened doors to hands-on tactile doing of projects as Francis does for his students.* What is a parent? A parent is a loving door-opener.

Do you have to have children to be a loving parent? No.

Mom bought me a dissection kit for my eighth birthday. Sixty years later, I dissected a squirrel, a rabbit, and a large striped bass with Nora during the Covid lockdown summer. This was after I got Nora her own dissection kit the year before when she was five. I did not come up with that idea. She did, but it resonated with me because of my mother's gift to me half a century before. Nora had found a dead squirrel and nonchalantly picked it up and declared, "Ba, I want to see its heart." She'd watched an open-heart surgery documentary a few days before in her "I want to be a doctor" quest.

I laboriously and messily cut the squirrel open with my pen-knife and said, "We really need a scalpel and tweezers to do this right."

"Will you get me one?" asked Nora, as she held the heart in her hand and remarked, "It's not heart shaped."

"No. Hearts aren't heart shaped."

"Its heart is *much* smaller than I expected! How big is my heart?"

"About the size of your fist."

"Can I see its brain? When can you get me a scalpel?"

Some might think this activity was not age appropriate.

I think the words *child appropriate* are often used incorrectly. What's appropriate to me is to pass on to a child or grandchild (or to students as Francis does) lessons in being a hands-on, polite, kind, and capable *doer*. That way you aren't afraid to follow your interests. Maybe you even turn out to be someone who can build; start a fire; cook; build a wall; do CPR; swim, climb, and draw; skin a rabbit; look people in the eye; work hard and not whine (too much); and shake hands, make eye contact, and introduce yourself. Maybe you can even identify an artist or composer or two by seeing or hearing a bit of their work; know the difference between World Wars I and II; appreciate that China is an old and incredible civilization; and appreciate that all good roads lead to Black American music. Some computer coding and robot creation doesn't hurt either.

I think keeping a promise is important, including buying a dissection kit for a kid who is "too young," just like Francis is inspiring high school students "too young" to build and code in ways that rival what college students are doing in places like MIT. Who says life has to be lived in neatly packaged, "appropriate" stages? And by the way, Nora delivered a glowing obituary, then commenced to "sing a sad song" over the remains of the squirrel

—after she dissected it—and then she honored "This poor little lost forest creature" with a homemade tombstone and touching "He lived a good life" eulogy.

## I never fully succeed with my grandchildren, but I try

Lucy learned that cooking involves getting spattered with hot oil sometimes and that knives have to be sharp to be useful, and therefore used with care and yet confidence. *Child appropriate* in our house mostly means "allowed to try," with safe supervision, and to find what interests you and to go for it. Jack learned that working with mortar and concrete all day means you wear gloves but that still you lose some skin on your hands due to concrete burn, that the pH of wet cement is so high it can cause pain—the alkaline burn usually gets worse before it gets better—"But, Jack, you'll be okay." And he was.

What if the *doing* of life—say, by being a wide-awake seven-year-old awestruck at a poster of a great piece of art, or by being the sculptor who made it, or by watching a grandson and two granddaughters work next to you on a construction project while you are feeling boundless joy, or by wanting to be a "mother *and* surgeon *and* opera singer, Ba, and you can take care of my babies" —needs no justification?

When Nora takes it for granted that I'll be around to help raise her children, I don't point out the math isn't in my favor. I do think about dying, though, a lot more than I would otherwise if there wasn't so much love to miss out on when I die. Nora is quite matter-of-fact about this. She makes her own math calculations. One day after explaining how "I'll move in with you when I have babies," so that "You can help me like you help Mom and Dad," Nora paused, thought about it, and added, "Don't worry,

Ba, you'll live until you're one hundred and twenty-two, and if you die sooner I won't forget you because I'm going to name all my sons Frank."

"How many?"

"Three—Frank One, Frank Two, Frank Three."

"Okay."

"What if you have daughters?"

"I'll name them Genie. And when you're too old to walk, I'll carry you. Did you know you and Nana will *shrink* when you get very old? So there will be no problem carrying you like you carry me. And I can do chest compressions on you, too. Also, if I change my mind and call my son Jason, I hope you won't mind."

"Jason is fine."

The circle of life. Plus all the chest compressions I may need.

## We need to stop pretending we can do anything to kids and it'll all turn out fine

How is our model of a career-first, family-second culture that provides few-to-no social services—thus leaving countless parents with no good choices—working out for children? How are kids raised by parents who fit family into career rather than career into family doing? It's not the parents' fault. They've been offered few good options. For that matter, how is it working out for students who do not have teachers who treat them as worthy of staying up for them half the night while helping them build robots and code? In short, how is our utilitarian society serving our children?

## Uninspired, depressed children do not thrive

We need to stop pretending we can do anything to kids and offer parents no good choices or support and it'll all turn out fine. A study released May 1, 2019, first published in the *Journal of*

*Pediatrics*, offered evidence that suicide attempts—among *children* in America—have risen dramatically. Using data from the National Poison Data System, researchers found more than 1.6 million cases of ten- to twenty-four-year-olds attempting to kill themselves by poisoning from 2000 to 2018. More than 70 percent of the suicide attempts by poisoning were made by young women. There was also a significant spike in the number and rate of suicide attempts among ten- to fifteen-year-olds. This statistic alone should raise urgent questions: what the hell are we doing to provide stable and joy-filled, door-opening, beauty-drenched, art-loving, nature-exploring lives of discovery for today's children or, for that matter, for their overworked parents?

"From 2000 to 2011, [the rate of child suicide attempts] was relatively steady, but then after 2010 or '11, there was a dramatic change," Henry Spiller, the study's author and the director of the Central Ohio Poison Center told the *Huffington Post*. "Depending on the age group, [the suicide rate of attempted self-poisoning] goes up 200 to 300 percent. Something is happening in adolescents that hasn't happened before—and that isn't what was occurring in the 1990s or 2000s."

What's changed? Lots. Teens living in the ever-darkening shadow of their phones; degrading misogynist, often racist, and violent porn and rape-culture invading childhoods; disconnected online "life"; the continuing impact of divorce as a normal event for millions of children; the well-known pathologies of our disgracefully failing educational system.

That said, the limited choices offered parents resulting in a work-life imbalance is (in my view) a major key to understanding many of our children's (and grown-ups') distress. And since that has meant that kids face being raised by non-family strangers, since we don't accommodate, encourage, *let alone pay for* time off from work for *both* parents to care for preschool-age children, we've built a traumatizing trap for all concerned. Worse: not only aren't parents helped who want to stay home with young kids, many parents who opt for daycare can't even afford to pay for it. So the stress levels just escalate.

### Having mentioned *porn* let me be clear: I'm not anti-porn, but there's a problem: rape culture and porn are *NOT* the same things

It seems to me that nonviolent, non-misogynistic, non-abusive porn made by consenting adults for other consenting adults and enjoyed for stimulation in the context of a sexual relationship and/or alone by people needing something to masturbate to is fine. It's normal. Use of erotica has a long history. What is new and harming us all is acquiescence to our burgeoning modern rape culture for profit *masquerading as porn*.

Greed-driven, "respectable" tech companies obliquely enable this through their search engines and self-serving algorithms. They excuse this as the new normal in the name of free speech in the same way the NRA facilitates mass murder in the name of so-called gun rights. And our culture is too cowardly to draw distinctions, say, between owning a single shot rifle to shoot rabbits destroying one's garden and a one-hundred-round magazine attached to a military grade weapon of mass destruction used to murder a classroom full of children. We are also too cowardly to draw distinctions between porn and enabling rape culture. Maybe liberals don't want to be labeled as prudes. Maybe evangelical right-wingers don't want to admit they use porn, too. No one wants to talk about this.

## Time to be honest about our rape culture

One person who has stood up and taken on child rape and rape culture is columnist Nicholas Kristof. His writing has been shining a light on a very dark child-destroying corner of corporate culture. As Kristof points out in "With Help from Google, XVideos Lets People Leer at the Worst Moment in a Child's Life" (*New York Times*, April 16, 2021), Google and the other Internet giants have been notoriously cruel and irresponsible when it comes to protecting children.

"I've no problem with consensual adults making porn," says a Canadian student. "Who cares?"

The problem is that many people in pornographic videos weren't consenting adults. Like her.

Just after she turned fourteen, a man enticed her to engage in sexual play over Skype. He secretly recorded her. A clip, along with her full name, ended up on XVideos, the world's most-visited pornography site. *Google searches helped direct people to this illegal footage of child sexual abuse.*

. . . [S]he begged XVideos to remove the clip. Instead, she says, the website hosted two more copies, so hundreds of thousands of people could leer at this most mortifying moment of her life, preserved forever as if in amber. That happens all over the world: Women and girls, and men and boys, are sexually assaulted or secretly filmed, and then video is posted on a major website like XVideos that draws traffic through search engines. While the initial video assault may be brief, the attack on dignity becomes interminable. "The shame I felt was overwhelming," the Canadian student says. . . .

*Google is a pillar of this sleazy ecosystem, for roughly half the traffic reaching XVideos and XNXX appears to come from Google searches.* "The porn tube sites are obsessed with their Google rankings because Google is their lifeline," said Laila Mickelwait, the president of the Justice Defense Fund, which fights sexual exploitation [rape-culture child abuse] online. *"Google is the primary means by which they [child abuse vendors] drive traffic to their sites."* (Italics added.)

## Abandonment by any other name

How do Google and other tech giants get away with this? Because we have been brutalized. Surely we can find it within ourselves to cut the Internet tech giants down to size and set limits on their ability to enable those who abuse children? Surely we can come together to slap down the heartless gun lobby and reclaim a little decency for ourselves? It is time to admit that we've been betrayed, and so have our children. And our brutalizing goes way past rape porn to our entire entertainment culture.

In "What the Sexual Violence of Game of Thrones Begot" (*The Atlantic*, May 4, 2021), *The Atlantic* staff writer Sophie Gilbert writes:

> I don't have much tolerance these days for scenes involving the casual, ritualistic degradation of women, which is why deciding to rewatch *Game of Thrones* was such a colossal unforced error. Idiotic! Foolhardy! Own goal! I made it through the first episode, where a sobbing Daenerys Targaryen is raped by Khal Drogo on their wedding night in front of a romantic orange sunset. I got through the part where Daenerys learns to get her rapist to be nicer to her by being more of an engaged participant in her own sexual assault, and the moment where she subsequently falls in love with him and he with her. I watched as Ros is forced to violently beat another woman with a scepter to

gratify the sadistic sexual predilections of King Joffrey, and as Brienne is dragged away to be gang-raped by Roose Bolton's soldiers, until Jaime saves her. I stopped watching shortly before Jaime rapes his sister, Cersei, next to their son's dead body, and before Sansa is raped by Ramsay Bolton while Theon Greyjoy watches. It occurred to me at some point that this was becoming an ordeal. . . . A show treating sexual violence as casually now as *Thrones* did then is nearly unimaginable. And yet rape, on television, is as common as ever, sewn into crusading feminist tales and gritty crime series and quirky teenage dramedies and schlocky horror anthologies. It's the trope that won't quit, the Klaxon for supposed narrative fearlessness, the device that humanizes "difficult" women and adds supposed texture to vulnerable ones. Many creators who draw on sexual assault claim that they're doing so because it's so commonplace in culture and always has been. "An artist has an obligation to tell the truth," Martin once told *The New York Times* about why sexual violence is such a persistent theme in his work. "My novels are epic fantasy, but they are inspired by and grounded in history. Rape and sexual violence have been a part of every war ever fought." So have gangrene and post-traumatic stress disorder and male sexual assault, and yet none of those feature as pathologically in his "historical" narratives as the brutal rape of women.

## It's time to talk about betrayal trauma

Betrayal trauma occurs when someone you trusted (or someone who has power over you) mistreats you. What is betrayal trauma? For instance, it's a betrayal trauma when your boss, a father, or friend sexually assaults you. The same can be said when a company says it is going to do well by the world and then repeatedly betrays the defenseless. That includes mistreatment by the ever-more brutalized and brutalizing entertainment giants like HBO where rape is just another tool for getting eyeballs on screens.

Research shows that betrayal traumas are toxic. They are associated with measurable harm, both physical and mental, as Jennifer Joy Freyd, the founder of the Center for Institutional Courage and professor emeritus of psychology at the University of Oregon, has demonstrated. She points out that "institutional courage" is the only antidote to institutional betrayal. Freyd writes about institutional accountability and transparency, for instance when institutions respond appropriately to uncomfortable embarrassing disclosures or when institutions conduct surveys of victimization within their institution and then use the data to honestly change their behavior. It is this transparency that is missing when it comes to the tech giants.

## It's also time to rein in some of the childcare betrayal trauma we think is the "normal" price of parents having careers

Tech giants and the gun lobby as well as the entertainment conglomerates are not the only entities that have normalized brutality. Too many of us accept another kind of betrayal: childhood parent-inflicted separation trauma as our new normal. We have accepted the fact that society gives parents no good choices. So let's be honest and admit that scenes like this run counter to the way evolution wired adults and children alike for love: "Turns out, she didn't cry because she thought preschool was a one-time thing. On day two, when she realized that this would be her reality for the foreseeable future, she started wailing as we said our goodbyes. I can still hear the echoing, 'Don't leave, Mommy!!!' in the depths of my soul." (Jessica Grose, "How to Tackle Tough Drop-Offs: Expert Tips on How to Disentangle from Your Little Clingers Swiftly and Kindly," *New York Times*, August 20, 2019).

If we lived in a culture attuned to adults' and children's deepest emotional needs, where parents, grandparents, and children playing and learning together was deemed more important than our careers, then most of our businesses would not build in a parenting/young child separation trap. We would give rich and poor alike, single moms and divorced dads, nontraditional parents and married couples real choices and help them pay for those choices. With better choices and financial help for parents during the little child years, would anyone accept the idea that it is normal to find how-to articles advising us on "tips on how to disentangle from your little clingers swiftly"?

## "Do what Jessica did"

Perhaps in a culture revolutionized by adopting the survival of the friendliest ethos, rape and brutality would not be entertainment staples. Perhaps in a culture revolutionized by adopting the survival of the friendliest ethos, we'd also make it easier for more parents to do what my daughter, Jessica, and her husband, Dani, chose to do by swapping parenting and career roles until their two children were school age. Then again, they were lucky. They were living in Finland. Finland, somewhat like Iceland, makes it easy for one or both parents to stay home with young children: the government even pays them to do so. Healthcare is free. There are no prohibitive costs to having a child. The entire structure of their society is geared to making parenthood easier.

But even here in the anti-family, woman-trashing, betrayal-traumatized USA, maybe more of us with the means might want to try to do what my daughter-in law, Becky, did. Becky (now thirty-eight) bucked the prevailing one-size-fits-all career-first trend of her millennial generation. She says she did this because she'd become friends with my daughter, Jessica, (now fifty) and observed "how well Jessica's teenage children were doing."

Becky decided, as she's told me several times, "I wanted to do what Jessica did: get married youngish and have kids right away, and *then* start my career when they were in school. I really wanted both kids and career—but in that order." Becky did just what she decided to do. She found a man who wanted to pair-bond and have babies soon: my son John. They married. Becky went to work full-time a bit earlier than she'd planned to but other than that stuck with what turned out to be a good, if countercultural, plan. Friends (including some members of her family) were telling Becky she was crazy and should wait to marry, "at least get a master's degree first," and only after her career was established, "consider having children." Instead, Becky and John had their three children beginning in Becky's midtwenties, one after the other. John went to work full-time, and Becky stayed home with the children for four years, until Jack was six months old. Then John and Becky handed their kids over to Genie and me to care for five days a week. Both went to work outside the home full-time. Even before that, Genie and I were already helping Becky out on a daily basis.

## Thank you, Medicare and Social Security!

Thus began the most (and most unexpectedly) satisfying days, weeks, months, and years of my life. Soon after becoming nannies, Genie and I had Social Security payments coming in and, at last, were covered by Medicare, too. As self-employed people, our medical insurance coverage had been our major and most crushing expense. Now we could afford to turn our attention wholeheartedly to our grandchildren—*and* I got to play again! And John and Becky never had to leave a child begging them to not abandon them to strangers. Their kids grew up with Genie and me as a daily part of their lives, since birth.

Besides getting Social Security and Medicare (thank you, government!), I feel that the sort of entitlement as White upper middle class Americans that made our choices possible, as well as help from the feds, must be extended to all. Only a few of us have the means to even make a choice for family these days in the way Becky and John did. School debt weighs millions of us down. Social pressure to conform to career worship hurts our chances, too. And where is the support and the options for young parents that we got as oldsters?

Genie and I could help our children out. What about people with less family structure, less money, less options? What about young single moms? The fact they can't get the same level of support my children did is a national disgrace.

It is doubly disgusting that support is not there since it is "traditionalists" and self-proclaimed "conservatives" who have led the charge *against* extending family friendly help to others. They don't really want to help a woman keep her baby like the antichoice protesters scream at the traumatized women seeking abortions. If conservatives did want people to have a child, America and not Iceland would lead the world in family-nurturing social programs that (for instance) keep pregnant high school students *in school* and supported and helped with parenthood, a place to live, and income.

It would be American conservatives leading the charge for parents having interchangeable roles about who stays home, and getting government help to do so. There would be real choices for anyone with a child or wanting to have one or not have one to become a single parent, married, pair-bonded, pregnant, or not. Until that happens, those on the "pro-family" right should just shut the fuck up, die of shame, or, best of all, change their minds and join the fight for social justice and the joy of parenthood.

But America is falling so far short of helping women start families that the *number-one* way, statistically speaking, to descend into poverty for a young American woman is to have a child with no partner. That is just the shameful truth. And it's beautiful that Jessica and Becky met such supportive partners so young, but in our careers-first culture, that's not the case for most young women. We don't have a society like Iceland that promotes or supports young women in any way. Then demographers lament declining birth rates as if we were unaware that women have *zero* help.

As we have seen, there was very little support for Nicole Lewis when she attended college with a child in tow. Lewis is working to change that because so few others, let alone the government, stepped up. Generation Hope rallies around teen parents to help them earn college degrees and forge a path to economic opportunity. Generation Hope is now expanding its work with young parents beyond the DC region by sharing its best practices to help colleges and universities across the country better meet the needs of the nearly 4 million parenting students who are working toward their degrees. In just ten years, Lewis has created a unique and thriving organization that is gaining national attention for its whole-family approach to dismantling poverty. But why isn't this a program on the level of Social Security?

## Hello?!

And by the way, support for young women works. Project Hope is wildly successful. And Iceland shows that single parents raise children as happy in every measurable way as those kids raised in pair-bonded arrangements. So I love sharing these examples (yes, I'm proud of my daughter and daughter-in-law), but I think we need to recognize that in America we've built cultural norms and combined them with governmental neglect in a way that for most young women (and men and nonbinary people, too) mitigates against the life choices Becky and Jessica made.

That said, perhaps more young people who do have the means should be told that some joyful people like my daughter, Jessica, and daughter-in-law, Becky, did not play by the career-striving rules—and they still won (as it were) when it comes to both having kids *and* career. So, I'll share one other personal note about how my daughter, Jessica, dropped out of New York University to marry her musician/composer boyfriend, Dani.

At the time, Genie and I could not afford the school's tuition. And it would have taken Jessica at least six or seven years to complete college in a work/study program and taking a year here and there off to waitress and nanny. (She worked for a series of the richest people in NYC and the Hamptons.)

Jessica and Dani moved to Finland, where he's from, and had Amanda and Ben when Jessica was in her early twenties. Jessica stayed home with her children and supplemented Dani's income working from home making tiles—until their kids were school age. They were far from well off. Dani supplemented his income as a performer tuning pianos. Then Jessica completed her university degree at the University of Finland. The schooling was free. The medical care was free. They received money for Jessica being home with the kids.

Today, twenty-plus years later, Jessica is CEO of a New York–based venture capital firm specializing in green energy investment. Out of college she'd been hired as an intern. Jessica eventually took over the company. That company was in turn bought out by a bigger company. They eventually made her CEO of the entire parent company. Here's the ironic point: Jessica only got her break in American capitalism because the Finish government shared a little socialist bounty with her when she needed it most in her own free education and childcare. These days Jessica brings her own perspective to her work. In the context of discussing this book with me, Jessica emailed me this:

> No one talks about the way being a parent actually prepares you for the world of work. Because career has been a male thing what no one seems to want to talk about is how everything you need to succeed in management—fast reactions, dealing with situations, working with people, organizational skills, self-discipline, communication skills, turns out parenthood is an excellent preparation for. I found that lots of what works best related to leadership as a CEO draws on my parenting experience. Since in the world of work being a parent doesn't count and either draws a blank or rates as a minus no one wants to go there. Now I'm a CEO, people ask for my "how you did this" story, and

why I was able to so "quickly move up." When I attribute lots of my success to my parenting experiences
they become uneasy. In fact even using the word *parenting* let alone *mothering* makes them nervous. That's
because they aren't counting life experience of being
a parent as something that gives you management
skills. When I tell them that they should count parenting skills as management preparation other executives
tend to laugh nervously and/or move the conversation on.

Today Becky works as an academic administrator and assistant director in a private French/English bilingual high school.
She loves her job. She loves her children, and like Jessica, Becky
had her babies when fertility wasn't an issue. Of course both Becky
and Jessica were lucky: they had deep layers of family support.

Becky and Jessica, all things being equal and with a little luck,
someday will know why Genie and I make such a fuss about the
pleasure of finding ourselves as youngish grandparents and full-
time caregivers of our grandchildren at a time of life when, for
many people a bit older than us, life has been reduced to retirement doldrums and ill health.

As for me, I am as grateful to Jessica and Becky as I am to
Genie for their braving the bio-terror of giving birth, and for
their gift of children and grandchildren to our family when I was
still young enough to fully dive in as grandchild caregiver. I am
grateful to Finland for having supported families. I am grateful
to America for Social Security and Medicare that lets Genie and
me be full-time caregivers. I am grateful to Jessica and Becky for
braving the cultural winds that blow so cold on so many of us who
do want kids until it is almost too late.

## Kaiser Family Foundation survey: two in ten Americans report they often or always feel lonely

As I said, not everyone is as undeservedly privileged as Jessica and Dani and John and Becky, or as fortunate as Genie and I have been. According to a 2018 Kaiser Family Foundation survey, two in ten Americans report they often or always feel lonely. Adults younger than fifty were more likely to feel that way than those fifty and older. In 1985, the average American had about three close confidants, according to the General Social Survey. In 2004, that number hovered just above two; a quarter of respondents reported having no close confidants at all. And according to "Making Friends as an Adult Is Hard. Would You Pay $720 for Help?" by writer and editor for *Solo-ish* Lisa Bonos (*Washington Post*, November 8, 2019):

> Fifty-eight percent of Americans in the Kaiser study saw the increased use of technology as a major reason for feeling isolated (though other surveys are mixed on this issue). Remote work has been steadily rising. According to a 2016 Gallup survey, 43 percent of U.S. employees worked in a different location from their co-workers at least some of the time, up from 39 percent in 2012. *Americans are staying single longer; the median age of first marriage is thirty for men and twenty-eight for women, up from twenty-three and twenty in 1960.* (Italics added.)

In February 2018, the health insurance corporation Cigna surveyed 20,000 people age eighteen and older. The survey shows that loneliness has become worse in each successive generation. In the introductory overview, the findings of the sixty-page study were summed up thus:

- When asked how often they feel like no one knows them well, more than half the respondents (54 percent) said they feel that way always or sometimes.
- Just under half of all those surveyed report sometimes or always feeling alone (46 percent) and/or feeling left out (47 percent).
- At least two in five surveyed sometimes or always feel as though they lack companionship (43 percent), that their relationships are not meaningful (43 percent), that they are isolated from others (43 percent), and/or that they are no longer close to anyone (39 percent).
- Approximately three in five (59 percent) surveyed sometimes or always feel that their interests and ideas are not shared by those around them.
- A similar proportion surveyed report sometimes or always feeling as if the people around them are not necessarily with them (56 percent).
- More than a third of the respondents report feeling as if there is no one they can turn to.

## Murthy and Routledge: the loneliness epidemic

Former Surgeon General Vivek Murthy summarized his experience as a doctor dealing with the growing loneliness and alienation experienced by Americans in all social classes. Writing in the *Harvard Business Review* ("Work and the Loneliness Epidemic," October 16, 2017), Murthy notes, "During my years caring for patients, the most common pathology I saw was not heart disease or diabetes; it was loneliness." The behavioral scientist Clay Routledge echoes Murthy's findings in "Suicides Have Increased. Is This an Existential Crisis?" (*New York Times*, June 25, 2018):

I am convinced that our nation's suicide crisis is in part a crisis of meaninglessness. . . . A felt lack of meaning in one's life has been linked to alcohol and drug abuse, depression, anxiety and—yes—suicide. . . . How do we find meaning and purpose in our lives? . . . *Americans today are waiting longer to marry and have children, and are having fewer children.* This may be a desirable state of affairs for many people (though evidence suggests that American women are having fewer children than they want). *Nonetheless, researchers have found that adults with children are more focused on matters of meaning than are adults who do not have children, and that parents experience a greater sense of meaningfulness when they are engaged in activities that involve taking care of children.* (Italics added.)

## Sales: smartphones and disintegrating togetherness

One thing that is happening to young people is they are living at a time when family togetherness is disintegrating in whole swaths of our society. Parents are both at work and strangers care for kids. Another is the domination of tech addiction in their lives. Nancy Jo Sales, the author of *American Girls: Social Media and the Secret Lives of Teenagers*, writes, "The majority of eleven-year-olds own smartphones. And experts are worried" (*Guardian*, November 1, 2019). "Kids can't seem to put their phones down, which teachers say is disrupting class time and causing innumerable fights and misunderstandings." Sales continues:

Everybody wants to know: "What do we do?" They're all for limiting screen time—though it's hard, they say; their kids act like addicts when you try to take away their drugs—but when you raise the question of not giving kids phones at all, they balk. "How can we do that?" parents ask. "Our kids will have no social life. They won't be able to function in the modern world." . . . [L]et's look at all the other things kids won't be able to do if they don't have a phone. They won't be able to be part of a group chat, the site of hours of distracting discussions which arguably would be better had in person, where face-to-face interaction would elevate the quality of the conversation and deepen social bonds.

## Blakeslee: the hollowness of all substitutes for love

Loneliness is a killer because, as neuroscientists tell us, the *insula* is "a long-neglected brain region that . . . is the wellspring of social emotions. . . . It helps give rise to moral intuition, empathy, and the capacity to respond emotionally to music" as Sandra Blakeslee writes in "A Small Part of the Brain, and Its Profound Effects" (*New York Times*, February 6, 2007).

The insula is also activated when we're in physical pain. *And for humans, emotional pain is as real as physical pain.* That includes pain when toddlers (even newborns) are routinely separated from parents as the "normal" price of parental career "success" forced on parents by our culture.

Acceptance of pain as the new normal is drummed into us from nursery school to grad school. The message is: play by the corporations' rules. Accept the pain! Accept the disappointment! There are no options! After all, we're not socialists! Ha, ha! This playing by corporate rules now also includes the pain of delayed and/or derailed romantic pair-bonded relationships in favor of career-nurturing rather than loving. Again: no options, and few choices as the rich offer America a perpetual middle finger to our desire to be humans.

## The movie *The Terminator* got it wrong: the machines didn't take over—the assholes did

Bluntly: we've designed a society that inhibits our ability to fall in love when hormones, biology, and evolution are screaming at us to do so when we're young enough to take risks. And we've designed a society that even destroys our ability to have fun with our children. We're at work instead of entering into play as adults, to, as it were, wander a marsh with a child and reconnect with their ability to play and discover, rather than strive and scheme. We miss out on wonder-sharing childhoods with our own children and accept fake, delayed adolescence in "fun" companies that provide cool bikes to ride down hallways and sushi for lunch. This is the anatomy of a monumental rip-off. Conversely, love's wonder-inducing rewards can only found lifelong relationships that last. Dean Burnett points this out.

### Burnett: the happy brain

Dean Burnett is a doctor of neuroscience. He lectures at Cardiff University and is also a writer and a stand-up comedian. Burnett is the author of *The Happy Brain: Where Happiness Comes From, and Why*. He brings us up to date on what's known about our chemical neurotransmitters and their roles, such as dopamine (reward and pleasure), endorphins (a response to pain and stress), and oxytocin (the love hormone). In *The Happy Brain* he also explains the importance of love, sex, work, and friendship. When it comes to understanding why some people are able to stay in a long-term relationship, Burnett has this to say:

> Basically, because of how the brain works, if a relationship lasts long enough, our desire to maintain and prolong it becomes somewhat self-fulfilling. As ever, though,

the brain has a few things in place to help this process. Studies show that couples who have been together for decades who state they are still happily in love, have activity in the relevant dopamine reward centers of the brain that is basically equivalent to people newly in love, so it seems entirely possible for our brains to keep all the positive, pleasurable associations long-term.

Burnett makes clear that the benefits and rewards of establishing a lasting deep connection with someone, and the satisfaction of being part of a social group as an extension of that pair-bonded relationship, came late in our evolutionary passage. The profound satisfaction of experiencing love was something we began to feel only when our newer brains were more developed. And the most basic of all newer-brain prime directives from then on has not been canceled: *bond, love, be loved.*

# CHAPTER 5

# The Survival of the Friendliest: The Evolutionary Directive to Love and Be Loved— of Course—Brings Us to the Subject of Dogs

We can see our evolutionary prime directives reflected pretty clearly in the only animal species that co-evolved with us—dogs. Listen to dogs' wisdom. Dogs bond, love, play, and want to be loved. Dogs know how to live. If dogs wrote our legislation on family policy, we'd be living in Iceland. The word *supportive* hardly covers what dogs *are*.

Our dog Zip was left alone for five hours. When I came home, I knew he was hungry and filled his dish. Zip is an eager little rescue-shelter mutt combining dachshund, Chihuahua, and maybe a bit of Jack Russell terrier. We've had him for five years, and he came to us at nine months old. On this afternoon he was a year old. He began to eat. I sat down on the bottom step of our back staircase to untie my shoes. Zip left his dish, raced over to me, and jumped into my lap. He craves love more than food. Only after I'd held him, we'd nuzzled, and he'd licked my face and I'd scratched his neck, did Zip tear himself away and race back to his dish to wolf down the rest of his meal. Zip's idea of success is shared space, closeness, and contact.

As I sat at my desk revising this book for the last time before sending it to my agent, Zip was nestled inside my bathrobe sleeping against my chest. At night, neither of us sleeps very well without the other. Go figure—a descendant of wolves and an over-evolved, freakishly big-brained primate huddle contentedly together. Sometimes the more eccentric of this odd couple whispers to the other, "Big monkey *loves* little wolf!"

**Peace is not something that comes easily to me**

Each day during the Covid-19 spring/summer of 2020, Zip waited for Jack to arrive to work on our barn's renovation. They'd sit together "holding paws" as Jack once put it, while I had a third cup of coffee. As September 2020 began, I was feeling forlorn as I watched them together. Jack was about to go back to school part-time online and part-time in person, outdoors, at our local public school. I was already missing him.

The word *bonding* doesn't come close to describing all our feelings for one another. Jack's love for Zip is returned a thousandfold. I knew that when he was in school again and I was in the barn—alone!—finishing up the renovations, I'd miss him. Zip would, too. I knew when Jack was back at school and I was working alone on the barn that I'd also be kicking myself for the wasted times I got impatient and reverted to my dominating inner "born-again" idiot. Zip would keep me company, but he doesn't hand you buckets of mortar mix when you build chimneys.

## Fire in the kitchen: a confession

You were three, Lucy, the day I discovered I'd changed somewhat from total jerk to a fairly reasonable facsimile of kindness in action. You set a table napkin on fire while you experimented with a candle flame. I'd briefly left the room and our candlelit dinner table to do the dishes. Genie was in her sewing studio working on giant sets of triple-layer, fire-retardant blackout curtains for the school Becky works at and its new science lab. [Genie went to the Boston School of Fashion Design and can design and tailor anything from men's suits to stunning wedding dresses. She makes heart-stopping quilts, too, of incomparable beauty. She ran a small mail-order publishing company for many years, but her joy is found in her design/sewing studio.] Lucy, we were alone. You had no fear in your startled eyes when you looked at me to see how I'd react after you called me back with an urgent "Ba, you better come here!"

A blue sheet of flame curled up to the ceiling. You were curious about it but not afraid of my reaction. You had never been slapped by the hands that gently took that burning napkin away. And the voice that said, "That might not be a good idea, Lucy," spoke conversationally without yelling.

You were fearless in that moment because (unknown to you) your Ba has been playacting at NOT being the domineering, swaggering, angry fool he was raised to be—in other words, "a man of God." As I conveyed the flaming napkin to the kitchen sink—and then explained about fire and what it does—I was passing a sort of inner test and also passing on my gratitude for having been forgiven by another little girl now grown up—my daughter, Jessica.

I know the grim path of dominating, male, violent anger. I was hit with a belt as a child. It was "God's plan" for fathers to discipline. I walked far enough in Dad's biblical path of rage so that I get men who kill themselves or others. With one foot on the path to violence believing this was God-ordained, I have felt the pull of death by suicide. I want you to know that we can almost break but come back if we have love in our lives, Lucy. Never give up on love.

Lucy, by the time Jessica was a young parent herself, some twenty-plus years ago, I found myself in tears when standing in front of her while we were walking in a forest near where she was living in Finland. I'd come to visit Jessica and her children when Amanda and Ben were little. I'd already long since apologized many times for the way I treated her when I was a teen father, a child raising a child. But seeing how kind she was to her own children, in contrast to my poisonous memories, opened my guilt wounds anew. We'd talked during our walk about how I had worked to change and my regrets.

"I am so sorry," I said.

Jessica spoke the most luminous words there are in the English language, "I forgive you."

We walked on hand in hand. Your aunt Jessica is such a luminous presence in my life. Jessica calls me several times a week, often between meetings, just to tell me what she's doing. We are honest with each other and, to use the overworked phrase, tell each other everything. I have been forgiven and so am transparent to Jessica. There's no place left to hide. So I don't. When she spoke in Brussels at the European Union about new green energy technologies she was putting together for the EU, she put her phone on the podium so her very proud, very undeserving forgiven father could watch his daughter in action. When my projects are going badly (or well), I tell Jessica. When Nora says something funny, Jessica hears all about it.

That's why I'm who I am to you, Lucy—Jessica forgave. Jessica loves. Jessica advises. It's why you and I are best friends, too, Lucy, and, best of all, why fewer guilt feelings darken my friendship with you as those feelings used to do with my children. In short: my malignant narcissistic evangelical cancer has (almost) been excised. Thank you, Jessica. Thank you, Francis and John. Thank you, Genie. And thank you, too, Lucy; I owe you my life, darling.

## Breaking the bondage to generational cycles of hurt

To identify with beauty, forgiveness, and cooperation is to identify with a clear perception of what the evolutionary point of life is. But sometimes the condition we experience is the opposite of clear perception. It's a state of bondage to generational cycles of hurt and loss.

I can't undo the damage I did even if I am forgiven. The good news is that we can choose to break that cycle. Other people can't change us, but we can do the hard work to change ourselves. Love is a powerful motivator. When our bad ideas that run counter to evolution's message of cooperation assail us, such as fundamentalist Nationalist Hinduism, White evangelical Christianity, fundamentalist Saudi-style women-trashing Islam, some versions of fundamentalist Judaism, or rape-the-Earth capitalist achievement greed cults, we can choose to fight back. We can repent. We can change. We can rebuild. We can demand changes from our government. We can do this by going back to that childlike place of wonder within ourselves and reviving our natural chemistry of curiosity to find a kinder, fairer, and better way forward.

## The material world will crush you if seen only as itself

Joy-filled life begins where our slavish dependency on our material ambition and belief systems promoting the domination of others ends. Kindness is made possible by accepting paradox. Let our entire existence be a protest against servitude to a worldview devoid of mercy on the one hand and unquestioning addiction to the delusion of certainty on the other hand. Embrace paradox! Be happy! Embrace the humility of *not* knowing! Do not believe in any promise based on anything less than the experience of unconditional love. In other words, adopt the canine spiritual philosophy of life!

## Lee: dogs evolved alongside humans into something else—love addicts like us

We evolved mercy and forgiveness because we evolved the ability to feel empathy, and we aren't alone. Love is a thing but not only a human thing. Love is bigger than just us. Dogs, too, evolved the capacity to crave love and to return love and service to others.

According to scientists, dogs actually feel measurable emotions similar to ours. Like human children left with strangers, dogs, too, feel the pain of separation and loneliness deeply. Brain scans and other tests show that dogs get the same rush of dopamine we do and sense the same kind of emotions when greeting a loved one. And these days, dogs also suffer from humans' career-first idolatry.

The coronavirus aftermath produced articles on how to leave dogs alone again when going back to work, very similar to the ones on how to help a child survive being put in daycare again after the home life of lockdowns ended. One article came right to the point: "How to Prepare Your Dog to Be Left at Home Alone (Again)" by Jen A. Miller (*New York Times*, May 27, 2020):

> Did you get a new dog during the coronavirus lockdown? Or has your long-time four-legged companion gotten used to having you home? "Dogs are highly

social, which is why we get along with them so well," said Patricia B. McConnell, certified applied animal behaviorist and author of *The Other End of the Leash: Why We Do What We Do Around Dogs*. "If all of the sudden, they go from 'everybody home all the time' to 'nobody home all day long,' it can lead to some serious behavioral problems."

Jane J. Lee notes in "Dog and Human Genomes Evolved Together" (*National Geographic*, May 14, 2013) that researchers from the University of Chicago and a number of other international institutions have found that several groups of genes in humans and dogs have been evolving in parallel for thousands of years—including those related to diet and digestion, neurological processes, and even disease. The authors cited a study suggesting that dogs were domesticated thirty-two thousand years ago, earlier than former estimates. They found that domestication is often associated with large increases in population density and crowded living conditions, and that these communal environments might have been the "selective pressure that drove the rewiring of both species." For example, they point out, living in crowded communities with us may have conferred an advantage on less aggressive dogs, leading to more friendly canines evolving and eventually to pets "whose puppy-dog eyes gaze at us with such unconditional affection."

A recent study shows that dogs share humans' stress levels on a molecular level. In "Long-Term Stress Levels Are Synchronized in Dogs and Their Owners" (*Scientific Reports*, June 6, 2019), Ann-Sofie Sundman, Enya Van Poucke, Ann-Charlotte Svensson Holm, Åshild Faresjö, Elvar Theodorsson, Per Jensen, and Lina S. V. Roth write:

This study reveals, for the first time, an interspecific syn-chronization in long-term stress levels [between dogs and their "owners"]. Through assessment of cortisol concentration in hair of both dogs and their owners, we found an interspecific long-term stress hormone synchronization within the dog-human dyad. . . . Our results show that long-term stress hormone levels were synchronized between dogs and humans, two differ-ent species sharing everyday life.

## Hare, Woods, Wong: *the survival of the friendliest*

According to Brian Hare and Vanessa Woods of Duke University, authors of *The Genius of Dogs*, we tend to give ourselves too much credit when telling the story of how dogs came into our lives. Discoveries from the Duke Canine Cognition Center, where they work, reveal how dogs think and how and why humans have deep relationships them. Breakthroughs in cognitive science have shown dogs have a kind of genius for getting along with people. Why? When we look back at our relationship with wolves, their ancestors, throughout history, "We have a long history of eradicating wolves." (That long history is why Hélène Grimaud opened her wolf sanctuary and spent so much time trying to educate the public about top predators.)

So how, Hare and Woods ask, was "this misunderstood creature tolerated by humans long enough" to evolve into . . . Zip? "The short version," they write, "is that we think of evolution as being the *survival of the fittest*, where the strong and the dominant survive and the soft and weak perish. But essentially, far from the survival of the meanest, the success of dogs comes down to *survival of the friendliest*." (Italics added.)

It turns out that this survival of the friendliest tactic is passed on through genes and by instruction and example. It's what human learning is all about, too: a lifetime *process* of education in how to get on with others. In other words, we learned to forgive. We learned to feel sad when we abandon one another.

Kate Wong, in "Why Humans Give Birth to Helpless Babies" (*Scientific American*, August 28, 2012), notes that this evolutionary friendliness is inherited and also taught. The sort of intense nurture we need to give our big-brained babies and for how long, compared to other great apes, is what makes us humans what we are. In other words, communities and families aren't optional for learning to survive. They are our schools. More than that, they are the setting where we *become human* as our newer brain learns how to get along with others and how to experience empathy and then use it in what amounts to our very own *self-domestication process* as we turn from retribution to repentance and forgiveness.

*Science Daily* (February 15, 2018) reported on a Universidad de Barcelona (UB) study on human self-domestication: "It is a hypothesis that states that among the driving forces of human evolution, humans selected their companions depending on who had a more pro-social behavior." Kate Wong quotes Karen Rosenberg of the University of Delaware (an expert on the evolution of human birth) to the same effect that, given how difficult human birth is, one would think that if the female human pelvis could have gotten bigger without compromising locomotion, it would have. It didn't. Why?

## Gopnik: the hungry, hungry brain

Rosenberg says that perhaps because the timing of human birth actually "optimizes cognitive and motor neuronal development," evolution selected to stick with long-term childhood learning rather than evolving wider pelvises. That idea seems to fit with self-domestication/survival of the friendliest theories as well and "is worth pursuing," Rosenberg says. "Maybe human newborns are adapted to soaking up all this cultural stuff and maybe being born earlier lets you do this. *Maybe being born earlier is better if you're a cultural animal.*" (Italics added.) Or as Alison Gopnik, professor of psychology and affiliate professor of philosophy at the University of California, Berkeley, puts it in *The Gardener and the Carpenter: What the New Science of Child Development Tells Us About the Relationship Between Parents and Children*, while talking about our childhoods in the context of brain development:

> In fact, our brains are most active, and hungriest, in the first few years of life. Even as adults, our brains use a lot of energy: when you just sit still, about 20 percent of your calories go to your brain. One-year-olds use much more than that, and by four, fully 66 percent of calories go to the brain, more than at any other period of development. In fact, the physical growth of children slows down in early childhood to compensate for the explosive activity of their brains.

## Konner: the way of the bonobos

The evolutionary advantage of being a cultural animal might be described as the learning of *altruism*. This idea is explored by Melvin Konner. Konner teaches anthropology and behavioral biology at Emory University. He is the author of *The Evolution of Childhood*, and *Women After All—Sex, Evolution, and the End of Male Supremacy*. Konner's work provides evidence for the idea that humans, from early on in our development, became the most cooperative species. In the March 2019 issue of *The Atlantic*, Konner writes:

> Put apes and humans in situations that demand collaboration between two individuals to achieve a goal, as a variety of experimenters have done, and even young children perform better than apes. . . . Classic work on chimps has been complemented by new studies of bonobos, our other close relative. No more removed from us genetically than chimps are, they are a radical contrast to them, often called the "make love, not war" species.

Now that we're self-aware, how we *choose* to live can make parts of our evolution self-directed, a point Konner made in *Women After All*. Konner believes that our species is still evolving and will go either the way of chimps (warring assholes) or the way of bonobos (loving). It will all depend on how much we choose traits that are generally called "feminized," such as caregiving, to thrive in our culture.

In bonobo society, females, particularly mothers, play key social roles. Bonobo males do not use sexual coercion against females, and female bonobos form strong social bonds and effectively cooperate to keep male aggression down. Primatologists note that bonobos are in significant respects smarter than chimpanzees, as demonstrated by their superior capacity to learn. We evolved to care for those around us. We evolved to *play* with children. We evolved to ask for forgiveness when we hurt people.

In other words, British naturalist Charles Darwin got it right, but maybe we got Darwin wrong. Many people assume Darwin was talking about physical strength when referring to "survival of the fittest," meaning that a tougher species always will win. But what if he didn't mean that?

## Humans are the most cooperative

The survival of the friendliest concept is even the title of a recent book, *Survival of the Friendliest: Understanding Our Origins and Rediscovering Our Common Humanity,* by Hare and Woods, who we met arguing their case for dogs' survival of the friendliest paradigm. Recently, they've followed the logic of their dog research and expanded upon it to suggest humans also succeeded not because we were the strongest but because (like dogs) we were cooperative.

What helped us innovate, Woods and Hare say, was our knack for coordinating *with* and listening *to* others. We find common cause with both neighbors and strangers because that's what we're built to do. They say that the study of evolution points our way not to domination but to cooperation, not to self-sufficiency but to community. In fact, they write, what allowed us to develop technology and culture was our self-domestication—character-ized by decreased aggression—which gave us an ability to coor-dinate and communicate with others. But Hare and Woods warn this gift for friendliness came at a cost. If we perceive someone to be a threatening outsider, we detach them from our empathic reactions to "the other" so they become subhuman to us, and "fair game for terrible cruelty." We are, Hare and Woods conclude, simultaneously the most tolerant and the most pitiless species on the planet. Some of us have been both of these things as Jessica could tell you about me. Some of us have spent lifetimes trying to self-direct our own spiritual evolution to a better place.

For humans to continue to evolve successfully (in other words, to survive our own chaos-inducing proclivity for veering into cruelty), Woods and Hare say friendliness is the winning strategy. In an interview in the *Washington Post* ("'Friendliest,' Not Fittest, Is Key to Evolutionary Survival, Scientists Argue in Book," July 20, 2020), Hare points out that:

> Social problems require social solutions. The secret to our species' success is the same as it is with dogs and bonobos. We are the friendliest human species that ever evolved, which has allowed us to outcompete other human species that are now extinct. When that mechanism is turned off, we can become unbelievably cruel. When it is turned on, it allows us to win. We win by cooperation and teamwork. Our uniquely human skills for cooperative communication can be used to solve the hardest social problems.

## Wrangham: how we evolved morality

But what if an individual in a community reduces their relationship with others to brute strength and/or to a career stepping-stone? What if we call for family values and then do everything we can to undermine them by refusing to support parents? Worse, what if those parents deprived of help inadvertently raise their children to be lonely domineering strivers instead of joy-filled individuals who know how to love? What if we need to find better standards of how to treat people that don't leave us racked by guilt as my early years as a parent did? What is the right standard to live by? Do we need God or a holy book to instruct us? Do we need a god? Where do we get our rules from? This brings us to the subject of morality.

## Morality was not invented by religion

Morality is real. It is absolute.

Morality does not need religion.

Morality came first and religion a very distant second.

In fact, religion often masks evil, i.e., evangelicals storming the United States Capitol in Jesus's name, or Orthodox Jews refusing to educate girls because a woman is seen as a baby machine, or Muslims doing honor killings for virginity issues, or the horror show Dad and I unleashed on America in the name of (most ironically) saving lives. And when religion does something good, all it does is reflect and reinforce evolution's absolute moral standards and remind us of them.

Morality is less right versus wrong than about what works out best for everyone. Morality is evolution's most essential message: be nice!

Morality slowly evolved as part of our trial-and-error evolutionary survival-of-the-friendliest strategy. Humans began to notice what worked and which behaviors were counterproductive. We eventually learned to speak and, in many languages, called those behaviors *wrong*.

We evolved institutions and taboos to enforce social tribal behavior that helped us survive so we wouldn't settle every dispute with a massacre. Then of course we killed one another anyway. But it could have been worse. Proof? Some of us survived. We survived only because of the evolutionary still, small voice. Be nice, it said—or die. Make neighbors, it said, you'll need them! Repent, it said. Find a better way, it said. We did. Not perfectly, but we did.

## Morality is an evolutionary survival tactic—deal with it

In *The Goodness Paradox: The Strange Relationship Between Virtue and Violence in Human Evolution*, Richard Wrangham (who teaches biological anthropology at Harvard University) writes, "Reduced reactive aggression must feature alongside intelligence, cooperation, and social learning as a key contributor to the emergence and success of our species." That's why we like living in closely connected, "childminding, friendly communities and tribes: we need each other, and that need is rooted in our physical survival." That's why someone like me eventually woke up to the fact that the domination evangelical male model I was raised on is (to put it nicely) counterproductive. That's why every urge and instinct we have to survive revolves around our desire to be part of a social group that obeys certain rules related to getting along. That's why males and nonbinary people evolved the same chemical responses to childcare and loving children as mothers and can mother. That's why solitary confinement is used as a dire punishment and considered to be a human rights abuse. That's why I found myself saying I was so very sorry to Jessica for slapping her as a child and apologizing to my sons for spanking them—and meaning it. That's why (no matter what we tell ourselves) we know that leaving a screaming child in daycare maybe isn't the right thing to do. That's why we know we have to unite to demand better choices from our society and government. And that's why we know in our gut when children get used to abandonment, evolution teaches us to ask, was this really a victory?

## Distinctively human society sustained by egalitarian norms

In other words, evolution taught us that we actually *are* our brothers' (and children's) keepers long before the idea was folded into religious concepts expressed in passages such as these: "Bear one another's burdens, and so fulfill the law of Christ" (Galatians 6:2), and "I was hungry and you gave me food, I was thirsty and you gave me drink, I was a stranger and you welcomed me"

(Matthew 25:35). In fact, such passages resonate with us as prophetic only because in some deep inner place we *already know they are true*. Put it this way: the best of religion reinforces what we evolved to be, and the worst of religion denies the inner truth whispering to us to have empathy. True spirituality is kindness or it is nothing.

### Boehm: moral origins

In *Moral Origins: Social Selection and the Evolution of Virtue, Altruism, and Shame*, social anthropologist Christopher Boehm argues that keeping the playing field level was a matter of "bear one another's burdens" survival to our ancestors. They could not have been selfish and survived. We're only here because someone stronger once shared with someone weaker.

Small-scale nomadic foraging groups could not stock surplus food, and given the high-risk nature of hunting and gathering, sharing was required to ensure everyone got enough to eat. Suppressing our earlier primate ancestors' dominance hierarchies by practicing more egalitarian behavior was a central adaptation of human evolution. Egalitarian practices enhanced cooperation and lowered risk as small isolated bands of humans spread into new habitats across the world.

When the playing field is level, it enhances chances of survival for everyone. In other words, empathy worked better for our ancestors than brute domination and bullying—that is, if they wanted to be successful in building communities and families.

### Curry: morality evolved to promote cooperation

In *Current Anthropology* ("Origins of the Human Predatory Pattern: The Transition to Large-Animal Exploitation by Early

Hominins," 60, no. 1, February 2019), a group of scholars from the University of Chicago argue that natural selection has favored genes for *cooperation* between individuals in a wide variety of species, including humans. "Anthropology has struggled to provide an adequate account of morality," they say, and then describe the evolution of our ideas of morality as an attribute of

> adaptations [that] can be seen as natural selection's attempts to solve the problems of cooperation . . . these biological and cultural mechanisms provide the motivation for social, cooperative, and altruistic behavior—*leading individuals to value and pursue specific mutually beneficial outcomes.* They also provide the criteria by which individuals recognize, evaluate, and police the cooperative behavior of others. . . . [I]t is precisely these multiple solutions to problems of cooperation—*this collection of instincts, intuitions, inventions, and institutions—that constitute human morality.* (Italics added.)

## Oxford's Institute for Cognitive and Evolutionary Anthropology: Is morality innate or acquired?

In 2012, Oliver Scott Curry (the lead author of "Origins of the Human Predatory Pattern") was an anthropology lecturer at the University of Oxford. He organized a debate among his students about whether morality is innate or acquired. One side argued that morality was the same everywhere; the other, that morals are different everywhere. Seven years later, Curry, now a senior researcher at Oxford's Institute for Cognitive and Evolutionary Anthropology, offered an answer to the question of what morality is and how it does—or doesn't—vary around the world.

Everyone shares a common moral code, says Curry: all agree that cooperating, promoting the common good, is the right thing to do. Curry's group came to their conclusions about evolutionary and universal morality after they studied ethnographic accounts of ethics from sixty societies, across more than six hundred sources. They reviewed seven well-established types of cooperation to test the idea that morality evolved to promote cooperation. They looked at group loyalty, why we form groups, and why we conform to local norms and promote unity and solidarity. The result was that the team found that seven cooperative behaviors "were considered morally good" in 99.9 percent of cases across all cultures:

**Help your family.**
**Help your group.**
**Return favors.**
**Respect authority.**
**Be brave.**
**Divide resources fairly.**
**Respect others' property.**

As Curry confirms, in all cultures it paid to embrace the daily obligations of family commitment and to integrate oneself into a coherent community. It paid to be trustworthy. Put another way, it pays any society to try to discourage the betrayal of trust by individuals and companies alike. It pays, as it were, to get other parents' kids safely to and from home because they, in turn, returned the favor. Fast-forward: it paid to band together when confronting Covid-19 and to wear a mask to protect others. It paid not to be idiots and deny science. It paid to get the vaccine.

## Brooks: the chains we choose that set us free

In "Five Lies Our Culture Tells" (*New York Times*, April 15, 2019), columnist David Brooks puts Konner's points about altruism and connection like this:

> People looking back on their lives from their deathbeds tell us that happiness is found amid thick and loving relationships. It is found by defeating self-sufficiency for a state of mutual dependence. It is found in the giving and receiving of care. . . . In reality, the people who live best tie themselves down. They don't ask: What cool thing can I do next? . . . By planting themselves in one neighborhood, one organization or one mission, they earn trust. They have the freedom to make a lasting difference. It's the chains we choose that set us free.

What makes us happiest relates to how we evolved to survive. It is to put the quality of our relationships, and thus the good of others, at the heart of our lives. Dogs know this. Some lucky people eventually also discover the best life offers is love, mercy, forgiveness, compassion, and sacrifice for others. Thus, in evolutionary terms, the phrase *to become a success* might best be defined as becoming a person who is the foundation upon which others have the opportunity to build their lives.

# CHAPTER 6

# A Path to Caregiving Joy

Genie and I learned about what makes life most meaningful from one of our toughest experiences: in 2002, our youngest son, John, was sent to fight in Afghanistan. We'd been surprised when, in 1999, John joined the Marines as a post–high school, "I don't know what I want to study in college" lark. I summed up my ambivalence in a long opinion article, "My Heart on the Line," published in the *Washington Post* (November 26, 2002):

> It had been hard enough sending my two older children off to Georgetown and New York University. John's enlisting was unexpected, so deeply unsettling. I did not relish the prospect of answering the question "So where is John going to college?" from the parents who were itching to tell me all about how their son or daughter was going to Harvard. At the private high school John attended, no other students were going into the military.

After the terrorist attacks of 9/11, John's lark became deadly serious. Genie and I lived in abject terror for the next two years

203

while John was deployed multiple times. We also found ourselves unexpectedly part of a community we'd known little about: the proud but traumatized parents, spouses, lovers, and children of those at war. Genie and I were reduced to helpless former protectors of a child now beyond our help. Yet the parents of "our" Marines gave one another encouragement. We gathered in Marine family meetings. While our children were at war, we swapped stories, notes, and emails. At that time I felt closer to strangers with a MY SON IS A MARINE bumper sticker on their car than I did to some of my oldest friends. I learned community and connection are not optional.

Following three wartime deployments and an honorable discharge from the Marine Corps in 2004, John attended and graduated from the University of Chicago with honors and a degree in modern European history. We couldn't pay those college fees either, just like we couldn't with Jessica at NYU. John got a 100 percent scholarship because someone caring in the school office pointed him to a fund for former Marines that had rarely been used. (The University of Chicago is many good things but not known as a place former enlisted Marines gravitate to!) And Francis? He did a work/study program at Georgetown School of Foreign Service, took a year off to earn money for school, and then completed his degree. He won the school's top academic award. (Yes, I am bragging.)

Against the advice of his more career-oriented friends, John married Becky halfway through college. "I learned one thing in Afghanistan: life's too short to mess around," John told me by way of explaining his "get married now—have kids soon" decision.

After graduation, Becky and John moved in with Genie

and me until they could get on their feet. Fortunately, we could accommodate them. Lucy was born and, as I've already mentioned, lived in our house until she was two. Having John's children with us began to cure the cold dread we'd lived with when John went to war. These were not only grandchildren but three luminous answers to many anguished entreaties to gods (real or imagined), to the universe, or to anyone else—for our son's safe return. I was thankful I embrace the idea of paradox and pray in spite of the fact that I do not always believe God is there, let alone listening, when I do.

## Lucy's heaven

Lucy, I think you were aware of death early in life because having had a dad go to war—even though it was before you were born—was a sort of background noise that, though rarely mentioned, colored your outlook with a sort of grown-up seriousness almost by osmosis. Maybe that's why, at age five, you'd lie on the floor playing your "a soul that just arrived in heaven" game.

I did not know souls "go to sleep when they die and then wake up in heaven" until you told me. I didn't invent this game; you did, after looking at a book filled with pictures of Italian frescoes and asking me who all those skeletons were pulling themselves out of the ground. It turned out that the resurrection of the dead art theme was something you thought was a most excellent basis for playacting.

You looked around the attic when your soul woke up in heaven and, sounding mighty pleased and somewhat relieved, you exclaimed, "It's just like it used to be at home!" Then you ran over to your Nutcracker ballet doll and, giving your voice a convincingly thrilled inflection, said, "Look, Ba, my nutcracker is here in heaven just like the one we used to play with!"

The combination of knowing your dad "was in a war, Ba," me reading Greek mythology and the Bible to you, you looking at art and finding dead fish, birds, and (once) a seal washed up on the marsh by the tides was all it took to enlarge the scope of your playacting to include the big themes of life and death. Then my mother, Edith, died and then Genie's mother, Betty, also died early in your childhood. I'd painted you a picture of Betty after she died, of her flying accompanied by her dog and by you flying next to her in your yellow rain boots. You had that picture on your bedroom wall.

You instructed me to "be the angel meeting me." I picked you up and carried you to heaven; you lay still for a moment, then woke up, looked around, and smiled. I said, "Welcome to heaven, I've been missing you," and we hugged. Then you told me it was my turn to be dead and you'd be waiting for me in heaven.

"How do I do that?" I asked.

"Ba, you just lie down and die."

"Okay," I said.

"Now go to heaven."

"I'm dead, so I can't move. How do I get there?"

"Crawl over to the basket of stuffed animals and lie there."

"But I'm dead, so I can't move."

Exasperated, you said, "This is just a GAME, Ba! So just crawl over there, and I'll *pretend* I didn't see you do that! Then lie very still and be your dead soul, and I'll wake you up, and you'll see me and be so happy."

You were starting to be interested in the fact that Greek mythological stories about the afterlife and the Christian conception of heaven were different. We were walking up the drive, and out of the blue you said, "If Greeks die, they go to the underworld with Hades, Ba, not like Grandma Betty."

"Yes, in the ancient stories they did, but actual Greeks these days go wherever everyone else goes—or not—whatever."

"But the Greeks in the old-fashioned days thought they would go to the underworld with Hades."

"But they didn't because, like you said, Lucy, Hades isn't real."

"I know *that,* Ba! But is heaven real?"

"I don't know."

I have no idea why you loved Greek mythology so much, Lucy, but you did, and you were always revisiting the stories in our conversations and weighing their veracity. "This isn't real" was a standard comment of yours, usually uttered after I'd been reading some long, involved episode involving murder, the creation of mythical beings, and bad endings for assorted mortals who had run afoul of the gods due to the gods' petty jealousies.

Your doubts about the Greek myths—"Are you telling me he married his *sister*?!"—began to bleed into your interpretation of the Bible stories: "Are you telling me God told Abraham to *kill his son*?!" We'd been reading from a toddler Bible, and then when you turned three we began reading a young adults illustrated Bible. I let you decide for yourself about which of your "this is real" and "this isn't real" verdicts you'd pronounce. When we read the story of Jonah, you (age six) announced that "Jonah isn't real, Ba, it's just a story, like Persephone eating the food of the dead." You carried this theme further. "Goldilocks *isn't* real, Ba!" you declared after I'd claimed she'd come into our house that morning and stolen all our breakfast cereal. "Dinosaurs were real, Ba, but they're extinct!" you said when I'd joked I'd seen one on the marsh.

You tended to buy into stories about Jesus as more or less real. You pronounced once, "This actually happened, Ba," about Jesus raising Lazarus from the dead. As you put it, "He made Mary and Martha so happy!" But many of the stories left you thrilled, yet (as with Isaac saying okay to Abraham fixing to sacrifice him) dubious.

While reading Bible stories to you in conjunction with Greek myths, I found your skepticism contagious. It had actually been a long time since I'd read the Bible. Over the years, I dipped in once in a while looking for references to attack evangelical hypocrisy, but until I started reading it to you, the Bible was like a house I'd once lived in and thought I knew well but hadn't revisited. Once I actually spent some time there again, the place seemed different from how I'd been remembering it. The way themes in the mythology we were reading kept replicating themselves in the Bible stories was disconcerting, at least from the point of view of the theology I'd been raised on. Universal floods, falls from grace, people going down into the underworld after death, sinners suffering torment, saviors, resurrections, and heavenly battles swirled through the Greek mythology as well as through the Bible stories. The experience of re-encountering these stories afresh through your eyes was very much like my first homecoming for the summer holidays after being at boarding school: my bedroom just seemed so much smaller than I remembered it.

Regardless of the kind of truth value you assigned each story, Bible stories and Greek mythology provided us with many a script for you to rewrite in your inimitable way, adapting various episodes for our never-ending theatrical productions. Besides, you began to pick up on the mythological themes in other stories and in art. The connections were multiplying. Soon after you turned three, you started to listen for longer and longer periods to what you called "chapter books," as opposed to short illustrated books for younger children. I marveled at your exponentially lengthening attention span and gave thanks that your parents were (mostly) keeping you away from electronic tech devices and letting you discover your world in real time and hands-on.

By the time you were four, you were good for up to twenty minutes of *Winnie the Pooh*, thirty minutes of Bible stories (from a DK Bible storybook for young people ages ten and up), and you'd push me to read for an hour-plus whenever Hera, Zeus, and the Olympian gang were involved. You also updated the stories. Once you commanded me to draw "a picture of Zeus throwing lightning bolts at a family having a picnic at the beach, Ba."

After you knew various stories well, you began to develop your own theology about them. You not only asked questions about the believability of the stories but also began parsing out their internal logic. For instance, you wanted to know why someone would turn to stone if they saw the Gorgons. "No one is really that ugly, Ba," you said. Then you decided the Gorgons weren't so bad after all. And Medusa might have had snakes for hair, but you said that would not have scared you because "I *like* snakes, Ba!"

Back to your heaven: Lucy, you had me die many times and "arrive in heaven" as "a dead spirit, Ba." You woke me with the words "Here are your wings." I'd never told you that anybody had wings in heaven but you'd picked up plenty of visual clues from art, not to mention the Greek myths. You'd seen various assorted winged Eros fluttering about as naked winged babies in paintings based on Greek mythology. Wings question aside, apparently in heaven your favorite composers would be directing their very own orchestras. One time after you got to heaven (my turn to wake you), while looking around with a thrilled surprised expression, you called me "Mr. Beethoven." Later you decided that I was "Mr. Monteverdi," and you sternly instructed me to "Conduct me, Ba! I'll be your choir." I did and you loudly sang, "Glory to the Father, the Son, and the Holy Spirit!" (you'd recently seen Monteverdi's *Vespro della Beata Vergine*). Unlike the choir we'd watched in a concert video, you ran around the room waving your hands in the air while singing. When we'd watched the fabulous production (English Baroque Soloists and Chorus, John Eliot Gardiner), you insisted that I read you the

English subtitles translating the Latin text with many a "What's he singing *now*, Ba?"

You loved the fact that a large children's choir was involved in the Monteverdi concert. Anyone who walked in while you were bellowing, "Father, Son, and Holy Spirit!" would have thought that I was running some sort of crazy charismatic amalgam of a worship service where spiritual revival was being oddly combined with ancient liturgical forms and language until, that is, a moment later when you yelled, "You be Zeus and strike this teddy bear with a lightning bolt! He's profaned the gods!"

## One reason I sometimes almost believe (or want to anyway) is because of the love I receive from my children and grandchildren

I'd leave a door open to the discussion of faith in Lucy's and my conversations with an "I don't know"—my tribute to the paradox of describing myself as an atheist who prays and a believer in God who doubts to the point of atheism most of the time, a doubter who seems to (sometimes) feel a loving direction in my life—in other words, someone comfortable with unanswered questions and the acceptance of spiritual/psychological paradox as *just the way things are*. Maybe that's why I came up with the title of one of my books: *Why I Am an Atheist Who Believes in God*. Go figure.

Why do I still pray? Because that's how Mom raised me. You got a problem with that? We are who we are psychologically. To be comfortable in my own skin is to admit my inconsistency and then live with it anyway. Do you have a better idea? Life without spirituality just seems silly to me.

### My second round of childcare

Having helped Genie raise our own three children—when I was home and not directing third-rate Hollywood movies and before that, being on the road as the nepotistic idiot shill for fake family values and sidekick to my evangelical evangelist father— and unlike first-time parents who often feel caught in a seemingly endless cycle of caregiving for babies and toddlers, I knew all too well that, in actuality, the years before school fly by terrifyingly quickly. My older two grandchildren, Amanda and Ben, were grown-ups already! I hadn't visited them nearly enough in Finland. So I knew that very soon our three youngest grandchildren would be at school all day and my days would feel horribly empty. I knew that as time goes by, all one's career accomplishments that at the time seem like such a big deal, fade, but that my hunger for love was growing stronger as I grew older and (perhaps) wiser.

Since this was my second round of childcare, and a second set of children do-over, I also knew that however stymied you feel with crying babies or feeling marginalized as your friends go off to cool careers and you are stuck at home for a couple of years, in reality, the little-child years are a *very short* stage in most actual lives (unless you have seven kids or something like that).

For example, these days Lucy can be found in our house curled up with a book, reading to the point where we have to pry her out of whatever book she's reading to come eat. Or she's in the art room in my barn painting or building bridges she's engineered with glue and Popsicle sticks (500 or more per bridge), testing the "structural strength of triangles, Ba" and "suspension designs" that interest her. Lucy needs no childcare at all these days. She wins poetry contests. And watching her dive into the river and swim while battling the current in order to cling to a jutting rock far from shore *while* she's following a striped bass is stunningly wonderful.

**If you can manage to take time to love, bond, and care for your children full-time through the young years, this choice gives you and your children rewards that don't fade**

Bonds form when you become home, protector, caregiver, nurse, best friend, teacher, and co-adventurer. Above all, a most constant and loyal figure in your child or grandchild's life can't be faked with "quality time" or visits. I'm sorry I didn't know this many years ago. I spent about six months a year (spread out over the year a week or two at a time) away from my family for about ten years at the height of my evangelical and then Hollywood striving years. More fool me! This is why, somewhat perversely, I regarded the Covid lockdown as a reprieve: seven golden months with the grandchildren *every day* morning, noon, and evening, with no goddamned schools or work intruding! I was not the only person enjoying an odd reprieve. There was Microsoft inviting its people back to the office—but 73 percent of their workers surveyed said they now wanted flexible working conditions to stay *after* Covid forced many to work from home. So I know I'm not the only person who learned something new about myself in the lockdown.

**What was a golden reprieve for me and, I suspect, many others from the rush to work, school, and money-making was a threat to some**

Not everyone was happy about parents wanting to recalibrate their childcare priorities. Nor did some executives like losing control of their workers' every waking hour. Goldman Sachs CEO David Solomon unequivocally stated that he wanted all his workers back at the office. Referring to the new family friendly sentiment in favor of working remotely, he said, "It's not a new normal. It's an aberration that we're going to correct as soon as possible."

## How else is a sixty-eight-year-old man to become six again?

But is *money* what counts? Is everything else "an aberration?" Nora was six in the Covid-19 spring and summer of 2020. By this time, she and I were relaxed and happy friends, more like twins than an adult and a child. We hung out together for hours on our muddy little river beach. We'd lose ourselves in unselfconscious play. I'd stand knee-deep in water as she snorkeled in the murky depths looking for treasures—rocks, fish bones, broken bottles, stuff to decorate our village of miniature imaginary people that Nora (the friendly colossus) ruled. Each day, Lucy was in my studio painting on my easel while I read to her or I was giving her cooking lessons, teaching her to cut with razor-sharp knives, fry with scary boiling oil. "Little burns and cuts are part of the deal; deal with it."

I felt like I was in a dream—the happiest I'd ever been, yet filled with sorrow and fear at the Covid cataclysm and the shadow of death looming all around: the best and worst of times. Mostly, I was grateful. My kids were grown, and the school years had recently snatched away my grandchildren for most of the day. Now they were back! Our childcare routine had carried on only after the school pickups and only for a few hours. Now I'd been Covid-reprieved! I wanted to take advantage of each and every moment, and I did. So did Genie to the point that when, on the day in early March 2021 *when we got our second vaccine shot,* Genie said to me, "Isn't it weird to admit that for all the ups and downs of this last year we've been so happy?"

**Too bad more parents aren't told how *few* years they will *actually* have with their children before school effectively kidnaps them**

As I mentioned before, lucky for us, Covid-19 brought our grandchildren home full-time *after* we'd hit sixty-five. Before Genie and I started to get Social Security payments, we never could have afforded not to work full-time, be that on the college-speaking circuit where I scratched out a living as a writer, or Genie working on her mail-order book business and her sewing/design jobs. Actually, before Social Security kicked in, John and Becky were paying us for some of the childcare. It was that or Genie and I would have had to take on more freelance jobs. That said, besides having to work, many of us misplace our priorities and perhaps only slowly realize we threw out the candy and ate the wrapper. Take the thoughts expressed in many essays like this: "The Mothers of America Need a Bailout. This Could Be the Answer" by Katherine Goldstein (*Huffington Post*, July 5, 2020). The author was writing about her Covid-19 stay-at-home-with-kids experience.

> While I have a robust and fulfilling full-time career, my husband earns more than I do, and his salaried job and health insurance are crucial to our family. Although neither of us feels that his work is more important than mine, it is less negotiable. So, like so many mothers in the past three months, I've had countless instances of losing my already frayed temper, finding my only moments of peace were crying on the way to the grocery store, and questioning whether I could survive one more day of the *Groundhog Day*—like monotony of tantrums and witching hours, refusals to do Zoom classes, and the endless grind to keep a highly social

four-year-old from bouncing off the walls while also feeding and caring for two newborns. . . . Mothers all around have shouldered more of the educational and childcare burden created by lockdowns and have reported the highest levels of psychological stress and severe anxiety compared to fathers and people without kids, as a LeanIn.org study found.

Which begs a larger question: Why aren't *both* parents' jobs flexible enough to accommodate parenthood during, say, the years one to four of any child? Why don't we pay parents, who want to, to stay home with preschool children? Why do we still think of childminding as something more women than men do? Why does the powerful White male boss of a company like Goldman Sachs describe those discovering the joys of working from home as an aberration? And why the need for any writer to validate themselves in the first lines of an article on the experiences of parenthood as *also* having a successful career? For that matter why doesn't the government pay for childcare of grandchildren by grandparents?

I'll tell you *why*—because we hate women and children. Too strong? Nope! How else to describe the richest country on earth with shitty maternal death rates? Where are the *real choices* about how best to have a family backed up with tax dollars? Why do single moms face poverty? Why do young people have student debts? Why aren't abortions free? Why isn't contraception free? Why were some college professors such jerks to Nicole Lewis because she was in college with a baby? And by the way—if White men had periods, all related sanitary products would be free and men would get the week off and collect workers' comp once a month. It's time to tell the men who shape our business world of values that always favor shareholders (not to mention planetary destruction via greed) to just fuck off.

Shouldn't everyone be respected whatever their job—be that CEO or full-time parent? Is the solution to the universal parental struggles with tiredness, repetition, boredom, anxiety, sleeplessness, and ennui that have *always* been faced by *all* parents of young children to spend *even less time* with their kids during their most formative early years than parents got with their kids on farms in the Middle Ages?

## Changed definition of success

What if we changed our definition of success so none of us faced social pressures or economic pressures during our children's little-child years (say birth to four years old and preschool) to conform to a pro-business, one-size-fits-all, Goldman Sachs'–style model of life focused on our job title? What if families stuck together so grandparents were there to help? What if we didn't see ourselves defined by "a robust and fulfilling full-time career" first, but rather by *the robust and fulfilling quality of our most important relationships and the FUN they spin off as surely as fire generates heat*? What if parents *also* received a baseline of financial Social Security–type support *while* their children were ages birth to four, so they (like Genie and I these days) could *afford* to stay home and have the pleasure of caring for their kids?

What if our society transformed into one that does not revolve around purchasing; one in which our primary role is not as consumers armed with our commonly deployed credit cards? What if we heeded the wisdom in the book *The Day the World Stops Shopping* by JB MacKinnon, who argues that consumption—of fast fashion, flights, Black Friday–discounted gadgets—has become the primary driver of ecological crisis? As MacKinnon points out, we are devouring the planet's resources at a rate 1.7 times faster than it can regenerate. The US population is 60 percent larger than it was in 1970, but consumer spending is up 400 percent (adjusted for inflation)—and other rich nations, including the UK, aren't much better. "Many people would like to see the world consume fewer resources, yet we constantly avoid the most obvious means of achieving that," says MacKinnon. "When people buy less stuff, you get immediate drops in emissions, resource consumption, and pollution, unlike anything we've achieved with green technology." That's not to mention the impact materialism has on our mental health, inducing feelings of inadequacy and envy, and encouraging a culture of overworking.

## To provide a protected space of love

With every passing day, science-based research into childhood development points to the fact that from birth to school age is the time when what a child sees, hears, and does, and how they are cared for is far more important to their entire lives (and thus to society) than previously thought. As Gopnik writes:

> So our job as parents is not to make a particular kind of child. Instead, our job is to provide a protected space of love, safety, and stability in which children of many unpredictable kinds can flourish. Our job is not to shape our children's minds; it's to let those minds explore all the possibilities that the world allows. Our

job is not to tell children how to play; it's to give them the toys and pick the toys up again after the kids are done. We can't make children learn, but we can let them learn.

## Hutchins: Does evolution favor a winner-take-all society?

Older, outdated evolutionary psychology literature depicts the evolutionary process as creating inherently selfish, competitive individuals—the so-called "survival of the fittest." It fits in all too well with the American view that we are just workers, and success is winning over others. This has contributed to justifying a pitiless, individualistic, career-worshipping (and planet-destroying), libertarian capitalist view of life and "childcare." It contributes today to the belief that jobs are somehow worth more than "mere" childcare. It contributes to giving up on parenthood and using electronic gadgets as joy-killing, creativity-canceling babysitters.

Seen through the prism of the survival of the fittest dominance systems, a meeting in the Beverly Hills Hotel with a studio executive must surely be more satisfying than "just" picking up children at school or giving foot rubs to wanna-be opera singer toddlers. Working for Google or Goldman Sachs might seem more of an achievement than "just" being a loving parent. After all, isn't this a brutal world? Doesn't the *survival of the fittest* paradigm justify the fight to *win*, not to mention the need for career validation? Isn't success all about domination? Doesn't everyone want to grow up to work for Google or Facebook or Goldman and thereby dominate the world through monopolies of power? Isn't *this* what any sane person wants? Maybe not.

## What Darwin found was not a justification of business-style winning but that organisms with the greatest ability to *adapt to their local environment* survived

Darwin found that *sensing, responding, adapting,* and aligning with and within local ecosystems are the keys to survival. For Darwin, not *domination of* our environment but *cooperation with* it (or with our human competitors) best sums up the key to understanding how we or any other life-form made it this far. We are talking about human survival here, not just happiness.

Giles Hutchins, author of the book *The Nature of Business: Redesigning for Resilience*, says that in fact nature is about cooperation, not domination. In his essay, "Distorted View of 'Survival of the Fittest': Business Beyond Reductionism?" (CSR Wire, August 23, 2013), Hutchins writes: "Our prevailing reductionist approach to science, technology and business . . . encouraged us to see ourselves as separate from nature, and to view the world around us as something to be analyzed and over-exploited for our own wants and needs, with scant regard for the consequences." Hutchins points out that our view of nature as "a battleground of competing species, each fighting to survive, is a narrow view of a more complex picture."

What Hutchins says about a more complex and cooperative picture of nature and our part in it as part of nature is even borne out in the life of trees. We find that trees feed a wounded nearby tree. Isolated trees experience stress as do isolated people because community sustains life. That's a point Peter Wohlleben, a German forester who writes on ecological themes, makes in his book *The Hidden Life of Trees*:

When trees grow together, nutrients and water can be optimally divided among them all so that each tree can grow into the best tree it can be. If you "help" individual trees by getting rid of their supposed competition, the remaining trees are bereft. . . . This is because a tree can be only as strong as the forest that surrounds it. . . . Weaker members, who would once have been supported by the stronger ones, suddenly fall behind. . . .

But isn't that how evolution works? you ask. The survival of the fittest? Their well-being depends on their community, and when the supposedly feeble trees disappear, the others lose as well. . . . Even strong trees get sick a lot. . . . When this happens, they depend on their weaker neighbors for support.

## Dawkins's faux science of ruthless nature

Enough of this sentimental claptrap about trees caring for one another, or parenthood being so great, or people working remotely from home, or a grandfather being glad school was canceled so he'd get a second bite at the joy of childcare, some might say. Isn't the world a cruel, fatalistic place, where sorting out the winners (Google) and losers (local newspapers and parenthood) is the natural order of things? Put it this way: wasn't Germaine Greer right and relationships and marriage are just a battle for survival between the waring sexes? Greer's *The Female Eunuch* made the odd case that "Women have very little idea of how much men hate them." Greer's opinion was that the entire social system is a conspiracy to keep women down. "Most women, because of the assumptions that they have formed about the importance of their role as bearers and socializers of children, would shrink at the notion of leaving husband and children, but this is precisely the case in which brutally clear rethinking must be undertaken." Greer's advice on relationships? Run! Abandon! Divorce! Fight to dominate those that once dominated you!

These days, Greer's 1970s ideas seem weirdly out of step with what women I know seem to want. But today there is another sort of glib stridency masquerading as liberation, too: corporate bootlicking. Shouldn't we all just "lean in" and get on with wealth creation? Not according to the most recent and best science.

Scientists have been changing their minds about the "inevitable" competitive genetic brutality of life and the science of domination that used to revere what were thought of as "selfish genes." Science that justified a survival of the fittest mentality made popular by some scientists, such as Richard Dawkins, and writers, such as Greer, is falling out of fashion. And our dying planet seems to be telling us that economic growth (as we describe the rape of our Earth) maybe isn't all it's been cracked up to be by the job creators.

Here's a quote from the preface and first chapter of *The Selfish Gene* by Richard Dawkins that's a good representation of the now-debunked faux science of domination: "We are survival machines—robot vehicles blindly programmed to preserve the selfish molecules known as genes. . . . They are in you and me; they created us, body and mind; and their preservation is the ultimate rationale for our existence. They have come a long way, those replicators. Now they go by the name of genes, and we are their survival machines."

## Buchanan and Powell: the fetishized Darwinian evolutionary theory

The old evolutionary psychology literature of the kind churned out by Dawkins interpreted behaviors like pair-bonding, love, altruism, and generosity, or one Marine parent reaching out to another, or my desire to cook for my grandchildren during a health crisis as a kind of veneer over the selfish drives of our genes. That view also reflected in Greer's version of a declaration of war on relationships as no more than a war of the sexes is being challenged. For instance, Buchanan and Powell seem to have Dawkins (and Greer's ilk) in mind when they denounce . . .

> . . . a tendency among some philosophers and scientists to fetishize Darwinian evolutionary theory and to assume that the possibilities for human morality are tightly constrained by the psychology that natural selection, working on the genetic components of thought and behavior, solidified in human beings many millennia ago. This mistaken evolutionary "determinist" view fosters an . . . [the] unduly pessimistic understanding of the possibilities for moral improvement based on a failure to appreciate how culture has . . . importantly, transformed our evolved moral nature.

## Roughgarden: life's about friendly cooperation

Evolutionary biologist Joan Roughgarden brings the perspective of both a scientist and a transgender person to the topic of sexual relationships and pair-bonding. She believes that evolutionary psychologists got something wrong about sex and the way that males and females interact. Her observations have implications for social, family, and business relationships. In *The Genial Gene: Deconstructing Darwinian Selfishness*, Roughgarden argues that during the 1970s many evolutionary biologists such as Dawkins or writers such as Greer mistakenly thought of sex as a kind of competition between ruthless males and ruthless females—each trying to exploit the other to pass along their genes.

But, Roughgarden asks, are selfishness and individuality—rather than kindness and cooperation—basic to biological nature? Does a "selfish gene" create universal sexual conflict, disruption, and chaos?

In *Evolution's Rainbow*, Roughgarden challenges formerly accepted ideas about gender identity and sexual orientation, upending the notion of the selfish gene by developing a compelling alternative theory called *social selection*. Roughgarden points out that older views imposed cultural gender stereotypes on scientific explanations, making them inconsistent with reasoning and empirical evidence.

Roughgarden proposes that we evolved to a place where "overall, sex is essentially cooperative—a natural covenant to share genetic wealth. Sexual reproduction is not a battle." In other words —what shaped human survival wasn't the survival of the fit test, or a competition between males and females à la Greer, but the survival of the friendliest, be that in sexual relations or one Marine mom calling another or neighbors during the coronavirus pandemic checking up on one another.

## Eisler and Fry: the expression of caring

Roughgarden's survival of the friendliest terminology of cooperation is similar to the ideas expounded by Riane Eisler and Douglas P. Fry in *Nurturing Our Humanity: How Domination and Partnership Shape Our Brains, Lives, and Future*. They write: "This [survival of the friendliest] frame makes it possible to identify the conditions that support the expression of our human capacities for caring, creativity, and consciousness or, alternately, for insensitivity, cruelty, and destructiveness." Eisler and Fry argue that based on findings from biology and social sciences, we know that the cultural environments we create affect nothing less than how our brains develop and hence how we think, feel, and act. How we relate to one another is defined by two larger cultural configurations at opposite ends of a continuum: what they call the *partnership system* (connection and loving) and the *domination system* (exploitation and oppression).

Eisler and Fry also debunk the outdated idea that we're hardwired for selfishness and the domination of others. They write, "Wherever we look, we can see the struggle between partnership and domination playing itself out in various aspects of culture." For example, despite the movement against the large economic inequalities of our time (inherent in all domination systems), top-down control still governs the world of business and corporations worldwide. Yet even within some of the most powerful corporations, some employees are starting to recognize that the move from domination to partnership—the fittest to the friendliest—is essential if the human race is to survive.

In *The Meritocracy Trap: How America's Foundational Myth Feeds Inequality, Dismantles the Middle Class, and Devours the Elite*, Daniel Markovits (Guido Calabresi Professor of Law at Yale Law School) writes that many well-off parents commonly apply to ten private kindergartens, running a gauntlet of essays, appraisals, and interviews all designed to evaluate—four-year-olds. Why? To prepare their kids for "success" in the all-consuming free market.

In "How Life Became an Endless, Terrible Competition" (*The Atlantic*, September 2019), Markovits sums up this joyless commitment to what we call success: "A person who extracts income and status from his own human capital places himself, quite literally, at the disposal of others—he uses himself up." Markovits adds that "Americans who work more than sixty hours a week report that they would, on average, prefer twenty-five fewer weekly hours." They say this because our capitalist system subjects us to a "time famine," which a 2006 study found interferes with the human capacity to "have strong relationships with their spouse and children, to maintain their home, and even to have a satisfying sex life."

## Cohen: the "hustle culture"

Some of us are pushing back against the careerist survival of the fittest time and soul famine. "The feelings of emptiness produced by watching a rigged globalized system deliver homogenization on a massive scale—one way to think, one way to work, one way to conceive of profit, one way to impose a brand, one way to be healthy, one way to deliver a gentrified urban neighborhood—has [sic] been underestimated as a source of disruptive fury," writes Roger Cohen in "The Harm in Hustle Culture" (*New York Times*, February 1, 2019). Cohen points out that the hustle culture is a ploy to extract ever more work from ordinary people—to the sole benefit of corporations and their shareholders.

## The question is this: can we change the way we've been co-opted by defining ourselves by our jobs?

Can we see our relationships as acts of cooperation, not as a competition? Why should it take a pandemic to remind some parents of the pleasures of actually being parents? Can more parents be freed to be parents and stay home for a few years even when there isn't a pandemic? Will society reorganize itself to make this possible? Will political leaders step up and fight for *actual family values* and real choices that empower families? Will they legislate and spend tax money accordingly? Will the next step in feminist thinking champion the right to be flexible in our approach to balancing commerce and family life?

Can we live in tune with what makes us happiest? Can we have fun with our children without someone telling us that life is supposed to be about "serious" work, or a war between men and women, or effectively screaming, "Everyone back to the office!"? Do we really want to be free from the inconvenience . . . of love?

## I become a member of the young mother's club

My ritual of childcare has made me compare the happiness I am experiencing as "just a caregiver" with the more socially acceptable and earlier career-driven stages of my life. This came home to me one day a few years ago when Lucy (then six) and Jack (then four) were in the kitchen painting on a roll of butcher paper stretched across the floor. Nora was on the kitchen table where I was giving her what I call baby rubs (glorified foot massages) while telling the older two a story.

My phone rang. It was a call from Seth (not his real name), an old friend of mine and a wildly successful entertainment lawyer in Los Angeles. I worked with him when I was directing the four feature films I made in Hollywood, South Africa, and Canada from the mid-1980s to early 1990s. This was before my first novel was published and I changed careers—again.

Seth asked me what I was doing. "I'm with the grandkids," I said, and then, without thinking, added, "I love hanging out with the other young mothers I meet at the dance studio Lucy goes to."

There was a brief pause as Seth processed my words. "The *other* young mothers?" he asked, laughing. "The OTHER young mothers?"

I laughed, too, though my remark made sense to me. Gender and age differences are no match for the shared experience of nurturing children. I "got" the "other young mothers" and other young dads, too, and they got me. When Seth added, "Why can't your kids hire a babysitter? When are you going to get back to writing your next book?," it seemed to me he'd missed my point and maybe the point of life, too.

The experiences in my life that I recall as most transcendent do not relate to work. They relate to shared love, like the time when Lucy was three, and a few days before Christmas she said, "Let's go outside and walk around in the dark."

We bundled up, and I put on my rubber boots and stuck a box of Swiss sparklers in my pocket. They'd been sitting on a bookshelf collecting dust when I discovered them a few days earlier—after sitting there, forgotten, for over thirty years since our family moved to America from Switzerland in 1980. We'd tried one to see if they had any sparkle left after all this time. It burned slowly and almost fizzled out a few times, but it did still work. Lucy loved it, and I let her hold the sparkler after I explained that she mustn't touch the red-hot part. It so captivated her that she wanted to try again, so out we went.

It was so foggy that we couldn't see the house after we walked out to the marsh. The lights across the river had misty halos. We stood on the muddy tidal flats by the edge of the river and lit the sparkler. The sparks were reflected on the dark water and in Lucy's eyes. "Happy Christmas, River!" Lucy suddenly called out as she waved the sparkler over the water.

When the sparkler burned out, I picked Lucy up. She lay back in my arms staring up into the misty air. As we walked home across the marsh, she held me close. At that moment, I knew the reason I was born.

# CHAPTER 7

# Using Ourselves Up Through the Capitalism of Disruption

Because of global warming, our entire marsh, front lawn, the crabapple trees, and the porch in front of our house will soon be covered by water. Lucy and I had been walking on the soon-to-be ocean floor. Human commerce, greed, all those terrific careers, and the need to dominate our planet are destroying my property in slow motion. Sure we all need to earn a living. But can human creativity and the desire to survive find ways to do that without trashing our home planet and/or drowning it?

The type of grasses growing by the edge of the lawn have changed over the forty years we've lived here as the level of the water and the frequency of high tides accelerates. Some fruit trees are dying. A one-inch rise in average tide might not sound significant, but it makes a huge difference when high tide coincides with the surge from a storm.

By the time Lucy is the age I was that night carrying her home through the fog, our lawn will be underwater all year. Lucy may someday return in a boat rowing above what once was our home and tell her children, grandchildren, or great-grandchildren that once upon a time, beneath the water, there was a little muddy shore on a river where, "When I was little, I lit a sparkler with my grandfather." If her children ask her what happened, she may answer, "Fancy careers happened to our planet rather than people doing the right thing and just earning a living."

## A nostalgic grandfather/granddaughter pilgrimage

When Jessica's child, Amanda, was nineteen, she came to live with Genie and me for four months. By then I didn't need the rising ocean level to remind me about the preciousness of time with my grandchildren. Amanda's visit was in 2012, while she was taking a year off after she'd graduated from high school in Finland. We revisited New York and made a grandfather/granddaughter pilgrimage back to the Metropolitan Museum of Art, "To," as Amanda said, "go back to where we always go."

Amanda led me straight to several of the pieces of art she'd fallen in love with as a child. Her must-see list included *Greek Bronze Statuette of a Veiled and Masked Dancer* (third–second century BC); *Madonna and Child* by Duccio di Buoninsegna (Italian, Siena 1300); and *The Crucifixion; the Last Judgment*, by Jan van Eyck (Netherlandish, 1430); not to mention the roomfuls of Impressionists, Degas dancers, and a stroll through the Japanese wing to reconnect with the amazingly beautiful screens.

Over the years, Amanda took several trips to be with us, either alone or with her brother Ben or her parents. Every time Amanda and Ben visited, we'd drive to New York City at least once. They visited us once a year, so this drive to NYC became a ritual. We sometimes stayed for a few nights, but if we wanted to save on the expense of a hotel and take several more trips we'd leave at 5:00 AM, arrive by nine or ten in the morning, find alternate side parking on the Upper West Side, walk across Central Park, and go to the Metropolitan Museum of Art. Then we'd drive home late that night. If I'd just sold a book and felt a bit prosperous, sometimes we'd stay in the city for a week. And since the Cloisters (an extension of the Met) is on the northern tip of the island of Manhattan, on the way home as we headed north we'd always stop there.

## The Cloisters

Besides being a faux monastic community reassembled from the bits and pieces of European architectural fragments bought by the Rockefellers in the 1920s and '30s, the Cloisters has an easy to see collection because there's not too much there. The collection includes Amanda's childhood favorite, the *Annunciation Triptych* from the workshop of Robert Campin (Netherlandish, 1375–1444). It was painted as an object for religious devotion but is now the centerpiece of the Cloisters' collection, sitting in a small room filled with antique items similar to the chests, boxes, and pots in the painting.

The middle panel depicts a demure Virgin in prayer. She's not yet aware of the Archangel Gabriel, who has just materialized. A miniature Christ Child bearing a little cross is descending on rays of light, preparing to enter Mary's womb. The painting is a snapshot of the fraction of a second just before the angel breaks the big news: You've got God in your belly. Or as the King James Bible tells the story in the Gospel of Luke: "Now in the sixth month the angel Gabriel was sent by God to a city of Galilee named Nazareth, to a virgin betrothed to a man whose name was Joseph, of the house of David. The virgin's name was Mary."

I'd sit off to the side in an alcove framing one of the deep-set windows overlooking the Hudson River and watch my enraptured granddaughter at various ages—eight, ten, eleven, twelve, on successive pilgrimages as she experienced the joy of reencountering something familiar in art. Rather than outgrowing it as she grew older, her love and understanding of the work deepened.

The other artwork in the Cloisters that Amanda loves is *Standing Virgin and Child*, a wood sculpture attributed to Nikolaus Gerhaert (Dutch, 1460–1473). Gerhaert sculpted with insane attention to detail. His thirteen-inch-high statuette is made of boxwood, and yet to my mind packs the punch of a monumental work in marble. The fine-grained boxwood is cut in stunning detail; for instance, the Virgin's fingertips press into the chubby flesh of the child and indent it in a way that every father and mother has witnessed as they lifted a child out of a bath.

### If every event with a child is being sandwiched into a "busy schedule," a parent misses a lot

If my mind had been on the next meeting I was going to while Amanda looked at the art in the Cloisters, would I have been able to notice the way she looked at an artwork and discover the beauty of watching her discovery? That's why I rarely told my agent and publisher I was in town. I kept those trips separate.

American-style capitalism is all-consuming, distracting, demanding, and loud. That's why American entertainment is also loud: it takes a theme park ride or endless stream of explosions or superhero adventures to even halfway distract us. News programs, which used to simply feature a news anchor calmly telling us the events of the day punctuated by some camera footage, now have banners flashing messages at us at the same time—"Breaking

News!"—so that you aren't really sure where to look. Anything quiet, contemplative, and lasting is shouted down. American capitalism tends to drown out the quiet moments when the best of life is experienced. It isn't working out very well for parents in this regard.

## Losing our balance-career vertigo

According to a comprehensive Pew poll on this subject ("Modern Parenthood," March 14, 2013), among all adults, over half (53 percent) of working parents with children under age eighteen say it's difficult for them to balance the responsibilities of their job with the responsibilities of their family. One third—33 percent—of parents with children under age eighteen say they're not spending enough time with their family. Fathers are more likely than mothers to feel this way. Some 46 percent of fathers say they're not spending enough time with their children, compared with 23 percent of mothers. Only 37 percent of today's working mothers say their ideal situation would be to work full-time.

There is no significant gap in attitudes between male and female parents: 56 percent of mothers and 50 percent of fathers say juggling work and family life is very difficult for them. Only 16 percent say the ideal situation for a young child is to have a mother who works full-time. A plurality of adults (42 percent) say mothers working part-time is ideal, and one third say it's best for young children if their mothers do not work at all outside the home. Among those with children under the age of eighteen, 40 percent of working mothers and 34 percent of working fathers say they always feel rushed and distracted by our fast-cuts distractions. That pace of "Breaking News" syndrome has invaded everything.

The Pew survey finds a strong correlation between financial security and "views about the ideal work situation." Among women who say they "don't even have enough to meet basic expenses," about half say the ideal situation for them is to work full-time. By contrast, only 31 percent of women who identify as people who live comfortably say working full-time is their ideal. A plurality of mothers, 45 percent, and about half the fathers surveyed say that "the best thing for a young child is to have a mother who works part time." Only 16 percent of all American men and women surveyed said that having a mother who works full-time is best for children.

To me, these statistics show that our society has failed families by forcing us to make a choice between family and work *instead of sensibly accommodating both, depending on THE STAGE OF LIFE in which we find ourselves.* Picture a distracted parent making a stop at the Cloisters, glancing at their cell phone to keep up with a flow of texts coming from their boss, oblivious to their daughter as she looks at an artwork and unable to interact with her and share in the experience. Picture a daughter absorbing the fact from her parent's example that there's no time to really *look* at anything, that everything we do is just a way station to big important things that have everything to do with making money, career status, and workplace relationships and nothing to do with savoring living life itself.

Thinking of children raised on an endless stream of mindless spectacle trying to enjoy art or listen to music or even learn about relationships and sex that is subtle, deep, and wonderful is a sad thought. Enter the younger people following tedious "influencers" selling them crap. Generational illiteracy in art, music, and the art of life itself, not to mention what good sex can be, is the price we pay for our entertainment culture where (to borrow from *This Is Spinal Tap*) the "amp" in our brain is turned up to "eleven" all the time.

## Sex

The same goes for sex. As an old lover (in every sense of the word) who relishes times of sexual intimacy with my best friend, Genie, I look at the frantic panic on display in most mainstream movie sex scenes (not to mention in all but the most intimate erotica) that is the opposite of what great sex actually can be—at least to me. Good sex (to me anyway) is the opposite of those clichéd first-encounter sex scenes where lovers are hoisted onto tables or slammed against walls and clothes are ripped off passionately.

Great sex is (to me anyway) relaxed, happy, and friendly and built on learning what another treasured person loves to do, feel, and *be*. Lying naked next to a longtime lover and lifelong best friend and talking while holding hands and then, at some point, beginning the slow tender process of stimulating each other takes time. The *time* good sex takes isn't just about time spent in any one encounter but about the time taken to *learn each other* during hundreds of encounters before. It's not about how to become some sort of generic great lover but about discovering what another person likes best and what you like best, too. And those likes and dislikes change.

## Monogamy is difficult, but it has a big payoff

You can become the world's greatest expert on one person's wants, their very individual body, and their very individual desires, moods, and rhythms. Every individual is an almost infinite bundle of distinct character traits, interests, quirks, and likes, and since those singular traits *keep evolving* as time goes by, if you love them—and stay together—you do not run out of interest in each other. That is because sex isn't static.

Your lover changes, and so do you. So questions about getting tired of sex with one person demonstrate a misunderstanding (and/or lack of imagination or experience) about how we all change. Genie never has been "the same person." She's many people. The woman I'm with now is not the teen I met. She's not the twenty-something mother. She's an altogether different lover now. And since I've been with her every step of the way, I have had a privileged ringside seat seeing the ongoing creation of a fabulous sexual being.

## Good sex takes time

It seems to me that the best sex is like haute couture, not off-the-rack. Sex, too, is the creation of an exclusive custom-fitted experience constructed by hand from start to finish, made from high-quality material, and for one client. An haute couture garment is always created for a singular person, tailored *specifically* for the wearer's measurements and body stance and taste. Or put it this way: I love to cook. I cook every day. But most of the time (now that the kids are grown) in the evenings I have only one client. I know she was raised on Irish stews. They hold a nostalgic place in her memory. So among many other things I cook I make Irish stews a bit more often for her than I would just for myself. Why? Because I'm not cooking generically.

Cooking isn't the point—Genie is. I am cooking *for* Genie. I never enjoy my food so much alone or with anyone else as I enjoy it when I'm *also* watching Genie delight in the tastes and textures of what I've made for her. Her pleasure is my pleasure. This isn't selflessness. It's sensible selfishness. I'm looking for validation and stimulation. And this is reciprocated because Genie knows me better than I know myself. Just to speak plainly: nothing makes me hornier and more aroused than me making Genie feel pleasure deeply and happily.

## Little to nothing is done to help families be families *at the same time* as navigating careers

What is true of hurried sex and bad cooking is true of hurried family life cut (as it were) to the pace of a TV commercial or a frantic sex scene. Nothing is done to allow for *time* for parents to take several years off from work to learn each *individual* child's wants, likes, and needs, and to care for their unique and evolving young children, let alone to accommodate an easy return to work. There is a blindness to how children change, too. And it takes *time* to learn each child's personality, to *be there* as they change and grow. To know them better than they know themselves. And they return the favor. To be known by a clear-sighted honest child is to be seen as you pretty much are.

As I mentioned in the Introduction, my daughter, Jessica, made a good point saying that men designed the business model as if families didn't even exist and women followed their lead—for a while. That dutiful following of the males' careerism was challenged when people started to work from home by millions during the pandemic. The cat was out of the bag. Families exist! Toddlers interrupt important meetings! Maybe living life at a slower, more intimate pace is good! Maybe more couples stuck at home could discover nice, slow, midmorning sex, too. Maybe there is more to life than work!

## Cronin: workplace diversity

Does it make sense that we're obsessed with measuring success by workplace achievement and workplace diversity? Is playing the corporate profit-earning and status game worth it? Does it make sense to teach our children by example that nothing (say, an afternoon at the Cloisters) has intrinsic value that can't be measured by economic gain? Darwinian philosopher and rationalist Helena Cronin from the London School of Economics thinks it doesn't.

Cronin first achieved prominence with her book, *The Ant and the Peacock: Altruism and Sexual Selection from Darwin to Today* (1993). These days Cronin speaks about the fallacy of measuring equality based on job titles and work status. On the BBC Radio 4 program *Thought Cages* (November 22, 2018), in an episode titled "For Greater Diversity, Be Less Fair," host Rory Sutherland interviewed Cronin, who took the opportunity to poke a stick into the eye of today's corporate received "wisdom," first designed by men and then all too often copied by women, willingly or unwillingly as they entered the workforce.

Cronin described the subject of equality between the sexes as a "third-rail issue—touch it, and you die" because her views are contrarian to the faux feminism of shilling for capitalism. Cronin argues against our obsession with trying to measure gender diversity only by "rational metrics" (capitalist success stories) and claims that "this narrow definition of equality has made society *less equitable*." It did this, Cronin says, because such metrics are predicated on the lie that no needs are more basic and important to our happiness than career status.

According to Cronin, corporate neoliberal "empowerment"

contends that if elite women succeed in the halls of corporate power, this will trickle down to benefit all women. But, Cronin asks, is what we define as career success—Money! Striving! Fame! Prestige! Power!—really the overriding vision we should have of what gender equality should ultimately be? Should job status be the definitive goal of any authentic social justice movement?

Job status is not just about the job but about happiness, too, not to mention linked to planetary survival. According to the Carbon Majors Database CDP Carbon Majors Report 2017, the top one hundred companies are responsible for 71 percent of global greenhouse-gas emissions while the poorest half of humanity are responsible for just 10 percent of global emissions. All those sexy careers are adding up to global destruction as the Carbon Majors Database illustrates.

The Carbon Majors Report is the first in an ongoing series of publications aimed at using this database—the most comprehensive available—to highlight the role that corporations can play in driving the global energy transition. Large-scale greenhouse gas emissions data has traditionally been collected at the country level. In fact, these emissions can be traced to a smaller group of commercial decision makers. And these decision makers include many of the leading companies that many strivers measure their success by working for.

Cronin points out that media interviewers often ask why more women don't want to sit on this or that corporate board, or don't fight hard enough for those seats, many of which are in the very companies destroying the ability of our planet to sustain life. What the media asks less often are questions many of us are asking that reflect another set of priorities: Does anyone really believe that shareholders are the only constituency that matters, not customers, not employees, not the community, or the Planet Earth—*not even our families' lives and our children's well-being?*

## Warzel: the total collapse of work-life balance

In the aftermath of the coronavirus shutdowns, some of us discovered that our old habit of being consumed by work followed us home. Instead of taking more time with kids, having more morning sex, and so forth, we just worked more. As Cronin might put it, our workplace status quest is consuming us—even when at home. Charlie Warzel writes in "You Are Not Working from Home" (*New York Times*, May 26, 2020):

> The WFH [Work from Home] revolution promises to liberate workers from the chains of the office. In practice, *it will capitalize on the total collapse of work-life balance.* . . . Increased productivity—but at what price? Back in April [2020 during the height of the first Covid lockdown], *Bloomberg* reported on a U.S. employee survey administered by Eagle Hill Consulting, which found that just a month into the pandemic, "about 45 percent of workers said they were burned out" after working from home. "*America's always-on work culture has reached new heights,*" the *Bloomberg* article warned. "*Whatever boundaries remained between work and life have almost entirely disappeared.*" (Italics added.)

## Obhi: power over others is a brain changer

What types of people venerate the joy-smashing cult of career? The answer seems to be: people into gaining power over others. What happens to us when we get power over others? Are power-hungry people the kind of people we ever want shaping our lives? Are they driven by the survival of the friendliest ethic? And how does power over others change us?

The answer to these questions was the subject of an informative National Public Radio (NPR) segment, "When Power Goes to Your Head, It May Shut Out Your Heart" (*Weekend Edition Saturday*, August 10, 2013). The program's thesis was that power is a brain changer and never for the better. The segment might have been accurately titled, "Why Are So Many Bosses Jerks?"

Neuroscientists have found evidence to suggest that feeling powerful inhibits a part of our brain that encourages empathy. Even the smallest dose of power can change a person. Sukhvinder Obhi, a neuroscientist at Wilfrid Laurier University in Ontario, Canada, says that power fundamentally changes how the brain operates. Obhi and his colleagues, Jeremy Hogeveen and Michael Inzlicht, produced a study giving evidence to support that claim. According to NPR:

> Obhi and his fellow researchers randomly put participants in the mindset of feeling either powerful or powerless. They asked the powerless group to write a diary entry about a time they depended on others for help. The powerful group wrote entries about times they were calling the shots. Then, everybody watched a simple video. In it, an anonymous hand squeezes a rubber ball a handful of times—monotonously. While the video ran, Obhi's team tracked the participants' brains, looking at a special region called the mirror system.

What's called the "mirror system" reveals what happens to our neurons that become active, for instance, both when we squeeze a rubber ball and when we watch someone else squeeze it. (It's the same thing with other familiar actions like picking up a cup of coffee, hitting a baseball, or flying a kite. Whether you do it or someone else does, your mirror system activates.) In this way the mirror system places us inside a stranger's head. Furthermore, because our actions are linked to deeper thoughts—like beliefs and intentions—we may also begin to empathize with what motivates another person's actions. Feeling less powerful boosted the mirror system. The people feeling less powerful empathized highly with others. "But," Obhi says, "when people were feeling powerful, the signal wasn't very high at all. So when people felt power, they really did have more trouble getting inside another person's head."

The *Weekend Edition* story noted that other scientists corroborate Obhi's findings. "What we're finding is power [in both sexes] diminishes all varieties of empathy," Dacher Keltner, a social psychologist at the University of California, was quoted as saying. He added, "Whether you're with a team at work [or] your family dinner, all of that hinges on how we adapt our behaviors to the behaviors of other people. And power takes a bite out of that ability."

It seems that any social movement extolling the benefits of seeking power over others through career status is "taking a bite" out of our ability to empathize with others, beginning with a lack of empathy for our own children. Maybe that explains the hard-heartedness of pressuring parents to work around the clock in order to "succeed," even when their children are very young.

Writers who are a bit "successful"—and/or who also had spiritual guru parents with a global following!—meet rich and powerful people. From childhood forward I've met and known folks in the USA, the United Kingdom, South Africa, Switzerland, Italy, and Asia with scads of money, a few with titles, many with political power, three US presidents, one European prime minister, and some folks with A-list star celebrity status in the movie and music businesses. *But* I've only known one or two super wealthy, very powerful, and very famous people who have maintained the self-knowledge, self-discipline, self-love, and wisdom to live unpretentiously and thus to *stay* happy.

I know just one zillionaire who managed to stay married. I know just one zillionaire who it seems (sorry to put it this way) is still normal in the empathy department. Maybe he's that way because he never set out to become rich. He's an Internet entrepreneur who helped create a very successful online virtual world for kids. (It was Club Penguin, which he eventually sold to Disney.) Dave Krysko and his wife Donara celebrated forty-five years together in 2021. Money was never, and isn't now, their priority. Dave and Donara give lots of money away, and Donara funds and builds housing for homeless, neglected, and abused women.

Point being: With a few exceptions, money and/or fame seem to be among the worst things that can befall anyone, let alone happen to their kids. So it seems to me that if you love yourself and your children but have the extreme misfortune to acquire (or inherit) lots of money, to wield power over others, or to get famous, then live comfortably, but please for your own and your children's sake—choose to live well below the level of your means.

## Ayn Rand's "Neoliberal Theater of Cruelty"

How did we get to the place where seeking empathy-dulling power and money has become a quasi-religion? Put it this way: who shaped our values so that an afternoon with Amanda at the

Cloisters rates as less essential than some swanky job title? One answer is Ayn Rand.

Rand was the twentieth-century philosopher and author of *Atlas Shrugged,* who advocated for the right to selfishness and seeking power over others as a high male calling. Rand was a power-worshipping evangelist for empathy-crushing "success." This led to what New York University professor Lisa Duggan calls Rand's "Neoliberal Theater of Cruelty," wherein what happens to others just doesn't matter, say, like a search engine company enabling the makers of videos of child rape to proliferate and profiting from that in the name of free speech.

In her book *Mean Girl: Ayn Rand and the Culture of Greed,* Duggan asks, "How could a thousand-plus-page novel, featuring cartoonish characters moving through a melodramatic plot peppered with long didactic speeches, attract so many readers and so much attention? . . . Clearly, the fantasies animating the novel struck a deep chord." Rand's plots legitimize the brutalist effects of capitalism, creating what Duggan calls "a moral economy of inequality to infuse her softly pornographic romance fiction with the political eros that would captivate a mass readership."

While reviewing Duggan's book in the *New Yorker* ("The Persistent Ghost of Ayn Rand, the Forebear of Zombie Neoliberalism," June 6, 2019), Masha Gessen made this astute observation about Rand:

> Rand's novels promised to liberate the reader from everything that he had been taught was right and good. She invited her readers to rejoice in cruelty. Her heroes were superior beings certain of their superiority. They claimed their right to triumph by destroying those who were not as smart, creative, productive,

ambitious, physically perfect, selfish, and ruthless as they were. Duggan calls the mood of the books "optimistic cruelty." They are mean, and they have a happy ending—that is, the superior beings are happy in the end. The novels reverse morality.

## Rand/Nietzsche: shame-free disrupters

Rand defended male privilege as a reward for capitalist success and excess. In other words, she held up the sort of success I dreamed of during my most stupid and uninformed younger years chasing power in the evangelical subculture and later trying for success in Hollywood. Rand wouldn't get why I'm so thankful now for my failures that gave me *time* to just *BE* with my children during the downtimes when my striving came to naught.

Rand believed in crass supermen, not in men open to the inner stillness of contemplation, let alone finding happiness through nurturing others. She denied she'd modeled her brutal heroes on Friedrich Nietzsche's "Superman," but it's hard not to believe that she did. Rand reflects Nietzsche's rebellion against ideas of altruism and empathy altogether. Like Nietzsche, Rand advocates replacing the sacrifice of oneself for others by the sacrifice of others to oneself.

Nietzsche's hero was the Übermensch, the "superior man," who justifies the existence of the otherwise useless human race. (*Superman* is the word usually found in translations of Nietzsche's *Thus Spoke Zarathustra*.) This superior man (the "fittest" of all survivors) emerges when any man with "superior potential" masters himself and breaks away from the conventional "Christian herd morality." In other words, he becomes *a shame-free disrupter*—the ultimate male capitalist master of others. He gives free rein to his "selfish genes" (as it were), and abandons cooperative and "feminized" survival-of-the-friendliest traits as "weakness."

### Chang: Nietzsche's "real men" and Silicon Valley

We've recently had a plethora of supermen as poster boys for our idea of success. They are the types of people designing search engines that direct people to rape videos, deny they are doing that, and then switch gears and argue in the name of free speech that it's okay. We've been dominated by today's version of Nietzsche's "real men" but with a tech-age twist. Emily Chang, an American journalist and host of the TV show *Bloomberg Technology*, explores this twist in her book *Brotopia*. She says that Silicon Valley's "macho culture" fulfills the stereotype of the antisocial, male entrepreneurs: swaggering, risk-taking, sociopathic, insecure "bros." Whatever else these men are into, it's not the care and nurturing of, let alone protecting, others. It's no coincidence that Ayn Rand has a dedicated following in the ranks of these libertarian tech entrepreneurs, who celebrate their "successes" with dreams of migrating to Mars, leaving us losers in the unwashed mob of failures far behind.

### Warren: against the cult of self

Some American leaders have pushed back against the empathy-crushing onslaught. For instance, Massachusetts Senator Elizabeth Warren has explored the downside of our American version of capitalism as it has applied to families where both parents work outside the home when children are young—what Warren has called "the two-career pitfall."

In her 2002 book *The Two-Income Trap: Why Middle Class Parents Are Going Broke*, coauthored with her daughter, Amelia Warren Tyagi, Warren documented how from the 1970s onward, more women entered the workforce, transforming most middle class families into two-income households. But, say Warren and Tyagi, with that additional income came hidden liabilities. Both parents working meant paying for childcare became a necessity in a culture that provides none yet pushes both parents to work and won't help anyone stay home during the little-child years. The cost of commuting to and from work each day doubled. The cost of housing increased as competition to get into the dwindling number of good public school districts increased. So did the cost of paying extortionate college tuition. What made matters even worse was that while all this was happening, middle class wages stagnated.

In her campaign speeches made in 2019 and 2020 during her attempt to become the Democratic Party candidate for the presidency (disclosure: I voted for Warren in the primaries), Warren repeatedly said, "We do some things in the United States that just don't make sense. Not having publicly available childcare; not recognizing the burden of cost associated with two adults working; not having paternity leave; not having maternity leave; not having really effective health insurance that protects you from unexpected circumstances." And what of effective and equitable healthcare policy that is patient driven and not market driven?

In her book, Warren points out that as women entered the workforce from the 1970s forward, the economy grew dramatically. Workers were producing far more from each hour of work, with productivity nearly doubling since the late 1960s. If the minimum wage had been raised—at even the same pace as productivity growth since the late 1960s—by 2021, it would have been above twenty-five dollars an hour at a time when there was

Republican and some Democratic resistance to even raising it to the shamefully low fifteen dollars an hour pittance.

Speaking to voters during a campaign stop at the Veterans Memorial Building in Cedar Rapids, Iowa, on February 10, 2019, Warren told the truth as she thundered, "Millions of American families are struggling to survive in a rigged system that props up the rich and the powerful and kicks dirt on everyone else." She might have added, "Thank Ayn Rand!"

Even before Covid-19 hit, the middle class was shrinking, Warren noted, not because of necessity or economic forces but because "It has been deliberately hollowed out." Warren added: "When I talk about this, some rich guys scream 'class warfare!' Well, let me tell you something, these same rich guys have been waging class warfare against hardworking people for decades" while they are the ones freeloading on corporate welfare.

## Freeman: corporations cost American taxpayers billions

The powerful have made a habit of not telling the truth about the cost to others of their (mostly) tax-free wealth and power. For instance, safety-net benefits for low-wage workers (such as nannies, daycare workers, cleaners, food workers, and teachers) and their families made up more than half of spending on Medicaid, welfare (TANF), food stamps (SNAP), and the earned income tax credit even before Covid-19. In other words, many workers are paid so little that they have to apply for aid from the meager American "safety net," such as it is, even when they are working full-time at two or three jobs. Thus, ordinary workers and taxpayers bear a significant portion of the hidden costs of the low-wage capitalism of disruption that has enriched the powerful so they can launch their private space programs when millions of the children of the working poor go hungry.

Large corporations such as McDonald's, Amazon, and Walmart have reaped the rewards of what amounts to the welfare subsidy of their stinginess and lack of basic empathy for their workers. If there was any empathy or moral clarity left in America, we'd collectively vomit when confronted by pictures of Jeff Bezos's 417-foot yacht. The 417–foot superyacht is so massive that it has a yacht of its own, along with a helipad, reported *Bloomberg*. Developed by Dutch yachtmaker, Oceano, it has several decks along with three huge masts. Said to be the largest sailing yacht ever built, it nevertheless has a problem: because of the masts, Jeff's girlfriend can't land her helicopter on it! So a second boat was ordered to sail next to the main attraction and carry her helicopter.

Me? I'd like to ask this: "Hey, Jeff, if you could just manage to get along on only ten million a year and pay all the rest to your employees, what would they make an hour and what sort of benefits could you give them?" Or maybe the government should step up and ask that question backed by new tax codes because Jeff Bezos made around $321 million *per day* or $3,715 per second in 2020. Bezos earns approximately $149,353 a minute. For perspective, the median US worker earns $19.33 per hour, according to the Economic Policy Institute. Bezos pays his workers a whopping $15.00 per hour. Amazon spent millions to defeat attempts to unionize one of his plants.

## A high priestess of the career cult: Sheryl Sandberg

*Question*: What kind of role models inspire some of us to venerate career, money, and power as the ultimate goal, with the price of admission being not just the loss of all empathy for others but even inhibited or delayed personal relationships? *Answer*: Sometimes it is another Ayn Rand, a traitor-to-women woman putting forth how-to tactics for "success."

In her book *Lean In*, Sheryl Sandberg offered herself as a role model for the male capitalism-of-disruption dominance model masquerading as feminism. As a reward, Sandberg was briefly promoted to a high priestess position in the career cult. The talk show hosts lined up. She'd figured a way to have it all! But then actual feminists attuned to women's actual interests pushed back. In "The End of Leaning In: How Sheryl Sandberg's Message of Empowerment Fully Unraveled" (December 20, 2018), Caitlin Gibson, a feature writer at the *Washington Post*, wrote:

> The Lean In movement launched by Facebook Chief Operating Officer Sheryl Sandberg is officially over. Done. *Fin*. Sandberg's self-empowerment philosophy hasn't aged well: Research shows that pervasive issues—such as gender-based pay inequality, the disproportionate burden of domestic responsibilities on women, and the number of US companies offering paid family leave—remain largely unchanged. . . . "We're just in a moment culturally where we're starting to say: maybe it's an underlying structure problem. Maybe it's not just about a mom working as hard as she can, or a person of color working as hard as they can," says Audrey Kingo, the deputy editor of *Working Mother* magazine. "I think basically what we've learned is that Lean In hasn't worked."

Former First Lady Michelle Obama also offered pithy feminist criticism of the corporate-friendly neoliberal empowerment

Sandberg was shilling for. Obama made her remarks at an appearance at the Barclays Center in Brooklyn in early December 2018 while appearing on a book tour. "That whole, 'So you can have it all—' nope, not at the same time," she said. "That's a lie. It's not always enough to 'lean in,' because that shit doesn't work all the time."

## Zuboff: conglomerated corporate power of the surveillance state

The irony of a woman writing a book telling other women to imitate the White male domination system of empathy-crushing, family-smashing, brain-changing, power-hungry corporate power must be the high-water mark of the capitalism of disruption's hypocrisy. Shoshana Zuboff thinks so anyway.

Zuboff is the Charles Edward Wilson professor emerita at Harvard Business School and has made the depth of Sandberg's hypocrisy stunningly clear in her book *The Age of Surveillance Capitalism: The Fight for a Human Future at the New Frontier of Power*. Zuboff offers a chilling exposé of the brutal business model that underpins the digital world and the entire edifice of its unchecked, one-dimensional, conglomerated anti-family, anti-woman, anti-human corporate power that Facebook has come to epitomize.

Zuboff points out that it was Sandberg who helped develop Google's manipulative ad business before joining Facebook as chief operating officer in 2008. She calls Sandberg "the Typhoid Mary of Surveillance Capitalism."

Zuboff explores how vast wealth and power have been accumulated in ominous new "behavioral futures markets," where predictions about our behavior are bought and sold and the production of goods and services is subordinated to a new "means of behavioral modification." While the tech-manipulative, sociopathic, empathy-free general modus operandi is widely known, what was missing—and what Zuboff brilliantly provided—was the insight to situate them in a wider historical context.

As a reviewer at the *Guardian* noted in "'The Goal Is to Automate Us': Welcome to the Age of Surveillance Capitalism" (January 20, 2019), Zuboff demonstrates that while most of us think we are dealing merely with algorithmic inscrutability, in fact what confronts us is the latest phase in capitalism's long evolution. It's gone from the making of products to mass production to managerial capitalism to services to financial capitalism and now to the exploitation of behavioral predictions—covertly derived from the surveillance of us "users."

Zuboff summed up the capitalism of disruption's onslaught on individual freedom—and by extension our ability to form relationships and have families—in an interview, "Ten Questions for Shoshana Zuboff" (*Guardian*, January 20, 2019):

> We were caught off guard by surveillance capitalism because there was no way that we could have imagined its action, any more than the early peoples of the Caribbean could have foreseen the rivers of blood that would flow from their hospitality toward the sailors who appeared out of thin air waving the banner of the Spanish monarchs. Like the Caribbean people, we faced something truly unprecedented. *Once we searched Google, but now Google searches us. Once we thought of digital services as free, but now surveillance capitalists think of us as free.* (Italics added.)

Besides Zuboff, many other women are speaking up about this "neoliberal theater of cruelty." For example, in the context of our elitist corporate welfare at the expense of ordinary Americans, Abigail Disney (granddaughter of Walt's brother Roy) threw down a challenge to the status quo. In "It's Time to Call Out Disney—and Anyone Else Rich Off Their Workers' Backs" (*Washington Post*, April 23, 2019), she excoriated "the naked indecency" of Disney's chief executive Robert Iger's pay:

> Iger took home more than $65 million in 2018. That's 1,424 times the median pay of a Disney worker. To put that gap in context, in 1978, the average CEO made about 30 times a typical worker's salary. Since 1978, CEO pay has grown by 937 percent, while the pay of an average worker grew just 11.2 percent. This growth in inequality has affected every corner of American life. We are increasingly a lopsided, barbell nation, where the middle class is shrinking, a very few, very affluent people own a great deal and the majority have relatively little. . . . What is more, as their wealth has grown, the super-rich have invested heavily in politicians, policies and social messaging to pad their already grotesque advantages.

It's no coincidence that the person who spoke out about how executives have given in to untrammeled greed was a woman. Women have paid the highest price for our libertarian, career-centric, corporate–welfare coddled, so-called free market. Women are made to delay starting families up to the cusp of infertility by being pressured to put their educations and jobs first and only then consider family. The government offers no funding for parents to become parents. Even when they play by the male corporate and university culture rules, women are still abused and discriminated against in countless workplaces. And women are still paid less than men. Why? Because corporate America fears that "they" (52 percent of the population) might get pregnant and thereby jeopardize the 100 percent demands made of workers from cradle to grave.

The cry goes up: women are risky! They risk loving their children more than work! Pay "them" less! Why? Because women are perceived as just ever so slightly less easily fooled by American business models of one track, money-grubbing, power-hungry, status-seeking, Earth-destroying, child-neglecting, relationship-trashing "success."

As Jordan Kisner, author of the essay collection *Thin Places*, writes in "The Lockdown Showed How the Economy Exploits Women" (*New York Times Magazine*, February 17, 2021), "Mainstream feminism—not to mention mainstream economics or politics—has mostly ignored domestic labor. Instead, it has measured women's empowerment by their presence and influence in the workplace, which is attained by outsourcing housework and childcare to less economically advantaged women for a low wage." Kisner describes how women remain "mired in housework" and how it's common now to hear the term "the second shift," which describes how the work of maintaining a home and caring for children still falls disproportionately to women, even if they have full-time jobs and pay for help.

What's more, people who are paid to do domestic labor or care work (like eldercare or housecleaning) are, as a group, badly compensated and denied workplace protections or benefits. These jobs are held mostly by women of color and immigrants.

In 2020, Oxfam published research showing that if American women made minimum wage for the work they did around the house and caring for relatives, they would have earned one and a half *trillion* dollars in 2019. Globally, the value of that unpaid labor would have been eleven trillion. Kisner notes that in a 2019 speech, Marilyn Waring, a public-policy scholar and long-time advocate of revising economic measures of "productivity," derided "the absurdity" of defining activities like caring for elderly relatives or newborns, shopping, and cooking, as having no value, or as leisure. "You cannot make good policy if the single largest sector of your nation's economy is not visible," she said.

## Michelle Obama offers a personal, cautionary tale

Former First Lady Michelle Obama pushed back against the Sandberg/Rand "lean in" fiction that ignores family and actual work women and men do for their families—"the single largest sector of your nation's economy." Michelle Obama has also been refreshingly candid about some of the collateral damage spawned by the career-worshipping cult. She uses her own struggle to become a mother as a cautionary tale.

The Obamas had waited to have kids and so were only able to have their daughters through IVF. In a clip shared on *Good Morning America* (November 9, 2018), Michelle Obama revealed that before resorting to IVF she suffered a miscarriage, which left her feeling "lost and alone. . . . I felt like I failed, because I didn't know how common miscarriages were because we don't talk about them." She added, "So that's one of the reasons why I think it's important to talk to young mothers about the fact that miscarriages happen, and the biological clock is real."

# CHAPTER 8

# Grandparenthood and Fertility Clocks

Nagging obsession whispered in my mother's voice: "Shouldn't Christmas include more Jesus than you're teaching *my* great-grandchildren?" You have to have been raised evangelical (or Mormon or conservative Roman Catholic) to "get" why the "am I doing enough Jesus at Christmas?" question can be such a guilt-inducing issue for a "backslider" like me. Of which more in a moment . . .

## Winell: religious recovery

My friend Marlene Winell is author of *Leaving the Fold: A Guide for Former Fundamentalists and Others Leaving Their Religion*. She has been working in religious recovery for over thirty years and originated the term "Religious Trauma Syndrome." I published an article by Marlene: "It's Not Just Personal: The Collective Trauma of Religion" (*Frank Schaeffer Blog*, February 21, 2021). Winell writes:

> Fundamentalist Christianity actively teaches that people are born bad and will always lean toward sin;

they can never be trusted. . . . Individuals are taught from early childhood that they are empty of goodness, strength, or wisdom, and must always rely on God for anything of value. Feelings and intuitions and conversations that cast doubt on religious teachings or leaders cannot be trusted, and thinking for yourself is dangerous. People with a different understanding of the world are seen as a threat to be destroyed or converted.

Winell talks about how children are taught to be afraid: of burning in hell, of living in a sinful world, of spiritual warfare, of other people, of life itself. Fundamentalists teach magical thinking and trust that a "superior being will resolve everything at the end of time." Most seriously, they promote black-and-white paradox-free thinking, with their group (be they American evangelicals, Saudi Muslims, Hindu Nationalists, whatever) having the Truth, and all others being damned.

Marlene has made a long study of how the psychological results of fundamentalist beliefs can be devastating. "Individuals may lack a sense of intrinsic self-worth or personal identity—identifying instead with their religious group. They may suffer anxiety because they can never be good enough and they can never have certainty about their ultimate salvation," she writes.

Some former evangelical believers like me face major struggles because discarding specific beliefs no matter how ridiculous they are does not erase the associated toxic assumptions and feelings about self and life. In addition, leaving this kind of faith brings with it the trauma of having one's entire worldview upended. Vital social support systems of church and family are disrupted, and the ex-believer feels lost in a foreign world of secularism.

Then there is the guilt at what you did that you thought was right at the time you were still a believer. My friend Brian McLaren has written an entire wonderful book about this: *Faith After Doubt*. As McLaren explains, in fundamentalist religions, parenting is often authoritarian and punitive, advocating corporal punishment. Children experience isolation in the religious group as they are kept in closed environments in church, family, mission, and school.

Winell writes about how those who flee a religious background ". . . may suffer serious developmental delays as information and experience are kept from them, and they are unable to mature in the wider community." Upon leaving a religion "with this in-group/out-group perspective," survivors like me strive to catch up socially, cognitively, and emotionally.

## Make Scrooge look like Mother Teresa

Thinking about the fundamentalist ghosts that still haunt me brings me to Amanda's post–high school extended stay with us, which lasted until a few days before Christmas 2012. Amanda and Genie took pity on me and decorated the tree when I was out of town. I'd been complaining to Amanda since mid-November. Christmas is a time when the full weight of the evangelical insanity I was raised in seems most omnipresent. I feel the nostalgic guilt-ridden pull of the certainties I've given up. Besides fighting off my religious holiday mixed emotions (where I enjoy the family time but still hear the echo of all the religious indoctrination I reject these days), I was also teasing Amanda. I was joking about how thoroughly they celebrate Christmas in Scandinavia with their so-called Little Christmas and their Saint Lucia's Day and all the rest that spreads the holiday out over weeks and weeks, even months.

"You do so much Christmas stuff because you live in the dark for six months of the year. I mean, who were the first humans to wander up to the Arctic Circle, spend a first winter there, and say, 'Goddamn! *This* is great! It's freezing and dark. Let's stay!'"

Amanda teased me back about "Your anti-Christmas attitude, Grandpa. You make Scrooge look like Mother Teresa!"

After Amanda decorated the tree that year, Genie and I had a lovely week winding up her four-month visit while I read *The Hobbit* out loud to them, thus reviving part of Genie's and my Christmas season tradition of reading works by Tolkien out loud to Jessica, Francis, and John. When Amanda left two days before Christmas to rejoin her family in Finland, Genie and I were very sorry to see her go. Amanda, Jack, and Lucy were sorry, too: they had become such close friends during that extended visit.

My son Francis arrived on Christmas Eve relaxed and happy, having been assured by Genie that "Dad's almost cheerful this year; Amanda worked wonders." Francis lives only a forty-five-minute drive away, near the school he teaches at. His Christmas Eve arrival is always an occasion. Francis brings us a case of a dozen assorted red wines that we'd never buy for ourselves. Genie and I parse these costly well-chosen bottles out over the year to break up the monotony of the table wine we drink most evenings. We only drink "Francis's wine" when we have something to celebrate.

## Coffee with John: a Marine father's reprieve

Many Christmases had passed since John came home from his last of three wartime deployments in 2004. We spent so many sleepless nights imagining the worst that Genie and I still feast our eyes on John any time we see him as if it's the first day he came home. Before Covid-19 ended his commuting, some of my best times were when John (knowing I get up at 3:00 AM every day to write) called me at 5:00 AM to ask for a ride to the train station. This was on the mornings it was too cold or snowing or raining too hard for him to walk or bike to the station to catch the train to Boston.

I normally hate when anything interrupts my early morning writing routine, but when John called, I loved it. Sometimes I'd say, "How about I drive you all the way in today?" Then we'd share the one-hour trip to Boston and stop for a cup of coffee together near where he worked. I'd soak in the sight of my former Marine, married, happy, and excelling at his job managing a team of software engineers. Sometimes I'd ruefully remember my dire predictions to Genie (when John was fourteen and not doing homework, and sneaking out to smoke) and how I'd scream that "He'll never do anything!"

Between the one-hour drive and the hour in the coffee shop, I'd get a luxuriously uninterrupted report on how John's job was going, the details about a bonus or pay raise, how he felt about his boss and the people he managed, about trying to balance work and family, and his frustration at how long the daily commute was. I once offered to move to Boston if John wanted to be nearer work so he could see the children more. He answered, "No, I want them to grow up like I did on the river and marsh." As his children's co-nanny with Genie, I'd share lots of information with John about our days together with his children and he'd talk about what he had done with the kids over the weekend or shared something funny they'd said. I'd do my best to wrap my mind around terms like *software algorithms* and *graph isomorphisms*. He'd describe his trips to New York and Chicago to meet with clients and how "some of these hedge-fund managers we write programs for just live in their own world and think they're having a bad day if they have to wait five minutes for a table in a restaurant."

We'd never talk about John's wartime experiences. I sensed this subject was off-limits. Once in a while, he'd choose to give me a glimpse of his sardonic post-combat humor. One day I said something offhand related to some news item about the never-ending war in Afghanistan. John came back in a split second with "That war was always lost; we just didn't know it then."

I kept thinking about a visit to one of John's bases where he was undergoing training soon after he graduated from boot camp at Parris Island. There was a sweetness to those half-grown anxious Marines putting on a brave face. I got to know one female Marine who was pregnant. The male Marines looked out for this pregnant Marine. She was a slender wisp of a White woman from West Virginia with black hair and fair skin and a soft accent. She must have been about twenty and looked twelve. The baby-faced hulking male Marines treated her like their little sister. I heard one of them offer morning sickness advice, "My mom used to eat crackers when she was pregnant with my little brother . . . " this from a huge Black Marine from the Bronx.

When I see young Marines trying to get home for a holiday, they are the ones standing in line for the standby pass. They are the ones who can't afford to eat in the airport. I never used to notice them. I do now. When need arises, the old-fashioned view prevails. Honor, courage, commitment are called upon to save the day—or at least satisfy the ambitions of the political class whose sons and daughters almost never serve. Then, once the day is saved, or more likely the lost war drags on and isn't newsworthy anymore, the cynics take over again and we send our defenders back to nowhere on the last flight, the cheap flight, and they feel lucky if someone gives them an extra bag of pretzels. We thank them for their service and then forget them in the same way we thank Black and Brown nannies when they leave some nice apartment on the Upper East Side of Manhattan to catch the subway home to their one-room studio in the Bronx.

### The Life and Times of the Thunderbolt Kid

Lucy, on Christmas Day 2012, my Marine, your father John, was smiling and lying on the couch by the fireplace with his head propped on pillows, watching you and Jack careening from gift to gift. Becky was enthusiastically handing out the presents. I don't know anyone who enjoys our family get-togethers with more gusto than your mother does. Sometimes she'll snatch back a book she's just given one of us to "just read you this one passage that you *have* to hear!" and then she gets carried away and reads the whole chapter (and once) even the whole book out loud to us. (Becky did this one year just after she married John, just before you were born, Lucy.)

Your mother, Becky, had given us Bill Bryson's hilarious *The Life and Times of the Thunderbolt Kid.* She reads out loud beautifully and she hijacked the entire day. It was one of the first (but not last) times I realized that the next generation was really taking over. The life force of my daughter-in-law surged into the room as proof that life was going to move on—with or without me.

I felt like a happy ghost given the chance to look in on some future Christmas when I'm dead and "the kids" are running the world. It came as a shock to realize that they'd be doing just fine without me (!) and doing things their way, not mine. They would do things their own way, just like Becky was doing that Christmas her way by picking up a book. She was also zapping my usual Christmas depression. Before I knew it, I was actually having a good time. The sky did not fall just because I wasn't reading the Christmas story out of the Book of Luke. Nor, Lucy, will it fall if you ignore some (or even all) of the advice I've offered you over the years.

Genie, still in her bathrobe, sat across from me on our big, old, brown leather couch with Francis leaning against her. We love your uncle Francis to crazy distraction just like you do, Lucy. He's so kind, so brilliant, and so trustworthy. Francis is the rock you must go to for refuge when I'm dead, Lucy. There's a reason he's the family executor of our will, even our living will, meaning that if/when it comes time to unplug Ba and Nana, Francis will sign the do-not-resuscitate order and let Genie and me die and/ or hand out our organs for transplant. Which is to say our loving trust in Francis is complete.

You grandchildren had finally settled down to play with your gifts. Lucy, you were wearing the John Singer Sargent *Carnation, Lily, Lily, Rose* replica pinafore Genie had designed and made for you and had just given you. I marveled at how stunningly beautiful you looked and how like the children in that great painting. I also marveled at how, try as I would, I couldn't prevent myself from feeling happy. My joy worried me. Nothing gets me down so fast as a hint of contentment. My Calvinist antenna went way up. I carry verses like this one deeply embedded in my brain: "But God said unto him, 'Thou fool, this night thy soul shall be required of thee: then whose shall those things be, which thou hast provided?'" (Luke 12:20).

I grew up cringing before our inexplicably disappointed, perpetually angry God. One of the miracles in my life is the way you and my other grandchildren have reached into my life to heal some of the trauma caused by my evangelical upbringing that haunts me to this day. And, most ironically, even when I try to describe how my children and grandchildren rescued me from my family's evangelical guilt hell, I reach for a Bible verse to do so! "The wolf also shall dwell with the lamb, the leopard shall lie down with the young goat, the calf and the young lion and the fatling together; and a little child shall lead them" (Isaiah 11:6).

## When we delay starting families to the cusp of infertility, there's a ripple effect that changes everything

As happened at "Amanda's Christmas," the grandparent experience has helped reground me in a reality-based life my parents' religious mania denied me. It is a healing experience everyone should have. But sadly, these days, instead of grandparents in their fifties, sixties, and seventies helping with grandchildren and discovering that "a little child shall lead them," it's more often their own children who must help the aging parent through their eighties and nineties.

## We've short-circuited the evolutionary cycle

By our career-first model we have effectively removed actively involved grandparents from the family reciprocity love-motivated childcare picture. This is insane.

Is *insane* too strong a word? No.

For a start (as we'll see in a moment), studies show that grandparents who care for grandchildren live longer. Bluntly: on average, older people who are not doing any childminding die sooner than they would have if they'd been caring for grandkids. Another consequence is that children don't grow up in a multigenerational environment. Old people are seen, if at all, during visits rather than as part of a daily comfortable routine. Separated from the cycle of family life and daily involvement with a cross section of age groups, older people have become the "other" to many Americans.

Covid-19 brought this "otherness" of the elderly home into sharp focus. In "The Pandemic Exposed a Painful Truth: America Doesn't Care About Old People" (*Washington Post*, May 8, 2020), Nina A. Kohn writes:

> When the novel coronavirus first emerged, the US response was slowed by the common impression that Covid-19 mainly killed older people. Those who wanted to persuade politicians and the public to take the virus seriously needed to emphasize that "It isn't only the elderly who are at risk from the coronavirus," to cite the headline of a political analysis that ran in the *Washington Post* in March. The clear implication was that if an illness "merely" decimated "only" older people, we might be able to live with it.

In Greece there was another story. According to a BBC analysis, one of the reasons Greece had an unexpectedly low death rate from Covid-19 in the first 2020 wave was because of the intergenerational mixing and family togetherness there that's taken for granted. In Greece families live together far more than in the USA. The elderly aren't so much seen as the other but are the familiar grandparents you were raised by. The result was that in contrast to America, younger people in Greece did all they could not to spread the virus to their grandparents. Thus the first shutdown was early, abided by, and accepted as necessary by younger, less vulnerable people.

## Pew: the "sandwich-generation" adults pressed for time caring for children and parents

We Americans are no longer an intergenerational community but live at a time when productive lives are seen strictly in terms of employment cycles, not family connection and all-important shared intergenerational connection. In fact, there were even Republican leaders who spoke in terms of "getting used" to the fact that "the economy starting up again" was more important than older people dying by the tens of thousands in care homes.

How did it come to this?

Children visit a grandparent from time to time. The rest of their lives are spent in hermetically sealed childcare, preschool, school, trade school or college, and then career age-specific bubbles. When older people are put at risk, this is accepted because they are so isolated from the rest of us. Many Americans have no grandparent living nearby or have had little to no childhood connection with older people. How come? According to research done by Pew in a 2012 study, the trend of Americans waiting longer to start their families (thus inadvertently eliminating younger, healthy grandparent childcare from their lives) began in the 1970s. The study offers a glimpse of what the future will look like for millennials: no one in their family will be at the right part of older age to help out when they have children. Maybe that's why the Pew researchers found that

> With an aging population and a generation of young adults struggling to achieve financial independence, the burdens and responsibilities of middle-aged Americans are increasing. Nearly half (47 percent) of adults in their forties and fifties have a parent age sixty-five or older and are either raising a young child or financially supporting a grown child (age eighteen or older) . . . Who is the sandwich generation? Its members are mostly middle-aged: 71 percent of this group is ages forty to fifty-nine . . . Among those with a parent age sixty-five or older and a dependent child, 31 percent

*say they always feel rushed even to do the things they
have to do.* (Italics added.)

## Berlin Aging Study: grandparents who care for grandchildren live longer

Grandparents pay a steep price for being cut off from child-care work, inspiration, and fun. They die sooner, according to the "Berlin Aging Study." It was first published in the journal *Evolution and Human Behavior*. Psychologist Ralph Hertwig and his colleagues at the Berlin-based Max Planck Institute for Human Development evaluated data from the study in which more than 500 people aged over seventy were interviewed between 1990 and 1993 and followed until 2009. They found that half the grandparents who looked after their grandchildren were still alive ten years after the first interview, while half of those who didn't—and also the non-grandparents in their control group—died within an average of five years. According to findings in the University College London 2020 study "Living Alone and Risk of Dementia: A Systematic Review and Meta-analysis," dementia risk leaps by 30 percent if you live alone in your fifties and sixties. Isolation takes a much greater toll than previously thought. The study surveyed 21,666 people over the age of fifty-five. The authors warned that there are a growing number of elderly people living alone and that loneliness seems to be a bigger factor than physical inactivity, even diabetes, obesity, or high blood pressure, in triggering dementia.

## Buchanan: active grandparents— a key to children's well-being

Kids who grow up with active grandparents involved in their daily lives do far better through their entire lifetime than those deprived of such contacts. Research by Professor Ann Buchanan, at the Department of Social Policy and Intervention at Oxford University, documented the fact that a high level of energetic grandparental involvement "dramatically increases" the well-being of children. Her study of more than 1,500 children demonstrated that those with significant daily grandparental involvement had far fewer emotional and behavioral problems than children deprived of everyday contact with grandparents ("Grandparents Contribute to Children's Wellbeing," *Oxford Research*, 2018). And a recent study by Boston College confirmed that an "emotionally close relationship between grandparent and grandchildren" is associated with "fewer symptoms of depression"—for *both* generations. So it seems I'm not alone in finding inner healing in my grandchildren's presence.

## Burnett: the positive influence of grandparents on longevity

It's not only the reality that individual grandparents who care for grandchildren live significantly longer and that grandchildren also do much better, but there's the matter of our species' overall life span. One factor in human longevity is "the positive influence of grandparents on the survival of young ones and the community at large," Dean Burnett writes in his book *The Happy Brain*. He continues:

> Older members of a primitive human community may not have been much good at hunting or the physical stuff, but they were still perfectly capable of looking after the babies and children, and didn't need to spend time pursuing mates or any of that other exhausting stuff. The children were cared for, learned wisdom

was passed on directly, extra hands were available for the day-to-day stuff. . . . The advantages of keeping your old folks around are many and varied. . . . Being a grandparent gives a new set of (ideally less demanding) responsibilities and focus to the older generation whose own children are grown and independent now. It's no wonder many of them are unashamedly eager for grandchildren, like my folks and in-laws were. But it's a two-way relationship; grandchildren get cared for, grandparents get to care for.

## Levy: how we feel about aging predicts our level of overall contentment

Our feelings about the aging process actually change how well (or unhappily) we age. When we think that older people are the other (and that maybe we should even sacrifice them to reopen an economy during a virus pandemic), this isn't just bad for the elderly. It's bad for younger people, too. In the *Journal of Personality and Social Psychology* (83, no. 2, August 2002), Becca R. Levy of Yale University and her colleagues found that "adults who developed positive attitudes about aging lived more than seven years longer than peers who had negative attitudes." The study investigated perceptions about aging and survival rates over a twenty-two-year period among 660 men and women ages fifty to ninety-four. Researchers gauged participants' attitudes about aging through their responses to statements such as "Things keep getting worse as I get older," and "I have as much pep as I did last year."

In an American Psychological Association publication's article, "Attitudes About Aging Affect Longevity" (vol. 33, no. 9, October 2002), we read, "Our study carries two messages. The discouraging one is that negative self-perceptions can diminish life expectancy; the encouraging one is that positive self-perceptions can prolong life expectancy. *Self-perceptions of aging had a greater impact on survival than did gender, socioeconomic status, loneliness and functional health.*" (Italics added.)

Younger people with callous or indifferent or (most likely) uninformed attitudes about the elderly are cutting their life spans shorter. Since attitudes about our aging process begin to form early in life, Levy and her coauthors believe that it's important to shape younger people's perceptions about getting older from an early age. Meanwhile, a study in Belgium showed that the best way to develop positive views of getting older is to have had a close relationship with a grandparent as a child. *Duh!*

### Put it this way: when Nora tells me that I am her best friend, she means it

As Nora and I rattle on together hour after hour about this and that and dive in and out of each other's stories, the bond forming is going to outlive me and provide Nora with a fear*less* attitude to her own aging someday. Me? It's fun to be a kid again and lose myself in long discussions with Jack, Nora, Lucy, Ben, and Amanda about the various stages of their lives. I don't feel old with them. And they don't associate the word *old* with anything other than feeling (mostly) safe, happy, and entertained by a person who is unconditionally on their side and more interested in them than in himself. When Lucy calls me after winning a poetry award or to tell me about what her friends are up to, I feel the most alive I ever feel these days. I also feel honored. This is what being trusted feels like.

I can't stress the point enough: by delaying starting families to the cusp of infertility in favor of education and career and because we've stripped people of real choices or help, or laws to protect them, or finances to stay home with little kids, we've hurt ourselves in so many unexpected ways. Again: this is not to say that getting into pair-bonding and baby-making at a very young age is a good thing. My kids suffered having a teen and then an angry, worried, striving twenty-something parent. *But* the opposite extreme today is not a great idea. That said, we all are stuck making the best of the decisions we usually don't even rationally make as life happens *to* us.

In any case we've cut down on our chances for intergenerational connection that contributes to all generations' longevity and well-being. We do not know how to age well or face death serenely. While younger people hear a lot about ideas like uploading their brain's memory bank to a computer to live longer, in the real world the best way to increase the odds in one's favor seems to have been right there all the time and has more to do with attitudes and connections related to aging and loving in the here and now than to science fiction.

### Getting old is hard; grandkids make it easier

Facing mortality, not to mention living in a body that can't do what it used to do, is tough. Confronting my aging became inescapable after my three youngest grandchildren went back to school part-time in September 2020. With the second wave shutdown looming in late 2020 and early 2021, John said, "Dad, you can't take care of the kids indoors now. You and Mom are in the 'older' cohort most at risk from Covid-19." And on a less dramatic front, ask me how I feel about aging some night when I've just woken up having to pee for the *third* time, knowing I'm scheduled for yet another prostate exam due to my rising

PSA numbers. That said, according to an American Grand-parents Association survey, 72 percent of grandparents neverthe-less "think being a grandparent is *the single most important and satisfying thing in their life*" (italics added). In other words, they (like me) feel some of the most gratifying relationships of their lives have been saved for last—enlarged prostrates, menopause etc., be damned!

### Life Itself

In the wonderful movie *Life Itself*, the character Isabel Díaz (played by Laia Costa) is a mother dying of cancer. She sums up my philosophy of parenthood, aging, and life when she tells her son:

> Listen to me . . . you have had many ups and downs in your life. Too many. And you will have more. This is life. And this is what it does. Life brings you to your knees. It brings you lower than you think you can go. But if you stand back up and move forward, if you go just a little farther, you will always find love. I found love in you. And my life, my story, it will continue after I'm gone. Because *you* are my story. You are your father's story. Your uncle's . . . My body fails me, but you *are* me. So you go now, give me a beautiful life. The most beau-tiful life ever. Yes? And if life brings us to our knees, you stand us back up. You get up and go farther, and find us the love. Will you do that?

If the multiple studies I've mentioned here are to be believed, Genie's and my childminding of our grandchildren and the daily intergenerational connection with our own grown children through the help we give their children are going to not only keep helping Francis, Jessica, and Dani, and John and Becky happily work but also prolonging all our lives in a way that helps us all to "get up and go farther, and find us the love." If multiple studies are to be believed, our grandchildren will live longer and more happily, too, because they have a positive hands-on view of what "getting older" means. *It is not only a time of looming decrepitude but can be a time of loving more purely and intensely than experienced at any other stage of life.*

## Only idiots are this annoyingly happy

Okay, I'm preaching. Sorry. What is more annoying than someone telling you how happy they are? Sorry. But even if you hate me now, my grandchildren will remember feeling safe and happy with this "aging" person. The associations with the words "getting older" will lose their sting. And since the older people they loved were happy in older age, aging won't seem so scary; in fact, growing old may even be a stage of life to look forward to.

If someone asked Jessica, Francis, John, Becky, Amanda, Ben, Claire (Ben's wife), Lucy, Jack, and Nora, "What do old people do?" they might answer: teach kids to ski; sit on the floor and draw with them at the Boston Museum of Fine Arts; dig the vegetable garden with the children; teach kids to fry shrimp calamari style; rebuild a barn and show a child how to use a table saw without cutting his fingers off; read books out loud; pick children up from school; come to every sporting event you're ever in; show you favorite movies; hug you and tell you that they love you; keep Band-Aids with pictures of mermaids on them for your cuts; explain why Maria Callas was a great singer and that Miles Davis's "Kind of Blue" is the greatest jazz recording ever; and be with you every single day.

I can also put this another way, and you'll hate me even more for this. On my sixty-eighth birthday in 2020, after months of childcare during the pandemic, Nora (then six) asked me, "Ba, why did you just have an ordinary day on your birthday?"

"You mean why didn't I take the day off and have some sort of treat?"

"Yes."

"Because my ordinary days *are* my treat, Nora. Being with you is what I'd rather do than anything else."

## Hrdy: motherhood is a minefield

It is in the context of delayed childbearing and frayed and broken biological evolutionary cycles of grandparent/grandchild life, that Sarah Blaffer Hrdy explores the fact that families have been set adrift. Hrdy knows a lot about childminding. She's a mother who teaches at the University of California at Davis and also an anthropologist and primatologist who has made important contributions to evolutionary psychology and sociobiology.

Hrdy gathered her hands-on childminding insights and combined them with her science chops to produce *Mother Nature: A History of Mothers, Infants, and Natural Selection.* Exploring anthropology and genetic "maternal instinct," Hrdy notes that parenting is being challenged by work-life imbalance issues. She writes:

> Today, mothers in developed countries, *and with them fathers and children,* enter uncharted terrain. Without anyone raising their hands to volunteer, we have become guinea pigs in a vast social experiment that reveals what women who can control reproduction really want to do. Children, too, are finding out what it means to be born to a complex and multifaceted creature who has an unprecedented range of options. It is an experiment-in-progress, with two outcomes

*already apparent. . . . Bluntly put, motherhood has become a minefield, and we are walking through it without so much as a map to guide us.* (Italics added.)

Hrdy points out what I noted before, that most primate mothers can rear their infants on their own because their babies are born fully ready as it were, but human mothers cannot now and never could and never will be able to. Big point here: *Today's need for childcare help has nothing to do with mothers going to work outside the home. Mothers have always needed help because (as we've seen) human parenthood is a long-term commitment.*

In other words, our American hatred of women is out of character with big chunks of human history. Proof? Women got help from entire communities. How do we know? Because the human race (mostly) made it this far.

Hrdy notes that throughout history mothers sought childminding help however and from whomever they could—from the father, other mothers, and grandparents; from siblings and cousins; and from one man or more than one man. In other words, while only females conceive and have our babies facing the bio-terror that involves, the skills, work, and duties of childminding have *always* been shared. That is to say, *normal* is community. Individualism is perverse. Libertarians are mistaken because without community dependent on service to others—we die.

## Intergenerational, gender-neutral childminding is the natural evolutionary mandate we thrive under

Our modern generational and gender-segregated way of life is a horror show. Picture the elderly locked in care centers at one end of the spectrum and babies separated from parents locked in daycare centers at the other end of life's spectrum. Both need each other. Both would have better lives if spent together. We've built a set of priorities that might as well have put them on different planets. Because it contradicts everything we evolved to be, this bizarre separation of the generations makes us all unhappy, even if we don't know why.

There's a reason infant and child mortality rates dropped when kids were with parents during the Covid lockdown rather than with strangers. There's a reason miscarriage rates dropped when women were able to care for themselves a bit better than they could working outside the home. There's a reason so many men got used to working from home, too, and many didn't want to go back to the "normal" world of business they now knew had actuality been the height of abnormality.

**Olmstead: Is It wrong to have a family?**

Parenthood is often delayed past what makes sense biologically. That's because people are given no good choices. Help from family evaporates into thin air when jobs change and people move far away. Some of us worry that pair-bonding and having children *at all* is a bad idea, maybe even "a choice for consumption." We've made it so hard to start a family, no wonder many people give up. Minimum wages are so low no one can live on that little well enough to have a child. Even when well paid, many of us are so unhappy with our present work-life imbalance we are (as it were) doubting our human future. Meanwhile, our fancy jobs are killing the planet, and we are, too, with our consumerism when everything we buy is shipped to us in yet another container from somewhere else. No wonder we fear doom! We're working hard to bring it about. Our American trajectory is starting to look less like an accident than a well-planned suicide.

We've made raising children without support systems and grandparents so "normal" that the entire process of having a family is understandably scary. Besides, some of us "wonder if our children will face planetary apocalypse," as the writer Gracy Olmstead puts it in her essay "Don't Let Climate Change Stop You from Becoming a Parent" (*New York Times*, September 19, 2019). Olmstead argues that the isolating selfishness of consumption is a far greater threat to our planet than the selfless sharing that having children and grandchildren encourages us to experience. Like Olmstead, based on my own experience I, too, think that isolated, lonely (not to mention angry, fearful) lives are less conducive to community connection and thus to providing the motivation to do what it takes to save our planet than lives filled with unconditional love.

### Higgins: we should not give up because it is true that every moment of human history involves crisis but . . .

Gareth Higgins writes in *How Not to Be Afraid: Seven Ways to Live When Everything Seems Terrifying*:

> . . . [T]hings may not be as bad as they may seem. The average human is living in arguably the most peaceable time we have ever known, at least since people emerged. . . . Terrible things have always happened; they happen today, and they will happen tomorrow. But these stories are often told either by voices or in environments that may seem authoritative but offer neither a context that explains them accurately nor wisdom about how to transform conflict. . . . The real news about your world does not begin with the flashing red strip across the bottom of the screen. It begins even before you engage any media or form of craft; it

begins in your mind, with the story you're telling about yourself.

Maybe, as Higgins says, the world is not ending quite yet. So the question is, who has the most motivation to press for good policies that might heal our Earth? My answer is many folks such as teachers, scientists, vaccine researchers, and the like, but also those of us lesser lights who are into childminding. It's those of us who are done with balancing careers and family and are into seeking meaning in loving others first, and money and prestige second, who offer a better way. It's those of us seeking joy rather than being cool (as it were) who care. It's those of us who reject malignant narcissism in favor of community. And that's not just parents. This cohort includes many single people and, many couples without children.

**When Covid-19 hit, my first thought was not about my survival, let alone writing career, but about how to circle the wagons around my family and grandchildren, how to prepare, how to survive for them**

How could I protect those I love? How could we protect not just their health but their ability to experience joy? In other words, how could Genie, Becky, John, and I unite to make Lucy, Jack, and Nora's childhoods—even during a pandemic—reflect Shakespeare's lines:

> Here will we sit and let the sounds of music
>
> Creep in our ears. Soft stillness and the night
>
> Become the touches of sweet harmony.
>
> (The Merchant of Venice, Act 5, Scene 1)

## Family: a firewall against individualistic striving

Love is the best firewall against individualistic striving and selfish, planet-trashing consumption. Tell me to save the planet "for the good of the Earth" or "for all humankind," and I have little evolutionary motivation to do so. Tell me to save our environment for myself, and I'm likely to do the math on sea level rise and looming scarcity of drinkable water and global warming and figure that at my age I'll be dead before all hell breaks loose. But tell me to save the Earth for Amanda, Ben, Lucy, Jack, and Nora, and my only question is, How do I do that?

That's not an expression of sentimentality; it's a hardwired evolutionary fact. Connection to those we love most is why (as we've seen) early humans banded together. It's what made us cooperate and build communities because we humans share a fearful solidarity: the fear of loss; in other words, the flip side of love. That's why I'll bet that there will be memoirs published about how the coronavirus crisis made some of us stop and reconsider our entire aim in life and reevaluate what we cared most about. Author and journalist Nina Burleigh, for example, writes in "Fomo Haunted Me for Years–but the Coronavirus Pandemic Cured Me" (*Guardian*, May 3, 2020):

> I have finally gotten over my Fomo, acronym for "fear of missing out." Fomo haunted my nights for years, a rat in the dark at 2 am, scratching up for review all the things I did not do to stay ahead of the game during the day. Now, Fomo, like the handshake, belongs to another age. . . . The pandemic has exposed how much of our previous lives hung on vanity.

To the extent that the pandemic made some of us reconsider our priorities and choose love more and striving less, we may even see it as a harbinger of renaissance.

Alison Gopnik again writing in *The Gardener and the Carpenter:*

> Love doesn't have goals or benchmarks or blueprints, but it does have a purpose. The purpose is not to change the people we love, *but to give them what they need to thrive.* Love's purpose is not to shape our beloved's destiny, but to help them shape their own. It isn't to show them the way, but to help them find a path for themselves, even if the path they take isn't one we would choose ourselves, or even one we would choose for them. (Italics added.)

In "Why, Despite Everything, You Should Have Kids (if You Want Them)" (*New York Times*, April 13, 2021), Tom Whyman, a philosopher and the author of *Infinitely Full of Hope: Fatherhood and the Future in an Age of Crisis and Disaster*, writes:

> In the wake of the pandemic, we must work to reverse the ways in which—both as a result of it, but also in the decades leading up to it—we have become increasingly isolated from one another, reduced to atomized cocoons of individuals and their families. And kids, if nothing else, can be a huge part of that resistance. Children, in truth, require many people, not just their parents, to help them flourish: Raising children need not mean (ought not to mean!) forming a private home to keep them safely contained in, away from the world. They must be raised to participate in it—through the care and guidance of grandparents, godparents, teachers, friends, community.

**This isn't altruism—it's informed selfishness**

Instead of feeling marginalized as I grow older, I have never felt more essential as I help my grandchildren and children "find a path for themselves." Nothing makes me genetically, psychologically, and evolutionarily happier than this sense that I'm pouring what's left of myself into the next generation. That includes some whimsical practicalities like planting more carrots in April 2020 as the virus closed in ("Will we even be able to go food shopping?!") alongside Nora, who by July 2020 was gleefully pulling them up every day, washing them in the rain barrel, and peeling them alongside me in our kitchen.

Walking from Nora's house to ours the other day, I asked her what she'd been doing earlier that morning. "I've been building a nest for homeless ants," Nora answered. She added, "Did you know ants are nice, even ones that bite?"

My heart sank. What would I do with myself when Nora was back in school full-time? Who would tell me about "homeless ants"? Who would argue with me and amuse me out of worry as Nora did with this exchange a few days before while walking down our drive from her house:

Me: "Nora, what are you chewing?"

Nora: "Nothing."

"I can see you *are* chewing something."

"I'm not."

"You have something in your mouth."

"No, I don't."

"Look in my eyes and tell me that."

Nora shooting me a direct I-know-you-hate-chewing-gum-but-I-don't-care LOOK: "I don't have *anything* in my mouth."

"I can see it! How can you *look me in the eyes* and say you don't have chewing gum when you do?!"

Pause for thought, then: "To be fair, I wasn't looking at your eyes but at your nose."

I was still laughing an hour later.

# CHAPTER 9

# Loveless Work, Childcare Deserts, and Intergenerational Connection in the Post-Coronavirus World

When Lucy was a toddler, I left *The Art of Florence*, a heavy, two-book set, open and propped against my missionary grandfather's (Mom's dad) old steamer trunk in the attic. Genie gave me the books decades earlier. While I valued them, I foolishly rarely opened them. Much like the good china that people never use, they were objects almost too precious to open. The books had remained in their box even when Amanda and Ben visited. Perhaps also because we had many other books on Renaissance art, I just never got around to opening them. Then one day, I finally took them out and propped both volumes against the old trunk. They became as much a part of Lucy's, and later Jack's and Nora's, playacting and daily rituals as our baskets of stuffed animals and the mounds of dress-up clothes and art supplies.

285

At first, Lucy (age three) turned the big glossy pages gingerly, rightly intuiting that these were expensive books. Then I told her, "There's only one wrong thing you can do with a book: not open it." I told her I didn't care if she tore a page, or wore the books out, or got fingerprints on the hundreds of fabulous illustrations. We left the books open to this or that picture for weeks on end, which exposed the pages to the sun and caused the colors to fade. I didn't care. The children were absorbing the art.

### Primavera

Lucy, you discovered that all Renaissance art roads eventually lead to the *Primavera* and Botticelli. Giorgio Vasari (Jane Smith first told me about him—"the first of all art historians"—and gave me a copy of his *Lives of the Artists** when I was twelve) describes Botticelli as having lost his great talent after he fell under the sway of the religious fanatic preacher Fra Girolamo Savonarola. Botticelli stopped painting his lyrical humanist tributes to love and turned to turgid religious works mostly devoid of the charm of his earlier work. Vasari said that . . .

> He printed many of the drawings that he had made, but in a bad manner, for the engraving was poorly done. . . . [Religious] Faith affected by Fra Girolamo Savonarola of Ferrara, of whose [extreme religious] sect he [Botticelli] became so ardent a partisan that he was thereby induced to desert his painting, and, having no income to live on, fell into very great distress. For this reason, persisting in his attachment to that [fanatical religious group], and becoming a *Piagnone* [Mourner, or Weeper] (as the members of the sect were then called), he abandoned his work; wherefore he ended in his old age by finding himself so poor, that if Lorenzo de Medici. . . . had not succored him the while that

he lived, as did afterwards . . . for his talent, he would have almost died of hunger.

In other words, Lucy, the religious right that handed America to Trump (with some help from Dad and me in terms of our evil influence in the 1970s and '80s) in 2016 wasn't some new thing. Fanatical fundamentalist Christianity has derailed many lives before—Botticelli's, for instance. The theocracy impulse of Fra Girolamo Savonarola is a religious form of anti-science, anti-art madness that's cyclical. The leaders of such outbursts, be they in America, Florence, or Iran, may change, but the impulse to join some close-minded, simplistic, reality-denying, conspiracy-addled cult is ever present.

Lucy, in the 1970s and '80s our family played a part in the rise of the American version of the Fra Girolamo Savonarola–style "conservatism." Your great-grandfather has been called a father of the religious right. So I figured telling you about Fra Girolamo Savonarola and the fact he made Botticelli burn some of his paintings was as good a way as any to get you thinking about the threat of stupid intolerance and bigotry and the veneration of ignorance that are still with us today.

We're lucky the *Primavera* wasn't burnt! Thus the gods of spring still gather in a woodland glade with you and me, Lucy, with Jack and Nora, with Amanda and Ben. And Venus is still queen of the season sixty years after I first met her in Jane's chalet. Spring still comes a-courting even in the midst of caring for you during the Covid-19 pandemic that struck like some re-enactment of the Black Death that preceded the Renaissance. The painting is still a guidepost pointing to the renewal we need, not just of the seasons but of every soul that forgets to embrace the intrinsic worth of beauty, truth, and love. Botticelli's message is still crucial: Live life seeking transcendent spiritual splendor. Seek what you find in your innermost place of stillness, and the rest will be added to you.

## What are grandparents "for"?

Providing a space for the inner stillness a child needs to contemplate the beauty of life—their very own encounter with the spirit of the *Primavera*—is what grandparents are for. And when I use the words *inner stillness,* I'm talking about more than moments of silence. I'm talking about being at peace within one's self, carefree play, a sense of security, of being loved; of always having arms nearby to swoop you up if you fall; a memory bank full of beautiful things, ideas, and experiences, tastes and smells, sounds and feelings to which a loving grandparent opened the door. A grandchild has the chance to start where I left off. I can work to pass on the best, not the depressions and regrets but the moments of light and grace. *I can choose* to *break the generational curse.* You can, too.

Furthermore, you do not have to be a grandparent to do this, or to have kids. You just have to have learned something on the way through this life so far. Know this: as Paddington (a bear from "deepest, darkest Peru" who comes to live in London, and who also starred in a series of books and an animated TV series) states, "If we're kind and polite, the world will be right."

It's in our rootless context of brutal, unkind, impolite lives that we Americans couldn't have prepared worse for Covid-19. When families needed help most, where could they turn? Everyone was somewhere else. Zoom calls weren't enough—even with a toddler running around in the background.

## We've achieved the "distinction" of re-creating a modern-era, pre-Renaissance "Dark Age"

While the virus caused a crisis, it also exposed the fault lines in our society. Today, parents face crises alone as a result of:

1. Providing no government-funded services for childcare while at the same time encouraging (actually, forcing, though social pressure about what is "cool" to do) both parents to work outside the home—even when they have very young preschool children.
2. Normalizing the idea of having children later so people can have big important careers and do big important educational things first, thus canceling or diminishing the availability of caregiving grandparents.
3. Making it normal to move "up" by changing where you live to chase new jobs, thus cutting ties that keep us rooted in community with its longstanding natural support systems.
4. Cutting grandparents out of the daily childminding cycle of life because they are sequestered, either by choice or by necessity, in senior "communities" that exclude anyone under fifty-five.

## Gallup study: parents on the move, chasing jobs

The Gallup study conducted in 2013, "Percentage of Respondents Who Moved Cities/Regions in the Past Five Years," characterizes the United States as one of the most geographically mobile (i.e., shortsightedly rootless and disconnected) countries in the world. "About one in four US adults (24 percent) reported moving within the country in the past five years," the report noted. This was a pre-Covid-19 study, but there is no reason to think that will change unless we want it to. According to data from the US Census Bureau, the average person in the United States moves residences more than eleven times in her lifetime.

Citing supplemental data from the Current Population Survey, a post on the blog of the New York Federal Reserve noted that between 1998 and 2013, "slightly more than half of interstate migrants said they moved for employment-related reasons—a category that includes moves undertaken for new jobs, job transfers, and easier commutes." But community, and thus by implication continuity in where we live, is what anthropologists like Meredith Small say is most necessary and most "species-appropriate" for raising children well. Of course if you keep moving away from family, or they move away from you, the most rudimentary childcare support systems evaporate.

Americans on the move, chasing jobs, leave behind family and other deep connections again and again and again. Then we wonder why our relationships and marriages go bad and why we feel lonely. Nothing drove this home more than the coronavirus: those cut off from family and from a support network were much worse off than those who had close nearby family ties. Our sense of being alone was exacerbated by authorities (the Republicans in the Senate, state houses led by Trumpists) who seemed determined to *not* help ordinary people but rather help corporations (and in Trump's case, his family and corrupt cronies) instead. The talk was all about "opening the economy," not about individuals' well-being, let alone kindness.

When we needed kindness—a safety net, free medical care, free childcare, deep community connections, and family more than ever—they were not there. It took the election of Joe Biden and a split Senate to even haltingly start a genuine bailout for American families. But maybe the March 7, 2021, $1.9 trillion Biden relief plan reflected a seismic shift in policy—and perhaps that was a start in a new direction, a first shudder of the pro-family and pro-love revolution we need. I hope so.

## We have an evolutionary survival instinct that's affronted when a crisis hits and the authorities do nothing to help

Evolution built us to expect help from others and to give it. That's the reason we instinctively wanted to know why our government "isn't doing anything" and expected someone to "do something" when Covid-19 emerged as our version of the Black Death. That's because, as Sarah Hrdy points out in *Mothers and Others: The Evolutionary Origins of Mutual Understanding,* while childcare methods vary from culture to culture, there is one universally true childcare baseline: we humans are "cooperative breeders."

We cooperative breeders evolved to expect help. Infant care is always social and the basis of every society—or it was until we backward, career-addled "moderns" came along. In our individualistic environment, the new "normal" before Biden was elected was for the government to say, "You're on your own." Call this the logical free enterprise outcome of the glorification of Ayn Rand's individualism.

## Mapping America's childcare deserts

We've made it hard for anyone to be there for us or for us to be there for them. We've made it unlikely that a grandparent lives across the road to be there to be a granddaughter's best friend when she needs to tell someone about the home she's building for "homeless ants," at a time when her own life has been upended by a pandemic.

## In two-thirds of families with school-age children, both parents work outside the home and they've also moved away from family

Talk about "burning the candle at both ends." We haven't even tried to offer a childcare Plan B Iceland-style. The result is summed up in a Center for American Progress study, "Mapping America's Child Care Deserts" (by Rasheed Malik and Katie Hamm, August 30, 2017). The study points out that in 2015 a national poll conducted by the *Washington Post* found that more than three-quarters of mothers and half of fathers were forced to move, switch jobs, or quit their jobs *due to a lack of paid leave or childcare*. Their "geographic study of childcare markets finds that approximately half of Americans across twenty-two states live in areas with an undersupply of childcare options."

As the first coronavirus lockdowns ended in May and June 2020 (only to come roaring back in July, August, and then in early 2021), already limited supply of childcare spaces contracted, even as demand skyrocketed. At the same time, school closures posing problems for daycare providers created an increased need for care among America's working parents.

As policy makers moved to reopen the economy, they needed to address this childcare gap. They mostly did not. The needs of parents and families—once again—were put second to the needs of the economy, i.e., shareholders. Companies (even cruise lines and bars) got bailouts but not families' childcare needs. Again, President Biden began to change this. The question he seemed to be asking was this: will America bring our families into the open (as it were) and make them our priority? Shouldn't Biden's pro-family entire agenda have instantly become law?

"Child care is an industry that has long been overlooked and undervalued," wrote journalist Emily Peck in "The Child Care Industry Is About to Collapse" (*Huffington Post,* May 15, 2020). "Taking care of young children—'women's work'—hasn't been seen as skilled labor. And when caring for children finally did become more of an occupation, it was something done by women of color in the homes of more affluent middle-class or higher-income white women."

In other words, a certain type of career-oriented faux corporatized White feminism was, in actuality, a race- and class-based system of exploitation of women of color by affluent, educated, entitled White (sometimes ironically self-identified "liberal") elites. And here's the dirty little secret: The White parents exploiting Black women and Brown women had themselves been exploited by the vicious Big Lie that career defines us. They, too, had been robbed of real choices.

Faux feminism was co-opted by male patriarchal business "values." Columnist David Brooks noted in "This Is How Wokeness Ends" (*New York Times*, May 13, 2021) that we saw this happen with other movements, too, for instance in the 1970s. American hippies built a bohemian counterculture. But they wanted to "succeed" in the American system. They sold their bohemian values to the market. Everyone could be a rock star! Year by year those bohemian values were diluted. Corporations co-opt. They and the universities they dominate send young people powerful signals about what level of dissent will be tolerated. They kill all revolutions against their system by embracing dissident values (the hippie culture, or feminism-whatever) and reduce them to a form of marketing. By taking what was dangerous to their monopolies and aestheticizing it, they turn it into a new brand. Feminism is welcomed and then put to work serving the male-dominated system. What is never allowed is any real challenge to the entire set of career priorities.

## As we have already noted, there's been historic, long-standing underfunding of childcare that is a byproduct of sexism

As Peck notes, "It's not hard to conclude that the child-care crisis is getting short shrift because it's a woman's crisis: 94 percent of child-care workers are women, and a majority are women of color." And also immigrants, many undocumented, make up the ranks of childcare providers to the more affluent. The whole industry is subsidized—not by government funds, but by the cheap labor Black and Brown women provide.

As of January 2021, the average hourly pay for a childcare worker was eleven dollars in an economy where earning less than twenty-five dollars an hour guarantees poverty. Many women earn the minimum wage or less, including many women with decades of highly sought-after but chronically undervalued childcare expertise. In other words, even an underpaid Amazon warehouse worker packing up lubricants and dildos is paid 40 percent more than most providers of childcare working for wealthy Americans. And how about the not wealthy Americans who also need childcare? Teachers, healthcare and other essential workers, blue-collar workers, retail and food service—where can they turn?

## We look at childcare entirely the wrong way

Childcare is undervalued because childminding itself is undervalued because *mothering* (by men, women, or by nonbinary people alike) is undervalued. As Jessica noted when she brings up the fact her experiences as a mother contributed to her management skills, her claims are met by awkward silences. *Anything* to do with caring for children is undervalued if not met with outright disdain. Mix in racial exploitation of nannies plus elite college-indoctrination and careerism, and you have a recipe for disaster.

To get respect, women with children or caregiving males or nonbinary caregivers must identify themselves as having some other job besides "just childcare" or being "just a houseparent" because childcare is regarded as unskilled labor. Yet for each undervalued woman working as a caregiver doing childminding-for-hire, several more women—in other words, America's other mothers—depend on her. So do their mates, husbands, and companies. Thus, the demotion of childcare is crazy. The demotion of parenting experiences is also insane. Of all the most essential of "essential" workers, childcare workers and parents should be at the top of the list, be they a stay-at-home dad or a professional at a daycare center. And far from childcare being "unskilled" work, it is a specialized field where experience is as rare and specialized as what goes into making a great thoracic surgeon.

We used to talk about childcare as if its purpose was to "free" women to get jobs. We updated that to "freeing parents"—men and women—to get jobs. But the real reason childcare is essential has nothing to do with parents' careers. It has to do with the meaning of life itself: the experience of love. Childcare is essential because children represent the entire destiny of human survival. In other words, parenting (by whatever gender) of children, be they our own children or grandchildren or someone else's, is *the only inarguably essential job there is.*

## Covid-19 provided a lens through which to see the built-in anti-childminding stupidity of our society

As Joan C. Williams, founding director of the Center for WorkLife Law at the University of California Hastings College of the Law writes in "Real-Life Horror Stories from the World of Pandemic Motherhood" (*New York Times,* August 6, 2020):

> Employers are using the pandemic to get rid of mothers, and our attempts to protect them are failing. . . . Between April and June [2020], caregiver-related calls to our hotline at the Center for WorkLife Law, which provides legal resources to help workers claim workplace accommodations and family leaves, increased 250 percent compared to the same time last year. . . . We're in this mess because, even before coronavirus, the legal protections for working mothers consisted of a convoluted matrix of federal, state and local laws, . . . [W]e need nationwide paid family leave and what many other advanced industrial countries also have: neighborhood-based, nationally financed childcare to replace the patched-together Rube Goldberg machine that just broke.

And what of the future of the children of all those Black women and Brown women raising tens of thousands of entitled upper-middle-class White babies? As Meredith Small, professor of anthropology at Cornell University, says in her book *Our Babies, Ourselve: How Biology and Culture Shape the Way We Parent:*

> We have no bigger crisis as a nation than the class barrier. . . . A child born to poor parents has a pathetic chance of growing up to be anything but poor. This isn't the way things were supposed to be in the United States. . . . Would it be different if all the children born over the last forty years had been given access to top-quality early education programs that not only kept them safe while their parents worked, but gave them the language and reasoning skills that wealthy families pass on as a matter of course?
> We'll never know.

I think that we *do* know. If we hadn't demeaned parenthood in favor of elevating career achievement to a quasi-religious cult, and if we hadn't in effect become nomadic, rootless, individualistic, disruption-venerating, thrill-seeking strivers, we might have our priorities straight when it comes to what a good life, a happy life, and fulfilling life actually can be. We'd be living in a country where it would be unthinkable that any preschool-age child would have less than topflight, parental stay-at-home care paid for by the government. Parents, family, friends, teachers, and grandparents would be teams of childcare givers so parents would not do this alone. Childminding (by men, women, and nonbinary people alike) would be seen as the highest, most-valued vocation of all. Parenting experience would be valued by corporations looking to hire and promote. Instead, we've trapped millions of the working poor parents in a cycle of low-wage, family-crippling struggle while the women in this cohort are caring for the children of the affluent.

**Until Covid forced our hand we kept families hidden and went to work pretending this was "just business" and we had no emotional lives**

We've got no national program of government-funded child-care subsidizing stay-at-home parents, let alone legislatively guaranteed fully paid family leave for EVERY SINGLE PARENT EACH TIME THEY HAVE (OR ADOPT) A CHILD to care for that child at home until they are four years old, an age when day-care is less traumatizing.

We've created family trauma. I think columnist Helaine Olen confirms my point in "Urban Baby Fell into a Trap All Too Common of Our Time" (*Washington Post*, July 10, 2020). She writes:

Mothers, fathers, and their children need more—more help, more support, more resources. This was true before the current crisis, and it's even more true now. When it comes to the online world of parenting, the biggest failure is not one of organization. It's that for all their complaints, all too many of the people doing the talking on confessional sites like the now-shutdown *Urban Baby* still believe that they can individually surmount the ever-increasing challenges of American life *rather than changing the system that underlies them.* Until that mindset changes, nothing else will. (Italics added.)

**Why some young Italians are leaving cities to start a new life (hint: it's not about the money)**

The dearth of good childcare options for most Americans and the fact caregivers are underpaid and parents made to feel bad about staying home while also getting no financial support to do so has underscored a hard truth: We Americans have been conditioned to care more about being seen to succeed than about experiencing joy. And we rarely admit this fact: Most jobs suck, even in "cool" companies. So all this "Do something you love, and it won't be like work" is utter bullshit. Even the sexy high-end jobs are repetitive wastelands compared to the joys of human connection.

**Can we change? I think we can**

Here's an example of how some people did change their minds about careers and their priorities. They happen to be Italian young people, but what they did is open to American young people, too.

A growing number of young Italian rebels have come back

from cities like Milano and Torino to the small villages. Often, they return to villages where their families used to live. The young rebels are trying to reestablish life as they imagine it once was for their grandparents. Many switched from business or tech studies and chose to study agriculture instead. Their return to the land (and to ancient skilled trades and crafts as well) has been deliberate. The Italian government has wisely been encouraging this trend through bipartisan legislation. (The Italians are not alone in promoting families. In France the government encourages people by giving a huge tax break to those who have children.)

It seems to me that those young Italians are on to something: reestablishing the aesthetic quality of family life. Americans have looked for what these young Italians have found (we'll go into more detail in a moment) while traveling as tourists. Consider the delight that many of the more fortunate of us Americans have experienced while exploring the streets of small Italian villages. We say things like "I wish I lived here!" while walking shoulder-width stone-paved paths winding between the solidly built stone houses that hug Liguria's coast. Something deep within us responds to the visual, aesthetic evidence of the kind of stability, continuity, sustainability, family ties, and communities we career worshippers can't (or won't) produce. Yet we respond to a visual reminder of another and better way of life. We marvel at the towns built by people who did not move so much, whose mothers, fathers, and grandparents lived within walking distance, who pair-bonded and had their children at an age when fertility was at its peak, who stayed put generation after generation, and who enjoyed enough stability in their lives to build stone houses crafted as artworks that would last hundreds of years.

Yes, I know, there's a bit of an irony here: In the nineteenth and early twentieth centuries, millions of Italians immigrated to the United States because of wars and poverty caused by disease and natural disaster and their aftermath. Like many of their American counterparts, many "modern" Italians who stayed in Italy also decided they were too busy with careers to pair-bond, let alone have a child, at least when young enough to begin a cycle of life in which they'd experience every stage, including an active and involved grandparenthood. Besides, their economy, like ours, became as weighted against ordinary Italians as ours is against ordinary Americans. Worse: the crafts practiced by Italian civilizations from the Etruscans onward, which made Italy the most beautiful country on earth (in my humble opinion), lost their place of honor when working for businesses came to be seen as more important than "mere" craftwork. So Italians, too, were swept along by domination system consumerism, which destroys what is central to the person—not to mention our planet's ability to sustain life. Unbalanced capitalism in Italy also turned people into utility-maximizing, striving workaholics with ever fewer permanent attachments.

By the late twentieth century the birth rate plummeted in Italy to below replacement level. Who had time for family when making money was the new religion? If the paths and terraces were maintained, it was by tourist boards or various European Union commissions eager to keep vacation destinations "authentic."

### *Forbes*: young rebels trying to reestablish life as it once was for their grandparents

But, as we read in *Forbes* magazine's "Why Young Italians Are Leaving Cities to Start a New Life as Farmers in the Countryside"

(April 21, 2019), some of Italy's youth are "breathing new life into the country's rural areas. In the past two years, the number of young graduates—often from urban centers—starting up their businesses in the countryside has increased by 35 percent. Many are driven by a deep appreciation of Italy's rich local produce and have a good understanding of environmentally friendly practices."

New forms of agriculture are now playing a significant role in youth employment. Migration used to go from rural to urban areas, pushing people out of the countryside toward cities. However, in the past few years, Italy has witnessed an important counterflow that has brought young, university-educated, green-minded, soil-regenerating, family-friendly, pair-bonded, and gifted metropolitan young people back to the countryside. *Forbes* notes, "Italy has become a country with the highest number of youths employed in [the agricultural] sector in Europe." This is good news for the Earth, too. What these young people are doing is a good fit with the call for change made in the movie *Kiss the Ground*. This is a fabulously made film about how regenerating the world's soils and farmland has the potential to rapidly stabilize Earth's climate, restore lost ecosystems, and create abundant food supplies. In fact, my grandson Ben is in this line of restorative work.

According to ISMEA (the National Institute for Agricultural and Food Market Services), the number of highly educated Italian young people moving to the countryside and building a life around regenerative farming has been growing. Data collected from the Ministry of Agriculture shows that every year the number of younger people in eco-conscious farming is increasing. Many of these new enterprises are managed by people under thirty. According to *Forbes*, "The protagonists of this phenomenon are young, usually overqualified, graduates" who had no farming experience before making their lifestyle change. "Through their education and lifestyle, they have acquired skills."

These young farmers and craftspeople may share a somewhat romantic desire of young metropolitans to be reconnected to Mother Earth. That said, enough stick with it so that the Italian government (through several administrations) has had sufficient faith in their prospects to encourage them. One out of ten entrepreneurs in Italy is now occupied in the new agriculture sector. (That sector was more crucial than ever during the coronavirus disaster that engulfed Italy in 2020–2021.) The slow food trend, along with consumers' growing preference for organic artisanal food, is enhancing the small, human-scale, family-friendly, and youth-oriented agribusinesses. During the pandemic this was no longer a luxury but a necessity.

Italian young people's return to the land has been re-creating stable communities. As I noted, they've also been practicing *regenerative agriculture*—farming practices that, among other benefits, reverse climate change by rebuilding soil's organic matter and restore degraded soil biodiversity, resulting in both carbon drawdown and improvement of the water cycle. These young farmers are making a profit out of the renewed attention to the idea of growing, trading, and eating food locally grown—staying put, and quite literally, trying to save all life on Earth.

## The way of life some younger Italians are trying to reinvent was traditionally maintained by their great-great-grandparents' generation

In the past, grandparents taught each generation how to build (or more likely extend) a solid stone house. The expectation was that their family would live there for generations to come. Parents and grandparents taught children how to keep the olive groves thriving, how to cut firewood without destroying the forest, how to fish without depleting stocks in coastal waters, and, of course, how to raise children. The same olive grove, the same path to it, the same landing for small boats, the same stone-flagged streets, the same communal oven, the same forest—these things were sustained and regenerative, generation after generation, as surely as a rain forest was once sustained by indigenous tribes. Civic pride in public spaces and an aesthetic way of life were also high priorities. The idea that some things are beyond price and have intrinsic worth in and of themselves was defended through actions that left entire tracts of countryside healthy and postcard lovely. The life of the village was an organic whole. These are the villages that younger Italians are returning to. It's the vitality of these places the young Italian farmers are reviving as they also work to regenerate the depleted soil . . . *and* start families.

One thing I am proud of is that (as I said) my grandson Ben is working in this area. He studied regenerative farming at university in Holland, which is where he and Claire met and lived together through their college years before marrying in January 2021. Ben has been working for several NGOs advocating for and pioneering new farming methods to restore the soil and making their documentaries, as well as working on farms himself. What Ben is doing at age twenty-six in the wake of the pandemic is being encouraged by European climate and environmental ministers from seventeen nations. They signed a statement in May 2020, urging governments to "make the EU's recovery a Green Deal" and "to build the bridge between fighting Covid-19, biodiversity loss and climate change." The big question is, "Will politicians stay the course and keep their eyes on the long-term crisis or short-term electoral considerations?" as First Vice President of the European Commission Frans Timmermans put it to a *New York Times* interviewer.

## The Finnish commitment to the educational philosophy of no dead ends

Regeneration of the soil and family life in the style of the young Italians and what my grandson Ben is doing in the agricultural sector is not the only sort of regeneration project we Americans should be promoting. Staying the course on a Green New Deal is not the only new deal we urgently need. If we're to tilt the work-life, fertility-childcare, and love-career balance back in favor of what is good for us and for our planet—small, loving, well-educated, close-knit extended families supported by eco-friendly, family-accommodating jobs, including restorative farming and green energy—we need to *also* completely rethink our public school system.

If young Italians becoming farmers and parents points the way to community, soil, and family regeneration, then, when it comes to seeking inspiration for educational regeneration, Finland is a good place for Americans to humbly study. Finland, by contrast to the USA, has the best school system in the world. Perhaps this was one reason, as well as Finland being led by a woman, that their Covid-19 response and recovery was so much better (that is, science-based and accepted rather than being politicized) than America's under Trump's pseudo leadership.

## Ironically, the Finnish school system was first copied from the original American public-school movement, which is now failing

Amanda and Ben grew up in Finland, so I have a personal connection to that educational system. Just like Ben was my introduction to what's going on in regenerative farming, so Ben and Amanda were my passport to an educational system that puts America to shame. What they got from public schools in Finland was better than what's offered by top private schools in America: good education but no entitled elitism.

In the nineteenth century, Finland suffered from famines and had devastating infant and adult mortality rates. Eisler and Fry note that as late as the 1940s, only 10 percent of Finns had a secondary education. But because of a determined nationwide effort that began with universal education for girls as well as boys and a strong women's movement, Finland gradually instituted high-quality education for all citizens, universal childbirth preparation for parents, free healthcare, and public support for families with children in the form of child daycare and home help services.

Today, Finland has the sixth lowest infant mortality rate in the world (the United States ranks fifty-fifth) and makes the top ranks of United Nations, measures of longevity, as well as the World Economic Forum's measures of global competitiveness. In fact, in 2006, Finland was in first place on the World Competitiveness Index, way ahead of the much wealthier United States. This has everything to do with their commitment to public schools, which are fully federally funded. Amanda and Ben went to school with a cross section of students from all social classes in their working-class farming and fishing village. As I said, their local school was paid for as a federal project, not with local tax money, which in America varies wildly from district to district.

My grandchildren's small rural school was as good as schools in the wealthiest parts of urban Finland. Each classroom had two teachers and no more than fifteen students. Their teachers had graduated from the top universities. Even average students leave public high school speaking three languages, playing a musical instrument, and able to get into just about any university or trade school they choose. This is considered normal. Private schools are illegal, as are religious schools, *so the elites concentrate on making sure their school system is great.*

## Tedrow: human beings as the most valuable resource

Mary K. Tedrow, director of the Shenandoah Valley Writing Project, led a group of American teachers to tour the Finnish schools and study them. Her report, "In Finland, I Realized How 'Mean-Spirited' the US Education System Really Is" (*Washington Post*, November 26, 2018), concluded by saying that in addition to keeping the door perpetually open to learning, the Finns include competence as a goal: helping students find what they do well. Since private schools (both secular and religious) are illegal, there is no opting out for the wealthy (or the antisocial religiously delusional). Thus, everyone is motivated to keep the public schools good. They've never heard of private universities either, let alone the scams we call for-profit universities so favored by the ilk of Trump's recent Secretary of Education Betsy DeVos—a woman who was never an educator and who favored the denuding of public education through the government support of private and religious school vouchers.

## Teaching is a high-prestige job in Finland, as is childcare for preschool children

Teacher training takes place in only the best universities, and entrance requirements are as competitive as for medical schools. That's because "The Finns know human beings are their most valuable resource," as Tedrow notes. And "Their budget reflects this belief." Plus the school system is not in the grip of a self-protecting teachers' union that the American left inexplicably backs at every turn as they often fight to defend mediocrity.

In Finland the public school system is free to all, for as long as they live, from preschool to PhD programs, from trade schools to physics. Compulsory education extends from age six to sixteen. After that, students may choose schools, tracks, and interests. They can take an academic or vocational trajectory, change their minds in midstream, or combine the two paths. There is no such thing as student debt. Adults may start families and then return to college or trade schools anytime and for free. Students can start a family before completing college, stay home with their children, or go back to work, or retrain in school and then change careers. Full paid family leave is *mandatory* and can last for several years as more children are born.

By contrast, in the United States we talk about arming our teachers with guns, not with better training. We do not talk about raising the level of respect for teachers by training them exclusively in our Ivy League schools. Instead we read stories about teachers having to buy their students supplies.

The quality of American schools depends on the zip code you live in. We only pay faint lip service to respecting teachers. We see news items of police officers handcuffing "unruly" eight-year-olds or worse. We watch videos of a handcuffed nine-year-old being pepper-sprayed while begging the cops to stop hurting her. A lot of teachers' time is consumed trying to make up for disintegrating families. We do nothing to put those families back together with a real minimum wage, say, at least $25.00 an hour plus full medical benefits. We do not have a wealth tax to strip the billionaires of their private space programs and invest in childcare and schools rather than their yachts.

## Shouldn't schools that serve poor children be the very best schools we have?

American students first enter the school system at age five and have only thirteen years to get a high school diploma. Failure to earn this diploma leads to a dead end. Kids can't come back to high school when they're older to try again. For those who do "make it," college debts crush dreams and close doors. In good neighborhoods, schools work, more or less. In poor communities, they might as well be in the Third World. Why? America dislikes, minimizes, and ignores children's real needs. Student debt also means that young people have to join the career cult more urgently than ever.

Who has time for starting a family when in debt? Who ever heard of medical students getting married during medical school, then taking time off with their young children from residency programs for three or four years, only to be welcomed back and able pick up the pieces with no loss of place, opportunity, or prestige?

Tedrow concludes her report with this:

> On one of our nights in Helsinki, the streets were filled with students celebrating the end of one of their

matriculation tests. We asked them: "What do you think is different between your schools and ours?" They were able to tell us in English—one of up to four languages most students have—that American students know they are all competing against each other for limited seats at university and that they will have to find the money to go there. "We are not worried about that, so we can just focus on learning," they said.

## Malaguzzi: the fight for quality childcare

The subject of good schools brings us to our American preschools. They are often rotten, exacerbating the cruel separation from parents and grandparents. They do not have to be. In "How to Build a Better Child Care System—the Coronavirus Has Highlighted How Necessary Good Child Care Is" (*New York Times*, May 29, 2020), Shantel Meek (founding director of the Children's Equity Project) and Conor P. Williams (a fellow at the Century Foundation) write:

> The Covid-19 crisis has crystallized the fact that childcare programs are essential to our way of life. But any infusion of resources now or in the future must be linked to a focus on supporting children's mental health, development and learning, raising standards and tightening accountability at both the federal and state levels. Child care shouldn't mean children roaming around while a babysitter sits idly by. It's where children's brains grow. We need to treat it as such. Yes, child care is about parents getting back to work. But, odd as it seems to have to reiterate, child care should also be about children.

Again, as with Finnish schools, there are great examples of

what we *could* have in the USA if we cared about families and drastically raised taxes on the wealthy to pay for compassionate, creative programs. Drawing on the great work of people like Loris Malaguzzi (the twentieth-century founder of the Italian Reggio Emilia educational philosophy), we need a childcare revolution. Malaguzzi participated in the building of Reggio Emilia's network of municipal preschools and infant-toddler care centers. According to Malaguzzi, children should have opportunities each day to be in a studio art space and also to explore the outdoors in all weather conditions. Mediums offered in the studio might include clay, watercolors, easel paints, sculpting wire, collage materials, recycled materials, and bits and pieces of nature. And *no* screens. As Alison Gopnik states in "(Hey, Teacher) Leave Those Kids Alone" (*Edutopia*, October 19, 2016) when interviewed by Andrea Cross:

> The typical notion is that there are things that parents or teachers can do to shape the child in a particular way. But from the point of view of evolution and psychology, especially in early life, simply providing a safe, loving space gives children a chance to invent and imagine and learn all sorts of new, unpredictable things. And children seem to be designed to be unpredictable and flexible. That's very different from the traditional educational approach. But it reinforces a point that progressive educators have made for a long time: It's the children who do most of the work. When we study children's learning mechanisms, we find that children—and especially very young children—are incredibly good at learning all by themselves, and are sensitive to even very subtle cues in their environment. They're much better learners than we could ever be

teachers.

Gopnik also reinforces the idea that the best childcare involves relatives and community. The results of such quality childcare are gratifying whether provided by a school or parent or (in our family's case) by a nearby Malaguzzi-based preschool where Lucy, Jack, and Nora romped several mornings a week after they turned four. Malaguzzi set up care centers that cater to the whole child with play outdoors, art, music, and a loving environment. Today these centers (and few care centers in the United States modeled on them) are screen free. Kids play together and create together. They thrive together while learning interdependence and creative kindness. When you think your children are important, it shows.

## The better lives we should bequeath the next generation

We still have a remarkable ability to seek stability, perhaps even sanity, amid our regressive, self inflicted social chaos. Think of the Italian young people or my grandson Ben, who have rejected the disruptive norm idealized in places like Silicon Valley (in other words, backward domination systems based on greed) and have headed back to the villages to try to make a go of eco-friendly lives while starting families. Think of the gay parents adopting children and putting family first and career second as parents trade off on who stays home and who goes to work. Think of the Greek families where grandparents live with their families and how the younger people's attitude about the elderly was such that it motivated them to abide by strict quarantine rules, thus saving thousands of lives. Think of the American grandmother who seeks custody of her grandchildren after her daughter overdoses on opioids, or the orphans in Mexico who are raised in family communities instead of in orphanages. NPR featured these family circles, describing how these orphans live in family units with an adult who cares for them as a parent. The system is so successful that many of the parents were themselves orphans who grew up in these *comunidades* and came back to raise the next generation. Think of intentional communities like one, I know about in Asheville, North Carolina, that my friend Gareth Higgins and his pastor/college chaplain husband lived in where fifty-four people are living in twenty houses.

## Intentional community

The houses (smaller than most of us are used to) and shared grounds, woods, common house, co-working space, catering kitchen, and shared dining area are designed to maximize the sanest use of space. Parking is removed to behind the row of houses so that paths between the buildings are free of cars. Gareth and his husband, Brian, lived so close to others that when one of the frailer people in the community had a need for something to be picked up, or if they fell, help was quickly on the way.

Folks ages zero to ninety-six, partnered, single, with and without kids, and with diverse family commitments helped one another. In this context the age at which people had had their children was irrelevant. Community made up for loss of intergenerational family life. Children could benefit from parents who were (unlike Genie and me) older and wiser and kinder. As Gareth wrote to me in an email:

> We used Slack—simple messaging software—with channels as follows: Announcements—things the whole community needed. This included:

- Individual Needs–from I need an onion to I need a ride to and from my cataract surgery

- Food Pantry (a couple of kind folk took orders for local farms/markets, and did a weekly shop and delivered to the neighbors)

- Activism (letting folk know about what's happening in common good-activism and how we can help)

Most people were on Slack and just checked for info periodically, and if we could help, we would and if we had needs, we would post them. It was wonderful. I think people could form pods like this everywhere, even if they didn't live together. All it takes is the will.

## Post-Covid-19: a time to reconsider

If the coronavirus taught us anything, it's what our actual needs are. College is nice, jobs are necessary—but we need connection. We need community. We need to be nurtured and supported. If we care about having a better future than the version sold to us by corporate bosses and anti-science evangelical and conservative Roman Catholic Savonarola-like clones, we will find ourselves demanding funding for well-paid, well-trained childcare givers when parents can't provide care. We will fight for real family values, including federal financial support for stay-at-home parents, free contraceptives, and easy access to free abortion. Unlike my father and I, who fought for misogyny in the name of "pro-life" activism in the 1970s and '80s, we will fight for an empathy-based baseline for all people. We will fight for the right to put foundational relationships *first* and careers and extended education *second*. We will fight for the time to enjoy parenthood and grandparenthood. We will fight the development of jobs that do not further destroy our planet's ability to sustain life. If we already earn enough to get by, we will refuse to move to another location for no better reason than earning more money. In other words, we will fight for the right to live like the deeply rooted social organisms we evolved to be, in balance with one another and our planet. We will regard the hording of extreme wealth as antisocial behavior right up there with child molesting. We are going to have to rethink our ideas of achievement and leadership, too. The patriarchal "traditional" model of individualistic striving needs to be rethought as my friend Matthew Barzun, diplomat and political fundraiser who served as the United States Ambassador to the United Kingdom, writes in his groundbreaking book *The Power of Giving Away Power*. Barzun says that our entire idea of leadership is wrong and that

> It's gladiatorial—us, alone in the arena, faces "marred by dust and sweat and blood," fighting an unnamed foe, surrounded by others who are critics at worst and neutral onlookers at best. It is highly romantic. But it can be highly toxic. It presents us with a false choice: fight it out or sit it out. In this mindset, good leadership means winning—winning against your opponent, winning over that crowd, or trying your best to win even if you end up losing. Who's in? Who's out? Who's on top? . . . Change the world. Listen to your inner voice. Work hard. Don't give up. Embrace failure. Okay, no big surprises. We've heard these many times. . . . The advice has all the makings of a great movie, but it is almost nothing like real life. . . . Of course, the reality is that our students [hearing this kind of individualistic advice] will not enter the solitary airlock chamber of a rocket when they take off the black robes and tasseled caps

after graduation. They will find themselves around a table that night probably thinking (and maybe drinking) with some uncertainty about the future. They will find themselves around tables with other people for the rest of their lives. They'll want to make things together. They'll want us all to end the false choice between dependence and independence.

## There will be trade-offs

That interrupted career will cost time and money and heartache. We will question ourselves. But the reward of a set of loving, sustaining relationships will more than compensate for the "What have I done?" moments. And as the people who were forced to wait to the cusp of infertility to have children will discover, in a more communitarian and intentional society of the kind Gareth describes, the deficits of having undermined the biological/evolutionary cycle of parent, child, and grandparent can be more than compensated for. We can find healing and start to heal our planet, too.

# CHAPTER 10

# We Can Change

It was Jane Smith, as I've told Jessica, Francis, John, Amanda, Ben, Lucy, Jack, and Nora, who first showed me Botticelli's *Pallas and the Centaur*. Sixty years later, Jane is still a big reason why art is so important to my children and grandchildren. As I said before, who says you have to have a child to be a parent? Childless Jane has been successfully parenting my children and grandchildren from the grave. Her epigenetic impact has outlived her by several generations already. She, like my teacher son, Francis, made other people's lives rich, better, more complete, and beautiful. In that sense, Jane was a parent. She was also a grandparent.

## *Pallas and the Centaur*

When you were six, Lucy, you asked, "Will she cut off his head?" as you studied Botticelli's *Pallas*.

"I think so," I answered, as I always did when you repeatedly asked me your favorite question about a painting that I thought of as "Jane's picture."

Lucy, you lay down on the floor to be at eye level with the book and said, "He looks like John the Baptist in icon. John the Baptist got his head cut off, too."

317

"The centaur's face looks like John the Baptist but not his horse's body," I said.

"Naturally it doesn't," you answered. Then you patiently explained, "The Centaur comes from a made-up story and isn't real, Ba. John the Baptist was a real person."

You lay in front of the huge art book, cupped your chin in your hands, and stared at the page for several minutes longer, lost in one of your art reveries. "She *is* going to cut his head off, Ba. She's pulling his hair. She looks sorry, and he looks scared."

"He has a bow so he could defend himself," I said.

"No, he can't. It isn't held up so he can't shoot. You have to hold a bow up to shoot it like Siegfried does in *Swan Lake* with his crossbow."

"Her dress is like the one in the *Primavera*," I said. "Look," I pointed, as I turned the page to the *Primavera*, "it has the same flowers."

"I want to look at *Pallas* some more," you said as you turned the page back.

"She's the same model he used for *The Birth of Venus*," I said. Then I launched into the story Jane had told me when I was about your age: "Simonetta Vespucci was the model for Athena, and she was Botticelli's model for at least one figure in the *Primavera*. After Simonetta died, he painted her from memory and finished *The Birth of Venus*. Or so it's said. Botticelli even wanted to be buried at her feet. She was his muse, like your Nana is to me."

"I want to be buried next to you if you die first, Ba," you said. "Or maybe I'll die first."

"I hope you won't!" I exclaimed, thinking that going to the Museum of Fine Arts in Boston, and looking at the Egyptian mummies, not to mention all those crucifixions, had opened the door to the contemplation of mortality a bit wider than made me comfortable.

Your interest in the order of who would die first was something you came up with entirely on your own, and sometimes it boiled over into you worrying, "What will happen if my mommy and daddy die first?" Once you cried when you asked me this. And that reminded me that I had cried, too, over this same question when I was a child as did your mother, Becky, who told me that she remembers crying when worrying about her parents dying.

"Probably you'll die first, Ba," you said in a disconcertingly matter-of-fact cheerful tone. "You're *much* older than me!"

I wanted to change the subject. "Pallas Athena is a god," I said, "sprung from the forehead of Zeus. Botticelli painted *Pallas* for the Medici family because . . . "

You covered your ears with your hands. I stopped talking.

You used this signal anytime you sensed that I was about to launch into Jane-style art history or Greek mythology over-drive. It had been my reaction, too, when my mother launched into the Fall from Grace, or the Nature of the Trinity, when all I'd asked was something like, "Did God know Jesus had to die even before God created us?" A simple yes or no was all I was looking for.

You jumped up from the floor and blurted, "Prince Nut-cracker, fight the rats!" Then you climbed onto a chair. "Get me a pillow to throw at you!" you commanded.

"Lucy, when you're directing ballets or movies, remember to ask your cast and crew to do things by saying 'please' first," I said.

"But you're not my cast, Ba. You're my friend."

I gave up on instruction. I lost every parental-style battle the moment you smiled at me. And anyway, I so disliked slipping into a grown-up role with you. It was just too much fun being five, six, or whatever age again and playing.

While playing, I had to keep a lot in mind. You called me Siegfried if we were about to jump from *Nutcracker* to *Swan*

*Lake* and moments later you'd call me Romeo, if you wanted to do a scene from the ballet. I was Joseph to your Mary when we played the nativity, including some crèche scenes that my mother would have called shockingly heretical, for instance, when you'd announced that you were *both* "the angel bringing good news" to the Shepherds (me) and *also* a Flower Fairy proclaiming "Peace on Earth!" Mom would have stopped the game abruptly and earnestly explained that "angels are real, darling, but fairies are just pretend and we mustn't confuse Bible stories with fairy tales by mixing the Things of the Lord up with worldly stories." But Jane would have been fine with your mixture of pagan myths with Christian doctrine, as I was.

In our games, you and I committed many cheerful heresies. We were *both* the Romans killing Jesus, *and* the Red Queen (from *Through the Looking-Glass*) at the foot of the cross. For that matter, you'd invite Pallas or Toad from *Wind in the Willows* into our resurrection dramas at the Garden Tomb. You'd sometimes introduce a Flower Fairy into the biblical narrative at the tomb of the risen Lord along with a fairy, goddess, or sprite "to give Mary Magdalene the good news."

## Genie and I were offered another chance at life after our children were raised and our son John returned from war

Genie and I ask ourselves: If opening a door for a child to something thrillingly beautiful doesn't epitomize the concept of *good*, then what does? What do we want to pass on to our grandchildren? How do we hope they define the word *success*? How can we become a Jane or a Francis, opening doors for others to wonderful things?

One way to start helping others is to really *see* them. This takes time. For instance watching my grandchildren's newborn faces as they slept in my arms became a moment of truth. I walked in circles around the kitchen table while holding them. I'd miss "important" meetings and (often) leave "crucial" calls unreturned and instead play them music as they slept in the cradle of my arms.

In Lucy's case, because she was living in our home, I became a sort of walking crib. This lulled Lucy into a trancelike state where her breathing would slow and her body relax. My arms ached from holding her in one position for so long. As she grew, I already knew that I could get tennis elbow by holding a sleeping baby in one position across my chest. I held her head cupped in one hand, for hours at a time, day after day. I was exultant when my daughter-in-law, Becky, called me her hero, simply because Lucy slept in my arms after she refused naps in her crib.

Besides this ego-boosting appreciation from a young mother (always a good thing), my reward for enduring the stress-position torture naps was beyond price. Lucy's translucent, delicately mauve-tinted eyelids would flutter in her sleep, and *I was there* to see this gorgeousness! I knew she could hear my heartbeat!

I've never cried for joy over a good review of a book of mine or when I'd been interviewed by Oprah and Terry Gross and Rachel Maddow and sales of some of my books (blessedly if briefly) spiked. But the sheer *beauty* of my undistracted closeness to my lovely grandchildren, side by side with me, swimming together, as it were, in our very own gene pool, made me tear up out of sheer gratitude. And I've also shed tears sometimes when thinking about how putting love first and working to quell my demons has been rewarded by a lifelong friendship with Genie—the mother goddess, buck-stops-here leader of our tribe.

## The hominin species *Australopithecus afarensis* ("Lucy")

The coincidence of one of my granddaughters sharing the name *Lucy* with the female of the hominin species *Australopithecus afarensis* (found in Ethiopia in 1974 and sometimes called the mother of the human race) is not lost on me. The continuing story of our evolution was quite literally in my arms for those long naps. My love, my empathy, my overwhelming desire to protect and nurture this little child was part of a vast and continuing story. Looking down at Lucy asleep in my arms, day after day, I recalled that when the team led by the French geologist and paleoanthropologist Maurice Taieb discovered the Hadar Formation in 1974 (in the Afar Triangle of Ethiopia) and found several hundred pieces of bone fossils representing 40 percent of the skeleton of a female, that besides doing their work they were also incessantly playing the Beatles' song "Lucy in the Sky with Diamonds." The team named their 3.2 million year old find "Lucy" because of that song.

When I'd run away from a British boys boarding school (as I mentioned earlier) the only possession I'd taken with me was my recently acquired *Sgt. Pepper's Lonely Hearts Club Band*. Thereafter (like the science team in Ethiopia), I had also been incessantly listening to "Lucy in the Sky with Diamonds." And now the most recent incarnation of the original Lucy was in my arms because music had been her grandfather's best excuse and most useful lure to entice a female into what amounted to an updated cave (my basement art studio). As I said before, I'd met Genie when she was eighteen in September 1969, only because I'd just bought the Beatles' new album *Abbey Road*.

**Art, biology, sex, lust, pheromones, and music were the primordial soup (so to speak) out of which John, Lucy's dad, and Lucy, too, eventually emerged**

The story of our human family's far distant beginnings in the plains of Ethiopia, the Beatles' music that influenced a whimsical name choice, the mystery of music that led to the first sexual couplings between Genie and me—in other words the force of aesthetics in our lives—seemed to come to a point as I looked down at "my" baby Lucy.

I was struck more deeply than ever by the overarching mystery of what it means to be a human. We might "only" be biological machines, but those machines look at the world through inexplicably spiritual eyes seeking aesthetic meaning. Put it this way: the mystery of being a human can be summed up by the fact that had Maurice Taieb named his team's find only as AL 288-1 (the official designation of the find in the catalogue) rather than *Lucy*, it's hard to see how the find would have so captivated our imaginations ever since. In Ethiopia, the fragment assembly came to be called *Dinkinesh*, meaning "you are marvelous" in the Amharic language.

Somewhere in the story begun by that other Lucy 3.2 million years ago, the consciousness and empathy that brought tears to my eyes as I contemplated my Lucy had evolved. We evolved from single-cell survivors to the creatures that play music in a base camp where geologists and paleoanthropologists gather to discover a link to our beginnings. We might "just want sex" when we desire to mate, but that need can turn into what we call love. Bone fragments are given a name and a personality. Facts are folded into stories. Carbon dating of bone fragments becomes one kind of truth, but so does the music playing in the science lab that inspires scientists to attach a whimsical name to their find. And a child's poem—as we shall see in a moment—can become a confirmation of an entire way of life, of sacrifices made, of being forgiven, of mistakes learned from, and of love turning our sorrows into joy.

### Marriage of Figaro

When she was a baby, I found that Lucy loved to listen to the classical music that I've played for her from birth. I picked several pieces we'd listen to again and again during our naptime stress tests. Lucy slept well to the music and, when awake, listened so attentively that she seemed to be holding her breath. Mozart became one naptime favorite. Nino Rota's scores for the films of Federico Fellini was another.

My view was of Lucy's face resting in the crook of my arm. Contemplating Lucy made every note sharper and every word more poignant. Beaumarchais's *Marriage of Figaro* (translated by Mozart's librettist and made into the opera) is a light romp, but make no mistake: the opera is not trivial. The sublime music carries a deeply felt story that ends with a paean to mercy—the survival of the friendliest prime directive set to music. And since *Figaro* was the second opera (as adapted for kids) Mrs. Parke marched me into, when playing it for the infant Lucy, my life seemed full, lovely, mercifully blessed, and meaningful. I'd come full circle: I was passing on to my grandchild the love a teacher gave me as a lost schoolboy.

That mercy-laden love was also preached by Mozart. A final ode is sung after the Countess forgives her husband, the repentant

Count. He's been involved in all manner of marital shenanigans, but finally he apologizes: *"Forgive me, my angel—forgive my transgression!"* The Countess responds, *"So frank a confession I answer with 'Yes.'"* Everyone onstage joins to sing Mozart's anthem to reconciliation and forgiveness, mercy and kindness.

> *From a maze of wild confusion,*
> *Full of doubts and of illusion,*
> *Comes domestic peace among us,*
> *As from darkness comes the light.*
> *Husband and lover, or married or single,*
> *Old or young, in pleasure mingle—*
> *Mingle with us in the banquet;*
> *Into day we'll turn the night.*

## Challenging the idea that our job defines us

We need to rediscover Mozart's survival of the friendliest version of Mrs. Parke's merciful truth: "As from darkness comes the light . . . Into day we'll turn the night." Mrs. Parke died. Her husband, Gordon, died three weeks later. They were both in their nineties in 2020 when they died. They'd spent seventy-three years together. They lived down the road from their daughter, grandchildren, and great-grandchildren in their home to their very last days, walking distance from neighbors that loved them and children and grandchildren who adored them and cared for them. Theirs was a good life in every sense of the word.

There's not a day I don't remember Mrs. Parke. Her favorite composer—Mozart—reaches into my life, too, just about every day with every note he composed, with music that so often reminds me that life is worth living not because of what I do for work but because of the gift of just being alive.

We remember people like Mrs. Parke because they made our lives more beautiful. And if we are smart, we'll work to do the same thing for everyone whose lives we touch. Put it this way: If you want to be happy and well remembered, never pay the minimum wage but always pay the maximum wage you can afford. Pay, share, and give the most you can to everyone. Give expecting nothing in return, and you just might get everything back ten times over in joy. That was true of Mrs. Eunice Parke: she was *fiercely* joyful!

## Be the light to others— you will be the one illumined

As we have seen in this book, before Covid-19 disrupted our lives, many of us were already trying to find the light by challenging the idea that our job defines us. Loneliness, frustration, and alienation were on the rise. Even the most successful of us felt too busy, too preoccupied, and too distracted to enjoy what we intuitively knew were life's greatest joys: deep lasting connection to others, involvement in our community, and the thrilling experience of love worth sacrificing for.

In "We Are Living in a Failed State" (*The Atlantic,* June 2020), George Packer writes: "We can learn from these dreadful days that stupidity and injustice are lethal; that, in a democracy, being a citizen is essential work; that the alternative to solidarity is death." And David Brooks notes: "The pandemic has been a massive humanizing force—allowing us to see each other on a level much deeper than politics—see the fragility, the fear, and the courage.... Everywhere I hear the same refrain: We're standing at a portal to the future; we're not going back to how it used to be" ("Why the Trump Ploy Stopped Working," *New York Times,* April 30, 2020).

## Now that we know pandemics are going to shape our future, should we just go back to the way things were?

A lot of people seem to be asking: Is so-called modern life all it's cracked up to be? Is being selfish really the way to declare your presence on this earth for the short moment you have on life's stage? Does our idea of what it means to be "a success" fit with our deepest spiritual, biological, ecological, and psychological needs? Can we get over ourselves and stop thinking we're *apart* from nature and embrace the fact we are *part* of nature? Can we listen to our own evolutionary biology and dare to embrace the truth about ourselves or will we listen to the next version of damn-the-facts ideology and start yet another cycle of unhappiness?

## The answer is found in our evolutionary history

Let's briefly recap our evolutionary history, which shaped us in a way that makes prioritizing career success above all else incongruous with genuine happiness.

- Human babies evolved to be born prematurely; otherwise our big brains/outsized heads would have killed all childbearing human females.
- Our children develop slowly compared to other mammals, and it takes ages to raise them.
- The females of our species that managed to survive the physical challenges of childbirth then found they needed to keep a mate or others around them long enough to raise children. So we evolved into animals that value community and connection above all else.
- Evolution gifted us all with a chemical/emotional motivation and reward for caring, sharing, nurturing, and childminding others: the experience of love.

- We became addicted to love via oxytocin, the "love hormone."
- We began to invent taboos, rules, religions, laws, and institutions to formalize and defend our discoveries about what works best to keep human society functioning: *mothering* one another from birth to death.
- Evolution screams: SHARE! LOVE! CARE!

## We can work together to reshape our society

Given who we evolved to be—*cooperators* who are happiest when caring for others and sacrificing for others, and in return being cared for—we can choose to direct our next step and the one after that toward a better, more humane life. We can make our *entire country* into an intentional community. We can reclaim the right to live as a "wayfinding experience of joy; an apprenticeship in meaning; a belonging and becoming in vibrant relationships," as my friend Samir Selmanović put it to me in an email about what he advises those people he coaches.

We may work for change so that someday, sooner rather than later, the list I put at the start of this book can be expanded upon. I think there is reason to hope for new, better, fairer American reality where:

- Relationship success is regarded as the highest human achievement.
- Sharing joy with our children is understood as the "point" of having children.
- Taking time off work or school to parent young children will become the norm for almost every parent when each child is born until they are at least four years old.

- When we leave work to care for young children and then return to work, there will be no social barriers (let alone stigma) inhibiting our careers.
- We will have strictly enforced anti-discrimination laws protecting parents returning to work.
- We will have strictly enforced anti-discrimination laws protecting the rights of college and high school students who get pregnant, allowing them to continue with their education while also caring for a child.
- More of us who pair-bond and decide to have children will do so when it makes biological and emotional sense rather than career sense.
- Those who do not wish to have children will be regarded as fully capable of shaping our future through sharing beauty, teaching, and interacting with others just as meaningfully as those with kids. They, too, will influence, shape, and create good lives for the next generation.
- Government-funded childcare for preschool-age children will be top-notch, child-centered, involve parents day-to-day, and be rooted in the hands-on experiences of nature, creative play, conversational skills, social skills, and making art and music (*no screens!*)—no matter the parent's zip code.
- We'll lead the world with the highest minimum wage, automatically adjusted for inflation—in other words, we'll have no more "working poor" struggling to just survive.
- We'll have no more billionaires because their wealth will have been shared through paying their employees a

*maximum wage* and earning far less themselves, as well as paying fair corporate and personal taxes.

- All corporations will pay taxes. (Ninety-one Fortune 500 companies paid *no federal income tax* in 2018!)
- Big money in American politics will be a thing of the past.
- There will be no way for any global company to shelter from taxes anywhere in the world because the USA will use the full extent of its power—trade, diplomatic, and military to eliminate this practice.
- Free medical care for all will be the norm.
- All government farm assistance to agribusinesses will end with the exception of assistance to organic, regenerative eco-friendly farmers.
- Our Social Security system will be revised to recognize stay-at-home parenting for very young kids as a national priority deserving of full benefits at retirement.
- Parents in all professions will have socially desirable options regarding who goes to work and who stays home with children, often swapping roles.
- Sex education will prioritize relationship education, kindness, and consent. Family will be taught as a subject.
- Violent, abusive, child-abusing (and privacy-abusing), misogynistic rape-culture "entertainment" will be a thing of the past. Companies that facilitate its spread through their search engines will be held responsible and shut down. So will companies that enable child trafficking. Top tech executives will face jail time as accessories to rape and child abuse if they do not prevent the dissemination of abuse and trafficking through their search engines.

- Schools, high schools, and colleges will not treat pair-bonding or sex as a side issue but encourage students to make their relationships succeed rather than take a back seat (no pun intended) to "more important things"—like preparing to earn the most money possible.
- Divorce and relationship breakups will decline as we work socially, politically, and economically to help make pair-bonded relationships succeed and thrive.
- Single parenthood outside a pair-bonded relationship will be supported and underwritten by social programs along the lines of the Icelandic model.
- Single motherhood will no longer be a route to poverty.
- Many more of us will become grandparents at a younger age so that grandparent childcare will be the usual experience of most children.
- Being deeply rooted in a community will be a social, moral, and "lifestyle" priority.
- People who have children later in life will be supported, helped, and encouraged through better pro-family policy decisions and financial aid that pays for all fertility procedures.
- We will move far less often.

**Based on a better understanding of our evolutionary selves, we can thrive in family life *and* in our work life, too**

We can't return to our childhood, but we can recognize the essentialness of childlike wonder. That truth is what my grandchildren have kept alive in me: wonder. Childlike wonder—for instance fully sharing in Nora's surprise, shock, and joy when her latest wiggly tooth came out: "I pulled it out all by myself, Ba!"—remains the only condition in which the value of everything else "important" makes sense to me.

## Cohen and Titus Lucretius Carus: love cheats time

Columnist Roger Cohen talks about what makes him tick in "Reflections on the Graduation of My Daughter" (*New York Times*, May 17, 2019): "Love cheats time because it's passed along, refracted through the generations; and it's the reason, with all its illusions, that we're here in the first place." Titus Lucretius Carus, the Roman poet and philosopher, sums up what I was saying about my grandchildren's love and about human connection this way: "Thus the sum of things is ever being renewed, and mortals live dependent one upon another. Some nations increase, others diminish, and in a short space the generations of living creatures are changed and like runners pass on the torch of life." Australian comedian, actor, writer, musician, philosopher, and director Tim Minchin adds his wisdom to that of Lucretius on how to pass on the torch of life: "Try to also express your passion for things you love. Be demonstrative and generous in your praise of those you admire. Send thank-you cards and give standing ovations" (commencement address at the University of Western Australia).

## Minchin: connection, commitment, and love

Minchin is best known for his satirical and unorthodox comedy. On the surface, he has a brilliant, angry edge, but Minchin, too, is turning into an old softie. His subtext is about the persistent power of kindness. Minchin riffs on the fact that we do not discover soul mates but co-create them—if we stick with someone long enough and persist through times of trouble. He talks about being a parent and spouse. He makes jokes about the touchstones of his life, but his writing most fundamentally revolves around what makes all of us tick: connection, commitment, and love. Minchin also casts a piercing gaze at our materialistic career-first society and our hollowed-out social values.

Through his comedy writing, Minchin tells his story about prioritizing parenting, art, caring, partnership, and deeper human connection. He tells his audiences that he married his high school girlfriend. He became a father early in life. He riffs on the fact that relationships take work but are worth it. Minchin references his deepest connections to family love, for instance, when he wound up a recent show in London's Albert Hall. Notwithstanding his being a rather militant atheist, he closed with his famous "Christmas Song" where he talks about the pleasure of liking Christmas anyway even as someone "not expecting a visit from Jesus." To him, the pleasure expressed in the song is all about drinking white wine in the sun with his parents and family.

I get Minchin because, like Minchin, Genie and I married so young. Like him, we're also not expecting a visit from Jesus—i.e., looking for magical solutions to life's quandaries. Rather, like Minchin, we're putting our pair-bonded relationship first and trusting that relationship to be worth the very hard work needed to make it thrive. We know that there are no perfect matches and that relationships don't just happen; they have to be chosen and then fought for. We know we fail a lot. And like Minchin and his wife, Sarah, if Genie and I had waited to meet "the perfect match" or waited to pair-bond until after we got some sort of secure career going, or until we had enough money, we might still be waiting. And if we'd walked away after fights and heartbreak, we'd have lost our best years together—the last twenty years out of our fifty-one-year journey, so far.

Minchin points out that there are no neatly packaged secure "stages" to life that give you all you want. There are no "safe spaces" or "trigger warnings." There's only one choice: either to live deeply, lovingly, kindly, and well or else to waste your life on materialistic dead ends and individualistic ego. But there's one drawback to the kind of choices Minchin, Sarah, Genie, and I and countless others have made: When you make the choice for unconditional love, it means you are vulnerable to loss. Love takes courage.

## Evolutionary history points the way to joy

Here's how I see it: We're animals who began by seeking patterns in nature around us in order to survive. Where does the ripe fruit grow? Where are the predators? From there we evolved further to seek more abstract patterns, in other words, to seek meaning. We never did find the meaning of everything or an answer to the question, "Why are we here?" Instead, we found love. I'll take that.

As a byproduct of evolving the capacity to experience love, we discovered that empathy is a thing that only becoming wealthy and/or powerful can destroy. In the light of the empathy "thing" and love, here's my starter kit; a "how-to" for anyone interested in living joyfully by the light of love:

- You can't guarantee happiness, but you can weigh your odds against disappointment. So begin by defining the best-case scenario of who you'd like to become. Then live that way *now*. For instance: Do you plan on having a serious relationship? If the answer is a vague someday even though there is a perfectly good someone right in front of you, then stop fucking around . . . now. Do you plan on being generous if you ever get rich? Then start now, and leave a better tip next time.

- Remember, your malleable brain is "you," so don't mess it up by treating your relationships casually. You might get used to living that way and wind up shallow, alone, and miserable.
- Treat sex as a precious gift.
- Unless you want to be single—and plenty of sensible people do—commit, pair-bond, live together, marry (whatever you want to call serious commitment) when you find someone to love. You'll never know enough to take such a big step until you do.

   All you need to ask yourself about someone you might commit to is this: Are they kind? Do I feel love for them? Do they feel love for me? Do we both know that relationships take hard work? Can we forgive each other? And if you've answered in the affirmative, do both of you understand that your relationship is more important than what either of you do for a living?

- All you need to ask about being qualified to be a parent is this: Am I creative and loving? If the answer is yes, give it a shot before you think you are ready because you'll never be ready until you try, fail, keep trying, learn, and move on.

## Babies or—not?

Life, as we Covid-19 survivors well know, gets interrupted. There are no in-between bits of life. There is just *now*. You have an infinite capacity to love. What you *do not* have is infinite *time* to get your love life (let alone baby-making) working.

The right time to love is *now*! If you want a child, go for it. If life's taught me anything, it's that parenting those around me, be they my children or grandchildren or even needy adults I'm not related to, is the only choice I never regret. For me these days, the only truth in life is what I read in the eyes of those I love. Everything else fades.

## Family time—or not?

If you are a younger person reading this, you are probably going to have a longer life ahead of you than most people did in human history. Trust me, a day is coming when you won't be able to remember all those important career "Should I get a master's first?" steps you took. So do not fall for the GDP-worshipping/growth myth. Lives lived according to the sterile "job first, life second" mantra end in regret.

## Here's how to make your pair-bonding work and maybe raise good kids, too

Maybe you already know that living in the moment with those you love is your best bet for experiencing joy. Maybe you already want to help start a social, legislative, political, and spiritual revolution that changes the way our culture puts work, money, and power ahead of love. So here are some ideas (in no particular order of importance) to help you change the world around us and maybe your daily life, too.

If my list (to follow) starts to feel daunting, hang in there. There's no way to do all I recommend, but what matters is this: embrace the chance to love and be loved.

Fight for legislation that takes family-friendly, relationship-strengthening steps in an enlightened *survival-of-the-friendliest* direction: family leave, federal Social Security–type financial support for every stay-at-home childcare-giving parent, laws protecting the rights of parents returning to work, federal funding for 100 percent of all public education, and free medical care for all—for a start.

Fight for legislation and regulation of the tech giants. Make them fully accountable on privacy issues, the spread of child abuse / rape culture masquerading as porn, not to mention child-trafficking. Bottom line: fix your algorithms—or go to prison.

If you want to make the most difference possible to our human future, then work for, donate to, fight for, and demand programs to educate girls and women worldwide. No girl, however poor, however desperate her country's situation, should be excluded from school. Education saves and improves the lives of girls and women, leading to stronger families, better services, and better child health for *all* people. Educating girls has the most wide-ranging impact on any society of any action for progress humans can take. It must become the number-one goal of all our foreign and domestic policy and spending to (quite literally) give peace a chance.

Go out of your way to be kind—even if you don't feel like it.

Think before you speak.

Put down that fucking phone!

We tend to look at the big events as important when it is really the small moments that matter most. Do the small things well. The rest will follow.

If you are able to, take a job that keeps you nearest your family.

Jobs come and go, but family is forever and can help you with both the routine things and the major life crises.

Take a job that allows you the time to do what will mean more as the years go by: building deep, human, loving, caring connections and working to better your community, caring for your neighbors, family, and planet.

If you work from home, when the workday is over, try to be there 100 percent for your family. The texts, calls, and emails can wait until tomorrow. If they can't—look for another line of work.

If you don't have a hands-on kind of job (such as being a farmer or carpenter), then do hands-on activities outside of your job, such as carpentry, cooking, gardening, baking, sewing, painting, designing, welding, knitting, stonemasonry—*anything* that connects you *kinetically* in *real time* to our beautiful world as a *physical being*. If you've always wanted to learn one of these or other skills—start now.

Instead of paying other people to clean your house, tend to your garden, or wash your car, do it yourself even if you have the money to hire people. Why? Because you need to *stop deluding yourself* about how "important" you and your job are as opposed to "just the regular stuff" and "ordinary" people. Knowing and acting like you are *not* special is the best definition of good *mental health*.

Concentrate on living life as a unified experience where even casual or unexpected relationships count. Here's an example: Next time you're stuck in an airport, don't treat those hours as "nothing time" or "in-between" time, let alone as "wasted time." Close your laptop, take out your ear buds, turn off the phone—and *look around*. Make eye contact. Talk to a stranger. You don't have to be upbeat and cheerful or wise. Just listen. That airport delay can become a turning point for you and someone else. That casual encounter may well be more important to you and to them than the big reason for your trip. You cared. The world just got better. You just got mentally healthier.

Enjoy the routines of daily life alongside your children. I'm always thrilled at how Nora loves doing small and ordinary things. Give her a dustpan, and she'll happily help me sweep up the sawdust left from our making birdhouses, home repairs—whatever—together. Children love to be given real tasks to do. When I ask Jack to help do the dishes, he happily works, turning our two kitchen sinks into harbors, pools, and soapy playgrounds. Lucy loves to set the table. After the children have peeled carrots, fried fish, cleaned potatoes, and swept the floor, they can sit down to eat feeling pride that they have participated in the meal. It's made even more special when they've planted and harvested some of the food on the table.

If kids grow up with maids and other people doing the daily jobs in their household and parents who think they are too important or too busy or too rich to mow lawns, plant gardens, cook, and clean kitchens themselves, of course the children grow into entitled pricks. They become unable to empathize with others and to do much besides a narrowly defined set of "important" educational and job tasks (if those). Being raised for entitlement is a curse.

Take nothing for granted, and maybe you won't be taken for granted.

You can't change another person, but if you love them, you *can slowly change yourself for them*. And if the person you commit to loves you back, they will see your effort and will reward you by making changes, too. It's called growing together instead of growing apart. And this takes sacrificing our malignant egos and self-destructive narcissism.

What is the surest way to ruin every relationship? Behave as if your idea of a perfect relationship is one where you'll find someone *already* the way you want them to be *and* prepared to put up with your bullshit—without you having to change anything about yourself for them.

If you've been together for a longish time and hit a bad patch lasting days, months, or even years, work through it. Why? Because you can't get the time of shared experiences back again. You can walk away—but you'll still be there with all your problems that contributed to the bad times. The person who has been with you all those years knows you. They don't have to have everything explained—again. They were *there*. You cannot make new old friends. And **NO—I am *not* urging anyone to put up with physical abuse! And NO I am not against divorce. I am against the sort of self-delusion that thinks that divorce will solve your problems.** So don't lie to yourself: the fact you don't always get what you want or that the person you are with annoys you or does not do everything you want is not abuse—it's called life.

Teach your kids to build things. Start slow and be patient. They love to learn and will thank you later for showing them how to get away from their screens and become more self-sufficient.

When someone asks you what you do for a living, tell anyone who will listen that what we *do* for a living should be our least concern—it's who we *are* and how we treat others that counts if (that is) we want to live joyfully.

Tell anyone who will listen that working to be rich is a squalid and disappointing life goal. Wealth is a curse.

Say "I love you" as often as possible.

If you think of something nice to say, say it now.

Tell anyone who will listen that wanting to be famous is as stupid as wanting to be rich. (There's a difference between getting famous as a byproduct of, say, being a great actor, and chasing celebrity for its own sake.)

Encourage love. Be a hopeless romantic. Play matchmaker.

If you are an employer, pay everyone who works for you the most you can and give less to yourself in order to make that possible. You might find you are even loved instead of hated and envied. When your children grow up, they might not be ashamed of you. You may die loving yourself rather than mired in loathing.

Stay put and make a home. Setting down roots is a good thing. You become part of a community, which enriches your life. You'll have people around you looking out for you. Example: a few nights ago I was up writing this book. I got a text at 4:00 AM. It was from my neighbor David. He'd seen the light on my barn flashing off and on. "Frank, your barn light is flashing; are you okay?" David thought maybe I was hurt or something and signaling for help. He was up getting a drink of water and noticed the light. He cared. It was just the wind making the branches move and setting off the motion detector switch on the light over the barn door. I've been in one place long enough so that my neighbors are friends. This takes time. *Stay put.*

Know your neighbors' names.

If you are in the supermarket and someone in front of you doesn't have enough to pay, and you have the money that day, pay. You'll feel good for weeks.

Shop locally.

Know where your food comes from.

Support regenerative farming and save our Earth.

Make sure you and everyone you know watches these eight must-see terrific and entertaining sustainable agriculture documentaries: *Kiss the Ground, Honeyland, The Pollinators, Before the Plate, The Biggest Little Farm, Follow the Food,* and *Rooted.*

Walk the dog.

Let your dog take its time sniffing around.

Stop to talk to other dog's companions.

Know when someone you know is ill. Give them your number and say "Call me day or night" and mean it. Call them if they don't call you.

Sit on your front porch and say hello. If you don't have one, sit in your driveway. If you don't have one, talk to people in the elevator.

Leave generous tips.

Leave a tip in your hotel room for the maid and a note thanking that person for cleaning your room. Stop in the hallway as you pass them pushing that cart stacked with towels and cleaning products and ask how they are. If they are having problems, try to help them. If you are rich, hand them a check for everything you earned that month. They can use that money more than you can.

Thank people delivering packages to your doorstep and tip them when they least expect it.

Move to eye level when you talk to someone in a wheelchair. Don't shout. They can hear you just fine.

Don't pet or distract guide dogs or other kinds of assistance and service dogs; they are working. That dog is a professional angel, so please respect them and their human partner.

Embrace this truth: many a plumber, carpenter, boatbuilder,

nanny, dog walker, farmer, gardener, garbage collector, bus driver, or arborist is as smart as any PhD from MIT or Yale. Our current standards of intellectual status are absolute bullshit. Many more people would have done better in every way skipping college and learning a trade. The people I respect most work with their hands; for instance, my boatbuilder neighbor Scott or the women who are the treasured *petites mains* (tiny hands), artisans in France and Italy doing the elaborate handwork that transforms a designer's dress into a showpiece. And what about my guitarist pal Daron Murphy, who accompanies Moby and can *play*!

The 8:8:8 rule could give us all a better work-life balance. Eight hours each for work, leisure, and sleep feels like a sensible balance—yet with home working and long-hours culture, it can seem like an unachievable goal. Proof? Some people working from home use the extra time they save by not commuting for . . . more work!

Bottom line: *Tell yourself and anyone who will listen not to become just another cog in the heartless grow-the-economy, money-worshipping, status-seeking, power-hungry, fame-seeking commerce machine inexorably squeezing the life out of our fragile planet—and the joy out of our lives.*

## To love takes work

Most of us know that it takes failure and heartbreak to do anything and do it well—from learning a new skill to working at a new job to managing our money. So how come we rarely admit that building good relationships—ones that thrive and pass the test of time—involve struggle and many sacrifices, too? Falling in love is easy. Staying in love is hard. Whoever said anything worth doing is easy?

## The redemptive power of *living nostalgia*

Repeated actions of loving lead to more love, tangled with sweet memory. I call this experience *living nostalgia*. Let me explain: Living nostalgia combines the past, present, and future into living in the moment with sweet memories illuminating that moment. This is the only defense there is against time's passage. Biting into a warm, homemade cookie "just like grandmother made" brings up timeless memories of sitting in a kitchen, enveloped in love. It's a bonus beyond simply eating something sweet and certainly carries far more satisfaction than devouring a fancy, overpriced pastry at a status-confirming restaurant. When people stuck at home called their grandparents looking for some intergenerational wisdom—such as how to do some actual cooking, maybe for the first time in their lives—they were doing what comes most naturally. They were, in essence, going home.

If you've ever watched *The Great British Baking Show*, you will see the embodiment of this: contestants tearing up when describing some particular cake, bread, pie, or scone as one that Nan or Gran or Dad or Mum "taught me to bake." That's because some things can't be improved. Good memories are among those things. That's why "Read it again" is a key phrase indicating that a happy childhood is underway. That is, there's been enough continuity and stability so that a child is beginning to treasure the familiar, comforting landmarks posted in her memory bank. "Take me to Cashman Park again!" "Play it again!" "Tell me again!" There's an *again* because there was a *before*—a trusted, undisrupted context. The beloved story, action, food, smell, sound, place, house, person becomes a memory, an anchor, a ritual, a place to go back to again and again in our minds. What is my job as a parent and grandparent? To give my children and grandchildren that mental nostalgia place to go to for the rest of their lives.

**Let's not let the discoveries that we all made and the life lessons that we learned in a time of great change and suffering go for naught**

The rewards of caring and sharing seem infinite. I have received a few rewards and ego-boosting awards over the years as a writer, artist, and activist. But I can honestly look you in the eye and hand on heart promise you that nothing ever came close to the joy the poem Nora wrote on April 5, 2021, gave me.

This was a few weeks after she went back to school in person for the first time in a year. She'd missed the second half of kindergarten. She'd played in my garden instead. Then the kids did online school stuff. Then it was masks on and back to social-distanced, in-person school. Then Nora found herself in first grade.

**About that poem**

When I pick up my grandchildren from school, I rarely multitask. They get my undivided attention. But not the day Nora wrote the poem; I was on the phone with someone who donates lots of money to a foundation I help when I can. This was an important call from a very wealthy person. They'd called me. I could not hang up—or so I told myself. So I broke every piece of advice I have just spent five years writing about in this book. I am a hypocrite.

Nora came to the car. She held out a sheet of paper and shot me an uncharacteristically shy glance.

"I wrote a poem, Ba."

"*Uh huh . . . Shhh*," I said, putting a finger to my lips and pointing to the phone.

Nora settled into the back seat, and I drove home. She was silent and clutching her sheet of paper as I talked . . . and talked . . . on the phone.

When we got home, I asked to see the poem. "Never mind," said Nora a bit glumly. "You can see it later." She put the poem on the staircase and walked into the kitchen.

A little later, Nora and Jack got into an argument out by the swing set. I wound up yelling at Nora, "Why are you such a pest to Jack?!" I shouted, "Snap out of it or I'll just take you home!"

Nora was not yet used to full-time school again and was a bit fragile and tired after a long day. I was used to her sunny, rested, morning-no-school self and had forgotten what after-school, little kid frazzled tiredness is all about. She'd gotten used to my all-day nanny self. We were both a bit in shock at the school routine intruding again.

When it was time to take her home, we walked to Nora's house in a post-getting-yelled-at silence. I was feeling guilty and sad. Why had I yelled at her?

Back home, at last I read the poem she'd held up so eagerly. Moments after I read it, I pulled a watercolor out of its frame and replaced it with Nora's poem. I placed it on a wall where I'll see it every day for the rest of my life.

I hope it's carved on my tombstone.

Once I'd put Nora's treasured words up on the wall, I ran out to the garden and picked a fistful of daffodils that had just bloomed that week. I walked to her house to say thank-you for the poem and to apologize for being mean. I told Nora that her poem "is now my most prized possession." I meant it.

Nora was fully restored and breezily joked, "You mean if there's a fire, Ba, you'll grab my poem *first*—before me?"

"No. I'll grab you first."

"I'll grab Zip *and* my poem, and then you can carry Zip, my poem, *and me* outside!"

Big smile! Shared laughter! Big hug! Redemption!

"Whose idea was the poem?" I asked.

"Mine. Miss Nell said to write any poem about anything I wanted to. And I wrote 'Ba Is.'"

### "Ba is"

Spelling and punctuation are as in the original laboriously "written in cursive, Ba," in pencil on a lined sheet of school paper. Nora's words offer me a vision of myself as I would love to be seen by others but have never measured up to. To put this in the evangelical language I was raised on: Nora's poem might be the best defense I can offer at the Last Judgment.

**BA is**

By Nora. S.

*Ba is creeatuv.*

*Ba is cind.*

*Ba is smart.*

*and Ba is my frend.*

*and Ba is Kumfrding.*

# ABOUT THE AUTHOR

Frank Schaeffer is a *New York Times* bestselling author of more than a dozen fiction and nonfiction books. Frank is a survivor of both polio and an evangelical/fundamentalist childhood, an acclaimed writer who overcame severe dyslexia, a homeschooled and self-taught documentary movie director, and a feature film director of four low-budget Hollywood features that he describes as "pretty terrible." Frank is also an artist with a loyal following of collectors who own many of his oil paintings.

Frank has spoken at dozens of major universities, libraries, and museums from the Hammer in LA to Harvard, Princeton, and Yale. Frank's three semiautobiographical novels about growing up in a fundamentalist mission, *Portofino, Zermatt,* and *Saving Grandma*, have been translated into nine languages. His video blogs posted on Facebook have had millions of views.

Frank has been a guest commentator on MSNBC with Joy Reid and has been frequently interviewed by Rachel Maddow. He has also been interviewed on almost every major TV news show from *Oprah* to the *Today* show to *20/20*. His memoir *Crazy for God* is used as a textbook in history of religion classes and courses in comparative religion and sociology in public and private universities.

In her extended NPR interview with Frank about his memoir *Crazy for God*, Terry Gross called it out as a very important book. Frank's book *Keeping Faith: A Father-Son Story About Love and the United States Marine Corps* was a *New York Times* bestseller and was described by the commandant of the Marine Corps as a new "Marine family Bible."

Frank is a progressive activist and in the 2018 midterm elections spoke on behalf of thirty-three Democratic congressional candidates in seventeen states.

**Blog** frankschaefferblog.com/
*Twitter* www.twitter.com/frank_schaeffer
*Paintings* www.frankschaefferart.com/
*Facebook* www.facebook.com/frank.schaeffer.16

**Book clubs** may contact Frank at frankaschaeffer@aol.com, and Frank will be glad to participate with your club as time permits.

## Books by Frank Schaeffer

*Why I Am an Atheist Who Believes in God: How to Give Love, Create Beauty and Find Peace*

*Sex, Mom, and God: How the Bible's Strange Take on Sex Led to Crazy Politics—and How I Learned to Love Women (and Jesus) Anyway*

*Patience with God: Faith for People Who Don't Like Religion (or Atheism),*

*Crazy for God: How I Grew Up as One of the Elect, Helped Found the Religious Right, and Lived to Take All (or Almost All) of It Back*

*Baby Jack: A Novel*

*AWOL: The Unexcused Absence of America's Upper Classes from Military Service—and How It Hurts Our Country* (with Kathy Roth-Douquet)

*Voices from the Front: Letters Home From American's Military Family*

*Faith of Our Sons: Voices From the American Homefront— The Wartime Diary of a Marine's Father*

*Zermatt: A Novel,* (Third of Calvin Becker Trilogy)

*Keeping Faith: A Father–Son Story About Love and the United States Marine Corps* (with son John Schaeffer)

*Saving Grandma: A Novel* (Second of Calvin Becker Trilogy)

*Portofino: A Novel* (first of Calvin Becker Trilogy)

## Films

*How Should We Then Live? The Rise and Decline of Western Thought and Culture* (1976)

*Whatever Happened to the Human Race?* (1979). A Christian response to abortion, euthanasia, and infanticide, narrated by Francis Schaeffer and former Surgeon General Dr. C. Everett Koop

*Wired to Kill* (1986). Writer/director. Post-apocalyptic action film starring Devin Hoelscher, with Merritt Butrick

*Headhunter* (1989). Director. Occult horror film starring John Fatooh, June Chadwick, and Steve Kanaly

*Rising Storm* (1990). Director. Futuristic action film starring Zach Galligan and June Chadwick

*Baby on Board* (1992). Director. Slapstick comedy starring Judge Reinhold and Carol Kane